FREE Test Taking Tips DVD Offer

To help us better serve you, we have developed a Test Taking Tips DVD that we would like to give you for FREE. **This DVD covers world-class test taking tips that you can use to be even more successful when you are taking your test.**

All that we ask is that you email us your feedback about your study guide. Please let us know what you thought about it – whether that is good, bad or indifferent.

To get your **FREE Test Taking Tips DVD**, email freedvd@studyguideteam.com with "FREE DVD" in the subject line and the following information in the body of the email:

    a. The title of your study guide.

    b. Your product rating on a scale of 1-5, with 5 being the highest rating.

    c. Your feedback about the study guide. What did you think of it?

    d. Your full name and shipping address to send your free DVD.

If you have any questions or concerns, please don't hesitate to contact us at freedvd@studyguideteam.com.

Thanks again!

GACE Early Childhood Education 001 002 Test Prep

GACE Study Guide & Practice Exam Questions
[3rd Edition Prep]

TPB Publishing

Written and edited by TPB Publishing.

TPB Publishing is not associated with or endorsed by any official testing organization. TPB Publishing is a publisher of unofficial educational products. All test and organization names are trademarks of their respective owners. Content in this book is included for utilitarian purposes only and does not constitute an endorsement by TPB Publishing of any particular point of view.

Interested in buying more than 10 copies of our product? Contact us about bulk discounts:
bulkorders@studyguideteam.com

ISBN 13: 9781628458381
ISBN 10: 1628458380

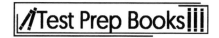

Table of Contents

Quick Overview

As you draw closer to taking your exam, effective preparation becomes more and more important. Thankfully, you have this study guide to help you get ready. Use this guide to help keep your studying on track and refer to it often.

This study guide contains several key sections that will help you be successful on your exam. The guide contains tips for what you should do the night before and the day of the test. Also included are test-taking tips. Knowing the right information is not always enough. Many well-prepared test takers struggle with exams. These tips will help equip you to accurately read, assess, and answer test questions.

A large part of the guide is devoted to showing you what content to expect on the exam and to helping you better understand that content. In this guide are practice test questions so that you can see how well you have grasped the content. Then, answer explanations are provided so that you can understand why you missed certain questions.

Don't try to cram the night before you take your exam. This is not a wise strategy for a few reasons. First, your retention of the information will be low. Your time would be better used by reviewing information you already know rather than trying to learn a lot of new information. Second, you will likely become stressed as you try to gain a large amount of knowledge in a short amount of time. Third, you will be depriving yourself of sleep. So be sure to go to bed at a reasonable time the night before. Being well-rested helps you focus and remain calm.

Be sure to eat a substantial breakfast the morning of the exam. If you are taking the exam in the afternoon, be sure to have a good lunch as well. Being hungry is distracting and can make it difficult to focus. You have hopefully spent lots of time preparing for the exam. Don't let an empty stomach get in the way of success!

When travelling to the testing center, leave earlier than needed. That way, you have a buffer in case you experience any delays. This will help you remain calm and will keep you from missing your appointment time at the testing center.

Be sure to pace yourself during the exam. Don't try to rush through the exam. There is no need to risk performing poorly on the exam just so you can leave the testing center early. Allow yourself to use all of the allotted time if needed.

Remain positive while taking the exam even if you feel like you are performing poorly. Thinking about the content you should have mastered will not help you perform better on the exam.

Once the exam is complete, take some time to relax. Even if you feel that you need to take the exam again, you will be well served by some down time before you begin studying again. It's often easier to convince yourself to study if you know that it will come with a reward!

Test-Taking Strategies

1. Predicting the Answer

When you feel confident in your preparation for a multiple-choice test, try predicting the answer before reading the answer choices. This is especially useful on questions that test objective factual knowledge. By predicting the answer before reading the available choices, you eliminate the possibility that you will be distracted or led astray by an incorrect answer choice. You will feel more confident in your selection if you read the question, predict the answer, and then find your prediction among the answer choices. After using this strategy, be sure to still read all of the answer choices carefully and completely. If you feel unprepared, you should not attempt to predict the answers. This would be a waste of time and an opportunity for your mind to wander in the wrong direction.

2. Reading the Whole Question

Too often, test takers scan a multiple-choice question, recognize a few familiar words, and immediately jump to the answer choices. Test authors are aware of this common impatience, and they will sometimes prey upon it. For instance, a test author might subtly turn the question into a negative, or he or she might redirect the focus of the question right at the end. The only way to avoid falling into these traps is to read the entirety of the question carefully before reading the answer choices.

3. Looking for Wrong Answers

Long and complicated multiple-choice questions can be intimidating. One way to simplify a difficult multiple-choice question is to eliminate all of the answer choices that are clearly wrong. In most sets of answers, there will be at least one selection that can be dismissed right away. If the test is administered on paper, the test taker could draw a line through it to indicate that it may be ignored; otherwise, the test taker will have to perform this operation mentally or on scratch paper. In either case, once the obviously incorrect answers have been eliminated, the remaining choices may be considered. Sometimes identifying the clearly wrong answers will give the test taker some information about the correct answer. For instance, if one of the remaining answer choices is a direct opposite of one of the eliminated answer choices, it may well be the correct answer. The opposite of obviously wrong is obviously right! Of course, this is not always the case. Some answers are obviously incorrect simply because they are irrelevant to the question being asked. Still, identifying and eliminating some incorrect answer choices is a good way to simplify a multiple-choice question.

4. Don't Overanalyze

Anxious test takers often overanalyze questions. When you are nervous, your brain will often run wild, causing you to make associations and discover clues that don't actually exist. If you feel that this may be a problem for you, do whatever you can to slow down during the test. Try taking a deep breath or counting to ten. As you read and consider the question, restrict yourself to the particular words used by the author. Avoid thought tangents about what the author *really* meant, or what he or she was *trying* to say. The only things that matter on a multiple-choice test are the words that are actually in the question. You must avoid reading too much into a multiple-choice question, or supposing that the writer meant something other than what he or she wrote.

5. No Need for Panic

It is wise to learn as many strategies as possible before taking a multiple-choice test, but it is likely that you will come across a few questions for which you simply don't know the answer. In this situation, avoid panicking. Because most multiple-choice tests include dozens of questions, the relative value of a single wrong answer is small. As much as possible, you should compartmentalize each question on a multiple-choice test. In other words, you should not allow your feelings about one question to affect your success on the others. When you find a question that you either don't understand or don't know how to answer, just take a deep breath and do your best. Read the entire question slowly and carefully. Try rephrasing the question a couple of different ways. Then, read all of the answer choices carefully. After eliminating obviously wrong answers, make a selection and move on to the next question.

6. Confusing Answer Choices

When working on a difficult multiple-choice question, there may be a tendency to focus on the answer choices that are the easiest to understand. Many people, whether consciously or not, gravitate to the answer choices that require the least concentration, knowledge, and memory. This is a mistake. When you come across an answer choice that is confusing, you should give it extra attention. A question might be confusing because you do not know the subject matter to which it refers. If this is the case, don't eliminate the answer before you have affirmatively settled on another. When you come across an answer choice of this type, set it aside as you look at the remaining choices. If you can confidently assert that one of the other choices is correct, you can leave the confusing answer aside. Otherwise, you will need to take a moment to try to better understand the confusing answer choice. Rephrasing is one way to tease out the sense of a confusing answer choice.

7. Your First Instinct

Many people struggle with multiple-choice tests because they overthink the questions. If you have studied sufficiently for the test, you should be prepared to trust your first instinct once you have carefully and completely read the question and all of the answer choices. There is a great deal of research suggesting that the mind can come to the correct conclusion very quickly once it has obtained all of the relevant information. At times, it may seem to you as if your intuition is working faster even than your reasoning mind. This may in fact be true. The knowledge you obtain while studying may be retrieved from your subconscious before you have a chance to work out the associations that support it. Verify your instinct by working out the reasons that it should be trusted.

8. Key Words

Many test takers struggle with multiple-choice questions because they have poor reading comprehension skills. Quickly reading and understanding a multiple-choice question requires a mixture of skill and experience. To help with this, try jotting down a few key words and phrases on a piece of scrap paper. Doing this concentrates the process of reading and forces the mind to weigh the relative importance of the question's parts. In selecting words and phrases to write down, the test taker thinks about the question more deeply and carefully. This is especially true for multiple-choice questions that are preceded by a long prompt.

9. Subtle Negatives

One of the oldest tricks in the multiple-choice test writer's book is to subtly reverse the meaning of a question with a word like *not* or *except*. If you are not paying attention to each word in the question, you can easily be led astray by this trick. For instance, a common question format is, "Which of the following is...?" Obviously, if the question instead is, "Which of the following is not...?," then the answer will be quite different. Even worse, the test makers are aware of the potential for this mistake and will include one answer choice that would be correct if the question were not negated or reversed. A test taker who misses the reversal will find what he or she believes to be a correct answer and will be so confident that he or she will fail to reread the question and discover the original error. The only way to avoid this is to practice a wide variety of multiple-choice questions and to pay close attention to each and every word.

10. Reading Every Answer Choice

It may seem obvious, but you should always read every one of the answer choices! Too many test takers fall into the habit of scanning the question and assuming that they understand the question because they recognize a few key words. From there, they pick the first answer choice that answers the question they believe they have read. Test takers who read all of the answer choices might discover that one of the latter answer choices is actually *more* correct. Moreover, reading all of the answer choices can remind you of facts related to the question that can help you arrive at the correct answer. Sometimes, a misstatement or incorrect detail in one of the latter answer choices will trigger your memory of the subject and will enable you to find the right answer. Failing to read all of the answer choices is like not reading all of the items on a restaurant menu: you might miss out on the perfect choice.

11. Spot the Hedges

One of the keys to success on multiple-choice tests is paying close attention to every word. This is never truer than with words like almost, most, some, and sometimes. These words are called "hedges" because they indicate that a statement is not totally true or not true in every place and time. An absolute statement will contain no hedges, but in many subjects, the answers are not always straightforward or absolute. There are always exceptions to the rules in these subjects. For this reason, you should favor those multiple-choice questions that contain hedging language. The presence of qualifying words indicates that the author is taking special care with his or her words, which is certainly important when composing the right answer. After all, there are many ways to be wrong, but there is only one way to be right! For this reason, it is wise to avoid answers that are absolute when taking a multiple-choice test. An absolute answer is one that says things are either all one way or all another. They often include words like *every*, *always*, *best*, and *never*. If you are taking a multiple-choice test in a subject that doesn't lend itself to absolute answers, be on your guard if you see any of these words.

12. Long Answers

In many subject areas, the answers are not simple. As already mentioned, the right answer often requires hedges. Another common feature of the answers to a complex or subjective question are qualifying clauses, which are groups of words that subtly modify the meaning of the sentence. If the question or answer choice describes a rule to which there are exceptions or the subject matter is complicated, ambiguous, or confusing, the correct answer will require many words in order to be expressed clearly and accurately. In essence, you should not be deterred by answer choices that seem excessively long. Oftentimes, the author of the text will not be able to write the correct answer without offering some qualifications and modifications. Your job is to read the answer choices thoroughly and completely and to select the one that most accurately and precisely answers the question.

13. Restating to Understand

Sometimes, a question on a multiple-choice test is difficult not because of what it asks but because of how it is written. If this is the case, restate the question or answer choice in different words. This process serves a couple of important purposes. First, it forces you to concentrate on the core of the question. In order to rephrase the question accurately, you have to understand it well. Rephrasing the question will concentrate your mind on the key words and ideas. Second, it will present the information to your mind in a fresh way. This process may trigger your memory and render some useful scrap of information picked up while studying.

14. True Statements

Sometimes an answer choice will be true in itself, but it does not answer the question. This is one of the main reasons why it is essential to read the question carefully and completely before proceeding to the answer choices. Too often, test takers skip ahead to the answer choices and look for true statements. Having found one of these, they are content to select it without reference to the question above. Obviously, this provides an easy way for test makers to play tricks. The savvy test taker will always read the entire question before turning to the answer choices. Then, having settled on a correct answer choice, he or she will refer to the original question and ensure that the selected answer is relevant. The mistake of choosing a correct-but-irrelevant answer choice is especially common on questions related to specific pieces of objective knowledge. A prepared test taker will have a wealth of factual knowledge at his or her disposal, and should not be careless in its application.

15. No Patterns

One of the more dangerous ideas that circulates about multiple-choice tests is that the correct answers tend to fall into patterns. These erroneous ideas range from a belief that B and C are the most common right answers, to the idea that an unprepared test-taker should answer "A-B-A-C-A-D-A-B-A." It cannot be emphasized enough that pattern-seeking of this type is exactly the WRONG way to approach a multiple-choice test. To begin with, it is highly unlikely that the test maker will plot the correct answers according to some predetermined pattern. The questions are scrambled and delivered in a random order. Furthermore, even if the test maker was following a pattern in the assignation of correct answers, there is no reason why the test taker would know which pattern he or she was using. Any attempt to discern a pattern in the answer choices is a waste of time and a distraction from the real work of taking the test. A test taker would be much better served by extra preparation before the test than by reliance on a pattern in the answers.

FREE DVD OFFER

Don't forget that doing well on your exam includes both understanding the test content and understanding how to use what you know to do well on the test. We offer a completely FREE Test Taking Tips DVD that covers world class test taking tips that you can use to be even more successful when you are taking your test.

All that we ask is that you email us your feedback about your study guide. To get your **FREE Test Taking Tips DVD**, email freedvd@studyguideteam.com with "FREE DVD" in the subject line and the following information in the body of the email:

- The title of your study guide.
- Your product rating on a scale of 1-5, with 5 being the highest rating.
- Your feedback about the study guide. What did you think of it?
- Your full name and shipping address to send your free DVD.

Introduction to the GACE Early Childhood Education 001 & 002 Assessment

Function of the Test

The Georgia Assessments for the Certification of Educators (GACE) is a test given by the state of Georgia to verify that applicants for Georgia's certification evaluation program have the required proficiency to be an educator in the Georgia public school system. GACE test takers include those looking to enter an education preparation program, those pursuing teaching certification in Georgia, and/or those hoping to attain qualification in a specific core academic subject area.

The GACE Early Childhood Education test is one of several assessments within the GACE program. It is intended to gauge the classroom competency of potential Early Childhood Education teachers within Georgia, based on existing criteria rather than on a comparison to the skill sets and results of the other examinees. It is meant only for teachers who have already finished an Early Childhood state-approved educator preparation program. Therefore, it is not designed for those who wish to include this specialty as part of his or her current teacher certification.

The GACE Early Childhood Education exam is on par with Georgia's P-5 curriculum standards and state and national subject standards. Like the other GACE exams, it was assembled by a wide range of Georgia educators. Three committees of Georgia teachers and test preparation faculty evaluated and approved the test questions. The passing score was assigned by the state agency of Commissioners based on their expert assessments and the suggestions of Georgia educators.

Test Administration

GACE tests may be taken several times a year at exam facilities in Georgia, other U.S. states, and internationally. They were created by the Georgia Professional Standards Commission (GaPSC) and Educational Testing Service (ETS). The Test Center Search tool found on the GACE website can be used to verify where the GACE Early Childhood Education assessment is offered: https://gace.ets.org/register/centers_dates

The GACE Early Childhood Education assessment is a combined test encompassing two parts (Test I and Test II). Test I and Test II can be taken separately or at the same exam appointment. The exam fee includes a registration fee and a test facility fee. Test takers incur a small fee to change the test location, date, or time after registration, and to cancel the test. Those GACE exams taken at international locations may require an additional facility fee. Test takers who wish to retake a test must wait thirty days. Therefore, the GACE online registration system (www.gace.ets.org) only accepts registrations that are at least thirty days after the original test.

Candidates who are disabled or have health-related requirements can register an accommodation request via ETS Disability Services: www.ets.org/disabilities.

Test Format

The GACE Early Childhood Education assessment comprises two tests of selected-response (SR) and constructed-response (CR) questions (typically two essay questions). Candidates may answer the CR questions via written word, speech, or signing. Each 75-question test may be taken individually or at the same time. Candidates are given four hours to answer the test questions (test time), and one additional hour is allotted to view any electronic directions included as part of the exam instructions (testing duration).

Each test is divided into the following content subareas: Reading and Language Arts; Social Studies; Analysis (constructed-response only); Mathematics; Science; and Health Education, Physical Education and the Arts. Each subarea contains a set of objectives and knowledge statements. Questions evaluate fundamental knowledge for these subject areas and the aptitude of the candidate to apply concepts.

Sections of the GACE Early Childhood Education Assessment	
Subject Areas – Test 1	Approx. % of Test
Reading and Language Arts	50
Social Studies	25
Analysis (constructed-response only)	25
Subject Areas – Test 2	
Mathematics	53
Science	30
Health Education, Physical Education and the Arts	17

Scoring

GACE Early Childhood Education test results are scored on a scale of 100 to 300. Scaled scores can be compared across all versions of the same subtest, but not necessarily across different subtests. A passing score is categorized in one of two ways: 220–249 (an induction-level score) or 250 and above (passing at the professional level). As per Georgia requirements, candidates who receive a passing score at either level achieve an Early Childhood Education certificate. However, since the GACE Early Childhood Education assessment is comprised of two tests, both tests must be passed to receive certification. If a test taker passes a combined test at different levels, the entire test is given an induction-level passing score. To pass the entire assessment at the professional level, the subtest that was passed at the induction level must be retaken with a score of 250 or greater achieved.

Graded right away by the computer, SR questions are each given one raw score point. CR questions are graded on a six-point holistic grading rubric. Since each test varies in the type and number of questions included, the percentage of correct answers needed to pass cannot be determined ahead of time. Conversion tables are used to adjust for difficulty among versions and ensure comparability. Not all of the questions on the test are typically incorporated into the final score. Most of the tests that include SR questions also include a mix of pretest questions that are not included as part of the final score. Instead, these are control questions used by ETS to substantiate inclusion on upcoming tests.

Recent/Future Developments

As of October 5, 2013, ETS took over as the supplier for the GACE assessments from Evaluation Systems (ES). Because tests offered by the two suppliers are scored differently, passing scores on GACE Early Childhood Education tests cannot be split between the two suppliers. Test takers must have passing scores from the same testing supplier on both assessment tests to be accepted toward certification. Test takers will receive credit for tests already passed as long as both parts of the assessment received passing scores.

[handwritten top margin: Reading education:
Phonemic Awareness   Vocabulary
Phonics   Comprehension
Fluency]

Reading and Language Arts

00) *Reading for Literature and Reading for Information*

A Promoting Students' Comprehension of Informational Text and Literature

Promoting Literacy Development

It is widely accepted that the more classroom opportunities a child has for listening, speaking, reading, and writing, the more these skills will strengthen. Educators, who frequently read to emergent readers using exaggerated pauses, inflections, tones, and pronunciation, report encouraging signs of progress in student literacy development and independent reading skills. *[handwritten: Inflection - rise and fall of person's speech]*

Directed Reading-Thinking Activities – *[handwritten: used before and after reading to improve critical thinking and comprehension]*

Prior to the introduction of a challenging text, educators may spend time with the class predicting what the text might be about. By paying attention to the features of the book or text, students can begin to formulate ideas about the overall content. Educators may try to extend this discussion, prompting children to consider what the setting of the book or written piece might be, what events might take place, and what types of characters they might encounter. When an educator focuses on prediction skills prior to reading, children begin to strengthen their ability to connect literature to real life.

After reading, educators may begin another class discussion, prompting children to consider whether their predictions were accurate and why or why not this was so. For instance, an educator may point out that a child's own life experiences may have prompted her to predict a certain outcome. When children relate literature to their own lives in this way, reading becomes a more enjoyable and meaningful activity. Post-reading activities may also involve small groups of children acting out various scenes or retelling the story in their own words, which also helps the educator to assess children's overall comprehension. Post-reading activities should include discussions regarding various literary elements such as cause and effect or the author's points of view.

Monitoring Comprehension – *[handwritten: a process in which students determine whether they understand what they are reading]*

Self-monitoring one's comprehension is a valuable lifelong skill for students to learn. Teaching self-monitoring takes advantage of students' natural ability to recognize when they understand the reading and when they do not. Students will need to learn to:

- Identify exactly the part of the text where the difficulty occurs
- Identify the specific problem and restate the difficult text in their own words
- Reread previous portions of the text to gain clues about the problematic piece
- Scan future portions of the text for information that helps resolve the question

[handwritten: Self monitoring Ex - jumping ahead in reading to find out why character did something]

Metacognition – *[handwritten: awareness and understanding of one's own thought process]*

Skilled readers have learned to think about thinking. This is called **metacognition**. Using metacognitive strategies is a skill that gives students control over their learning while they read and may involve the use strategies such as:

- Identifying purpose for reading the selection
- Previewing the text
- Matching their reading speed to the challenge level of the selection

[handwritten: Looking back at previous reading section is a metacognitive skill]

- Asking themselves comprehension questions
- Resolving comprehension problems independently or with help
- Checking themselves for understanding after reading the selection

KWL Activities
What I Know / What I Want to Know / What I Learned

Good reading teachers know how to help students activate their prior knowledge and draw from personal curiosity to set them up for the learning task. Students can create a **KWL (Know/Want to know/Learned) chart** to get ready for any unit of instruction. Teachers guide students to identify what they already know about a given topic. They then help them generate questions about the topic. After the instruction takes place, teachers help students analyze what they have learned.

Comprehension of Informational Text - *providing information about a topic*

Informational text is written material that has the primary function of imparting information about a topic. It is often written by someone with expertise in the topic and directed at an audience that has less knowledge of the topic. Informational texts are written in a different fashion from storytelling or narrative texts. Typically, this type of text has several organizational and structural differences from narrative text. In informational texts, there are features such as charts, graphs, photographs, headings and subheadings, glossaries, indexes, bibliographies, or other guidance features. With the aid of technology, embedded hyperlinks and video content are also sometimes included. Informational material may be written to compare and contrast, be explanatory, link cause and effect, provide opinion, persuade the reader, or serve a number of other purposes. Finally, informational texts typically use a different style of language than narrative texts, which instead, focus more on storytelling. Historically, informational texts were not introduced until students were ready to read to learn versus still learning to read. However, research is now suggesting that informational text can be developmentally appropriate for children at a much younger age.

One very effective strategy for increasing comprehension of informational text is **reciprocal teaching**. Reciprocal teaching is a method of small group teaching that relies on students assuming different roles to practice four reading strategies particularly helpful for readers of informational texts. Predicting, summarizing, questioning, and clarifying will lead students to understand and apply what they read. Skilled readers have acquired a set of techniques that make informational reading effective for them. They begin by previewing text selections and making educated guesses as to what the content will include. They then identify the purpose for reading the text and can explain why the content will be important to know. They are able to filter the reading selection to screen out the trivial points and focus on the most important facts. Using critical thinking skills, they monitor their own understanding of the information by asking themselves questions about what they have read. They use multiple methods to determine the meaning of unknown vocabulary. Finally, they can concisely and succinctly form an overall summary of what they have learned from the text.

Predicting
Predicting requires thinking ahead and, after reading, verifying whether predictions were correct. This method engages students with the text and gets them to pay attention to details that tell them whether their predictions might be coming true. The goal is to help students learn to base their predictions on clues from the text. They should not only state what they predict but also be able to comment on the specifics of the text that lead them to make those predictions.

Summarizing

Through **summarizing,** students learn to identify the main ideas and differentiate them from the less important information in the text. It helps them remember what they read and retell the central concepts in their own words. As students learn to break down larger chunks of information into more concise sentences, they use analytical thinking skills and hone their critical reading capabilities.

Questioning Techniques

Questioning has immeasurable value in the reading process. Answering questions about a text gives purpose for reading to students and focuses them on reading to learn information. Similarly, generating questions about a text for others to answer enables a student to analyze what is important to learn in the text and glean summarizing skills. Keeping Bloom's Taxonomy in mind, teachers can scaffold students toward increased critical thinking capabilities. Bloom's Taxonomy shows the hierarchy of learning progressing through the following stages:

[handwritten note: process in which teachers model or demonstrate how to solve a problem, steps back, offering support as needed. I Do, We Do, You Do]

- Remembering
- Understanding
- Applying
- Analyzing
- Evaluating
- Creating

Clarifying

This is the post-reading phase where students learn to clear up any misunderstandings and unanswered questions. Strategies for clarifying include defining any unknown words, rereading at a slower pace, reviewing previous segments of the text, referring to their summaries, and skimming future portions of the text.

Comprehension of Literature

Comprehension of literature comes through teaching students about story structure and the complexities of literary elements that comprise a good tale. Comprehension is enhanced when students learn to identify and analyze the characters, settings, events, problems, themes, and resolutions that are found in the stories. Teachers should keep in mind the following concepts when teaching story structure:

- Narrative Strategies
- Flashback
- Point of View
- Characterization
- Figurative Language
- Mood
- Theme
- Style
- Making Inferences
- Author's Purpose
- Generating Questions
- Main Ideas

Narrative Strategies

All narrative literature is centered on the plot of the story or the sequence of events that make the story happen. Authors use various narrative strategies to unfold their plot and make it grab the reader's attention. Writers give their stories action. Good authors are descriptive with their words. Narrative writers inspire readers to keep reading the story by adding an element of suspense. To help understand the characters and their relationships with one another, authors use dialogue between characters. The author may describe gestures and facial expressions to help develop the characters' personalities. These narrative techniques engage the reader, pull him or her into the story, and enhance the believability of the literature.

Flashback

Sometimes an author needs to give the reader more information about a character or the story's events, but the information doesn't fit well into the story itself. In such situations, the author might introduce a flashback into the plot. A **flashback** is a scene set earlier than the main story. → *Ex. character in car crash when younger*

Point of View

Writers can choose the point of view of one character (**first person**), a narrator who gives the point of view (thoughts and feelings) of one or a few characters (**third person limited**), or from a narrator who gives the point of view of all the characters in the story (**third person omniscient**).

1st Person - I/Me   2nd Person She/He   3rd Person - You/Yours
My   Her/His

Characterization

The writer wants the reader to be as connected as possible to the characters of the story. If the author directly makes comments about the personality of the character, it is called **direct characterization**. If instead, the author allows the reader to learn about the character naturally through the course of the story, it is called **indirect characterization**.

Figurative Language

Figurative language is used when a writer wants to illustrate a point that is not literal in meaning. Phrases that mean something other than what they literally state are called **figures of speech**. Examples of these are metaphors, hyperboles, similes, etc.

SHAMPO
Simile   Alliteration Personification
Hyperbole Metaphor Onomatopoeia

Mood

Authors use elements of literature to achieve a certain mood to their writing. The mood can be light and airy, comical, dark and oppressive, or any number of other emotions. The mood of a selection of literature will determine some of the meaning of the words and phrases.

Theme

In any selection of literature, the author is trying to convey a main idea or central theme. Sometimes the writer explains the main point clearly, while at other times, the reader must use critical thinking and analysis to determine the underlying theme of the writing.

Style

Each writer's own style is conveyed in his or her word choice, use of sentence structure, and the way punctuation adds to the story. The writer's style injects a certain personality, attitude, and voice into the writing.

Making Inferences — *Making a guess*

When readers put together clues from the writing to "guess" that a particular idea is a fact, it is called making **inferences**. Making inferences helps read "between the lines" of a selection to derive meaning that is intended by the author but not explicitly written.

Author's Purpose

There are endless reasons why authors might write a particular narrative piece to a certain audience. They might be simply trying to entertain readers, to enlighten them about a specific concept, to give information about historical or current events, to spark imagination, or to help readers resolve a problem.

Generating Questions

Asking questions as a reader reads requires an interactive relationship with the text and can deepen understanding. The reader is constantly honing metacognitive skills as more and more questions are asked.

Main Ideas

Typically, in a piece of narrative writing there are only a couple of ideas that the author is trying to convey to the reader. It is important to understand and discern the difference between a topic and a main idea. A topic might be "horses," but the main idea should be a complete sentence such as, "Racehorses run faster when they have a good relationship with the jockey."

Topic — thing
Main Idea — complete sentence

Integrating Knowledge and Ideas

Visual learning is a powerful tool for helping students integrate new ideas with their prior knowledge. Research shows that most students need to be able to see information to be able to learn it well.

Graphic Organizers

One highly effective method of integrating knowledge and ideas is the use of **graphic organizers**. These may be sequencing charts, graphs, Venn diagrams, timelines, chain of events organizers, story maps, concept maps, mind maps, webs, outlines, or other visual tools for connecting concepts to facilitate understanding. This strategy helps students to examine, analyze, and summarize selections they have read and can be used individually or collaboratively in the classroom.

Helping Students Identify and Evaluate Common Types of Text

The Importance of Teaching Varied Types of Text

Reading is fundamental to learning. Reading nurtures imagination, critical thinking, communication skills, and social competence. Many children are drawn to the allure of reading and often their attention is captivated by a certain type of book or books about a particular personal interest. It is important to introduce them to an eclectic selection of text types. Cultural knowledge, a more intricate worldview, and a host of new vocabulary can be built through the experience of diverse literature. Reading a wide range of writing styles brings students into contact with many characters and lifestyles. Reading varied texts sparks different emotions in a child and teaches a variety of means of expression. In this way, children deepen social and emotional skills. In short, reading a wide variety of texts produces a well-rounded education and prepares children for their experience of the world.

Literary Genre

Genre is a method of categorizing literature by form, content, style, and technique. When selections of literature share enough characteristics and literary elements, they are classified into the same genre. Genre is more than just a categorization system, though; genre identifies literature by its communicative purpose. Authors write to accomplish any of a variety of social purposes: to inform, to explain, to entertain, to persuade, to maintain relationships, and so on. All types of texts fall into one of the following five genres: fiction, nonfiction, poetry, drama, and folklore. Each of these has a variety of subgenres. A particular piece of writing may fall into more than one genre or subgenre.

Fiction

Fiction is imaginative text that is invented by the author. Fiction is characterized by the following literary elements:

- **Characters:** the people, animals, aliens, or other living figures the story is about
- **Setting:** the location, surroundings, and time the story takes place in
- **Conflict:** a dilemma the characters face either internally or externally
- **Plot:** the sequence and the rise and fall of excitement in the action of a story
- **Resolution:** the solution to the conflict that is discovered as a result of the story
- **Point of View:** the lens through which the reader experiences the story
- **Theme:** the moral to the story or the message the author is sending to the reader

Historical Fiction

Historical fiction is a story that occurs in the past and uses a realistic setting and authentic time period characters. Historical fiction usually has some historically accurate events mixed and balanced with invented plot and characters.

Science Fiction

Science fiction is an invented story that occurs in the future or an alternate universe. It often deals with space, time travel, robots, or aliens, and highly advanced technology.

Fantasy

Fantasy is a subgenre of fiction that involves magic or supernatural elements and/or takes place in an imaginary world. Examples include talking animals, superheroes rescuing the day, or characters taking on a mythical journey or quest.

Mystery and Adventure

Mystery fiction is a story that involves a puzzle or crime to be solved by the main characters. The mystery is driven by suspense and foreshadowing. The reader must sift through clues and distractions to solve the puzzle with the protagonist. **Adventure** stories are driven by the risky or exciting action that happens in the plot.

Realistic and Contemporary Fiction

Realistic fiction depends on the author portraying the world without speculation. The characters are ordinary, and the action could happen in real life. The conflict often involves growing up, family life, or learning to cope with some significant emotion or challenge.

Non-Fiction Literature

Non-fiction literature is text that is true and accurate in detail. Nonfiction can cover virtually any topic in the natural world. Nonfiction writers conduct research and carefully organize facts before writing. Nonfiction has the following subgenres:

- **Informational Text:** This is text written to impart information to the reader. It may have literary elements such as charts, graphs, indexes, glossaries, or bibliographies.

- **Persuasive Text:** This is text that is meant to sway the reader to have a particular opinion or take a particular action.

- **Biographies and Autobiographies:** This is text that tells intimate details of someone's life. If an author writes the text about someone else, it is a biography. If the author writes it about himself or herself, it is an autobiography.

- **Communicative text:** This is text used to communicate with another person. This includes such texts as emails, formal and informal letters, and tweets. This content often consists of two-sided dialogue between people.

Drama

Drama is any writing that is intended to be performed in front of an audience, such as plays, and TV and movie scripts. Dialogue and action are central to convey the author's theme.

- **Comedy**: Comedy is any drama designed to be funny or lighthearted.
- **Tragedy:** Tragedy is any drama designed to be serious or sad.

Poetry

This is text that is written in verse and has a rhythmic cadence. It often involves descriptive imagery, rhyming stanzas, and beautiful mastery of language. It is often personal, emotional, and introspective. Poetry is often considered a work of art.

Folklore

Folklore is literature that has been handed down from generation to generation by word of mouth. Folklore is not based in fact but in unsubstantiated beliefs. It is often very important to a culture or custom.

- **Fairy Tales:** These are usually written for children and often carry a moral or universal truth. They are stories written about fairies or other magical creatures.

- **Fables:** Similar to fairy tales, fables are written for children and include tales of supernatural people or animals that speak like people.

- **Myths:** These tales are often about the gods, include symbolism, and may involve historical events and reveal human behavior. Sometimes they tell how historical things came about.

- **Legends:** Exaggerated and only partially truthful, these are tales of heroes and significant events.

- **Tall Tales:** Often funny stories and sometimes set in the Wild West, these are tales that contain extreme exaggeration and were never true.

Helping Students Evaluate Literature

Teaching students how to identify quality literature is essential. Students need to know how to choose a good book and, after reading it, how to form sound judgment—based on solid evidence—about the book. Here are some questions that students can ask that will help them evaluate the books they've read.

- Did I enjoy the book? What made it enjoyable?
- Do I feel the story and characters were believable?
- Was the conflict resolved in a way that wasn't too simple?
- What was the climax and did it fit with the storyline?
- Did the action of the characters fit with their personalities?
- Was there a lesson or moral to the story? What was the theme?
- Were the characters well-developed? Did I get to know them and bond with them?
- What was the setting of the book and was it well-developed? Could I "see" it?
- Did the characters seem like they were from the time and location of the story?
- Did the book envelop my mind? Was I wrapped up in reading it?
- Did the author write with purpose and if so, what was that purpose?
- Did the dialogue between characters seem real, like what someone would actually say?
- Was it worthwhile to read the book?

Interpreting Words and Phrases Used in Text and Analyzing and Describing Text Structure

Interpreting Words and Phrases

Words can have different meanings depending on how they are used in a text. There are several methods for helping students decipher word meanings:

- Dictionary: Students should be taught to effectively use a dictionary and a thesaurus, including digital dictionaries and resources. Students need to know how to read the dictionary so they understand that there can be more than one meaning for a particular word. Dictionaries also help teach word pronunciation and syllables. A thesaurus teaches antonyms and synonyms. Once students know the correct meaning and pronunciation, they are able to better understand the context of the word in the text.

- Word Parts: Dissecting words into their word parts, (i.e., root word, prefix, suffix) will help determine the meaning of a word as a whole. It's beneficial to teach high-frequency Greek and Latin root words, since they comprise the majority of the English language. Some methods for teaching word parts include the following techniques:

- Analogies
- Word Play
- Word Association
- Syllabication
- Spelling Patterns
- Reading Context
- Writing Context
- Inventive Writing

- **Context Clues:** Students can look at other words in the same or surrounding sentences to help determine the meaning of an unknown word by the way it is used in the same sentence or paragraph. This kind of search provides context clues.

- **Author's Purpose:** Authors use words differently depending on what they want the reader to glean from the text. Some ways writers use words are as follows:

- **Literal:** the exact meaning or definition of the word
- **Figurative:** metaphorical language and figures of speech
- **Technical:** in-depth writing about specific subjects such as math or music
- **Connotative:** showing an opinion or suggestion within text as a secondary meaning

Determining Text Structures

There are different text structures used for various purposes in writing. Each text structure has key words and elements that help identify it. It is important to teach text structure because students who do not have much prior knowledge on a topic depend on structure to help assimilate new information. Readers use text structure to help find information within a text. Summarizing requires knowledge of the text structure of a piece of writing.

Some common text structures include:

- **Chronological Order:** Time order or sequence from one point to another. Dates and times might be used, or bullets and numbering. Possible key words: *first, next, then, after, later, finally, before, preceding, following*

- **Cause and Effect:** Showing how causes come before effects and how one leads to the other. Time order may also clarify cause and effect. Possible key words: *cause, effect, consequently, as a result, due to, in order to, because of, therefore, so, leads to, if ... then*

- **Problem and Solution:** Outlines a particular problem in detail and suggests one or more solutions to the problem and the pros and cons of solutions. Possible key words: *difficulty, problem, solve, solution, possible, therefore, if ... then, challenge*

- **Compare and Contrast:** Describes how objects, people, places, and ideas are similar or different from one another. Possible key words: *like, unlike, similar to, in contrast, on the other hand, whereas, while, although, either or, opposed to, different from, instead*

- **Description:** Explains a topic, including the main idea and details. Possible key words: *for example, such as, for instance, most importantly, another, such as, next to, on top of, besides*

Foundational Skills to Literacy Development, Fluency, and Comprehension

Foundations of Literacy and Reading Development and the Stages of Early Orthographic Development

Developing Language Literacy Skills

It is believed that literacy development is the most rapid between birth and 5 years of age. From birth until around 3 months, babies start to recognize the sounds of familiar voices. Between 3 months and 6 months, babies begin to study a speaker's mouth and listen much more closely to speech sounds. Between 9 months and 12 months, babies can generally recognize a growing number of commonly repeated words, can utter simple words, respond appropriately to simple requests, and begin to attempt to group sounds.

In the toddler years, children begin to rapidly strengthen their communication skills, connecting sounds to meanings and combining sounds to create coherent sentences. The opportunities for rich social interactions play a key role in this early literacy development and help children to understand cultural nuances, expected behavior, and effective communication skills. By age 3, most toddlers can understand many sentences and can begin to generalize by placing specific words into categories. In the preschool years, children begin to develop and strengthen their emergent literacy skills. It is at this stage that children will begin to sound out words, learn basic spelling patterns, especially with rhyming words, and start to develop their fine motor skills. Awareness of basic grammar also begins to emerge with oral attempts at past, present, and future verb tenses.

English Literacy Development

English language literacy can be categorized into four basic stages:

- Beginning
- Early Intermediate
- Intermediate
- Early Advanced

Beginning Literacy

This stage is commonly referred to as **receptive language development**. Educators can encourage this stage in literacy development by providing the student with many opportunities to interact on a social level with peers. Educators should also consider starting a personal dictionary, introducing word flashcards, and providing the student with opportunities to listen to a story read by another peer, or as a computer-based activity.

Early Intermediate Literacy

When a child begins to communicate to express a need or attempt to ask or respond to a question, the child is said to be at the early intermediate literacy stage. Educators should continue to build vocabulary knowledge and introduce activities that require the student to complete the endings of sentences, fill in the blanks, and describe the beginning or ending of familiar stories.

Intermediate Literacy

When a child begins to demonstrate comprehension of more complex vocabulary and abstract ideas, the child is advancing into the intermediate literacy stage. It is at this stage that children are able to challenge themselves to meet the classroom learning expectations and start to use their newly acquired literacy skills to read, write, listen, and speak. Educators may consider providing students with more advanced reading opportunities, such as partner-shared reading, silent reading, and choral reading.

Early Advanced Literacy

When a child is able to apply literacy skills to learn new information across many subjects, the child is progressing toward the early advanced literacy stage. The child can now tackle complex literacy tasks and confidently handle much more cognitively demanding material. To strengthen reading comprehension, educators should consider the introduction to word webs and semantic organizers.

Book reports and class presentations, as well as continued opportunities to access a variety of reading material, will help to strengthen the child's newly acquired literacy skills.

Stages of Early Orthographic Development: Learning to Spell

Orthography is the representation of the sounds of a language by written or printed symbols. Learning to spell is a highly complex and cumulative process with each skill building on the previously mastered skill. This is considered **orthographic development**. It is imperative for educators to ensure that each skill is taught in sequential steps in order for children to develop spelling capabilities.

Emergent Spelling: Pre-Communicative Writing Stage

Children may be able to accurately identify various letters of the alphabet but will likely not be able to associate them to their corresponding sounds. Children may be able to string together letter-like forms or letters without a connection to specific **phonemes** (the smallest units of sound in a given language). Nearing the end of this phase, children progress from writing in all directions to writing in standard convention from left to right.

Letter Name-Alphabetic Stage

At this stage, children begin to understand unique letter-sound correspondence and can begin to differentiate between various consonant sounds. Children may even be able to connect two and three letters together in an attempt to spell a word, but the letters they use will generally only consist of consonants. Most show a clear preference for capital letters.

Within-Word Pattern Stage

With a strengthening ability to recognize and apply letter-sound correspondence, children in this spelling stage can use their understanding of phonics to attempt full words that incorporate vowels. With repeated and consistent exposure and practice, children start to focus on letter combinations, spelling patterns, consonant blends, and digraphs. In this stage, students are becoming aware of homophones and experiment with vowel sound combinations.

Syllables and Affixes Stage

Just as the name suggests, children at this stage are focused on syllables and combining them to form words. Children begin to develop a deeper understanding of the need for vowels to appear in each syllable, and words begin to readily resemble the proper conventions of English spelling to them.

Derivational Relations Stage

In this stage, students learn how spelling relates to meaning. Generalizations about spelling patterns and rules of spelling start to be more readily applied, which allows the child to attempt the spelling of unfamiliar words. Children begin learning about root words and consonant and vowel alterations. It is during this stage that children begin to accumulate a much greater vocabulary base.

Effective Teaching Strategies for Spelling

There are several effective strategies that educators can introduce to facilitate each developmental spelling stage. Strategies focused on alphabetic knowledge, including letter-sound games, are of primary importance in the beginning stages. As spelling skills strengthen, educators may choose to introduce word families, spelling patterns, and word structures. There is some controversy surrounding allowing children to use invented spelling in their writing. Research indicates that, provided there is spelling instruction taking place, allowing invented spelling supports growth in the areas of phonemic awareness, phonics, and general spelling skills.

Roles of Phonological Awareness, Phonics, and Word Recognition Skills in Literacy Development

It is imperative that educators understand the five basic components of reading education. If there is any deficit in any one of these following components, a child is likely to experience reading difficulty:

- Phonemic Awareness
- Phonics
- Fluency
- Vocabulary
- Comprehension

Phonemic Awareness

A phoneme is the smallest unit of sound in a given language and is one aspect under the umbrella of skills associated with phonological awareness. A child demonstrates phonemic awareness when identifying rhymes, recognizing alliterations, and isolating specific sounds inside a word or a set of words. Children who demonstrate basic phonemic awareness will eventually also be able to independently and appropriately blend together a variety of phonemes.

Some classroom strategies to strengthen phonemic awareness may include:

- Introduction to nursery rhymes and word play
- Speech discrimination techniques to train the ear to hear more accurately
- Repeated instruction connecting sounds to letters and blending sounds
- Use of visual images coupled with corresponding sounds and words
- Teaching speech sounds through direct instruction
- Comparing known to unfamiliar words
- Practicing pronunciation of newly introduced letters, letter combinations, and words
- Practicing word decoding
- Differentiating similar sounding words

Phonological and Phonemic Awareness Instruction

Age-appropriate and developmentally appropriate instruction for phonological and phonemic awareness is key to helping children strengthen their reading and writing skills. Phonological and phonemic awareness, or PPA, instruction works to enhance correct speech, improve understanding and application of accurate letter-to-sound correspondence, and strengthen spelling skills. Since skill-building involving phonemes is not a natural process but needs to be taught, PPA instruction is especially important for children who have limited access and exposure to reading materials and who lack familial encouragement to read. Strategies that educators can implement include leading word and sound games, focusing on phoneme skill-building activities, and ensuring all activities focus on the fun, playful nature of words and sounds instead of rote memorization and drilling techniques.

Phonics

Phonics is the ability to apply letter-sound relationships and letter patterns in order to accurately pronounce written words. Children with strong phonics skills are able to recognize familiar written words with relative ease and quickly decipher or "decode" unfamiliar words. As one of the foundational skills for reading readiness, phonics essentially enables young readers to translate printed words into recognizable speech. If children lack proficiency in phonics, their ability to read fluently and to increase vocabulary will be limited, which consequently leads to reading comprehension difficulties.

Emergent readers benefit from explicit word decoding instruction that focuses on letter-sound relationships. This includes practicing sounding out words and identifying exceptions to the letter-sound relationships. A multi-sensory approach to word decoding instruction has also been found to be beneficial. By addressing a wide variety of learning styles and providing visual and hands-on instruction, educators help to bridge the gap between guided word decoding and it as an automatic process.

Role of Fluency in Supporting Comprehension

Fluency - rate, accuracy, prosody (expression)

When children are able to read fluently, they read with accuracy, a steady and consistent speed, and an appropriate expression. A fluent reader can seamlessly connect word recognition to comprehension, whether reading silently or aloud. In other words, reading fluency is an automatic recognition and accurate interpretation of text. Without the ability to read fluently, a child's reading comprehension will be limited. Each time a child has to interrupt his or her reading to decode an unfamiliar word, comprehension is impaired.

There are a number of factors that contribute to the success of reading fluency. It is important that students have many opportunities to read. Access to a variety of reading genres at appropriate reading levels and effective reading fluency instruction also play important roles in how successful children will become as fluent readers. The key is to have children repeat the same passage several times in order to become familiar with the words in the text and increase their overall speed and accuracy. Poems are an effective choice when teaching fluency, since they are usually concise and offer rhyming words in an entertaining, rhythmic pattern. Some other instructional strategies to consider include:

- Modeling reading fluency with expression
- Tape-assisted reading
- Echo reading
- Partner reading
- Small group and choral reading

Comprehension

Comprehension is defined as the level of understanding of content that a child demonstrates during and after the reading of a given text. Comprehension begins well before a child is able to read. Adults and educators can foster comprehension by reading aloud to children and helping them respond to the content and relate it to their prior knowledge. Throughout the reading process, the child asks and answers relevant questions confirming her or his comprehension and is able to successfully summarize the text upon completion.

Since reading comprehension encompasses several cognitive processes, including the awareness and understanding of phonemes, phonics, and the ability to construct meaning from text, educators should employ reading comprehension strategies prior to, during, and after reading. Reading comprehension is a lifelong process. As the genres of written text change and written language becomes more complex, it is essential that educators continually reinforce reading comprehension strategies throughout a student's educational career.

Some instructional strategies to consider are:

- Pre-teaching new vocabulary
- Monitoring for understanding
- Answering and generating questions
- Summarizing

The Writing Process and Using Tools and Resources Materials

Producing Clear and Coherent Writing Using the Stages of the Writing Process

Writing Skills Development

Children who receive regular and consistent encouragement to write and whose environment is rich with writing materials and resources will be more apt to strengthen their writing proficiency. Research suggests that at least an hour a day of writing practice, including skilled instruction, is necessary. Writing projects should be chosen that also involve the subjects of science, social studies, reading, or mathematics to give students well-rounded views of the purposes for writing. Piece by piece, students practice writing skills in all subjects, and collectively it should add up to more than an hour a day.

POWER Strategy for Teaching the Writing Process

The **POWER strategy** helps all students to take ownership of the writing process by prompting them to consciously focus on what they are writing.

The POWER strategy is an acronym for the following:

- Prewriting or Planning
- Organizing
- Writing a first draft
- Evaluating the writing
- Revising and rewriting

Prewriting and Planning

During the Prewriting and Planning phase, students learn to consider their audience and purpose for the writing project. Then they compile information they wish to include in the piece of writing from their background knowledge and/or new sources.

Organizing

Next, students decide on the organizational structure of their writing project. There are many types of organizational structures, but the common ones are: story/narrative, informative, opinion, persuasive, compare and contrast, explanatory, and problem/solution formats. Often graphic organizers are an important part of helping students complete this step of the writing process.

Writing

In this step, students write a complete first draft of their project. Educators may begin by using modeled writing to teach this step in the process. It may be helpful for beginning writers to work in small groups or pairs. Verbalizing their thoughts before writing them is also a helpful technique.

Evaluating

In this stage, students reread their writing and note the segments that are particularly strong or need improvement. Then they participate in peer editing. They ask each other questions about the piece. The peers learn to provide feedback and constructive criticism to help the student improve. Scoring rubrics are a helpful tool in this phase to guide students as they edit each other's work.

Revising and Rewriting

Finally, the student incorporates any changes she or he wishes to make based on the evaluating process. Then students rewrite the piece into a final draft and publish it however it best fits the audience and purpose of the writing.

6+1 Traits Strategy for Teaching Writing

6+1 Traits is a model for teaching writing that uses a common language to explain the standards for what good writing looks like. Students learn to evaluate whether these expectations have been met in their own writing and then edit, revise, and rewrite accordingly. The 6+1 Traits are the characteristics that make writing readable and effective no matter what genre of writing is being used. The 6+1 Traits are as follows:

- Ideas
- Organization
- Voice
- Word choice
- Sentence fluency
- Conventions
- Presentation

The Ideas Trait

This trait is the content of the writing. This is where students learn to select an important topic for their writing. They are taught to narrow down and focus their idea. Then they learn to develop and elaborate on the specific idea. Finally, they investigate and discover the information and details that best convey the idea to others.

The Organization Trait

This trait teaches students how to build the framework for their writing. They choose an organizational strategy or purpose for the writing and build the details upon that structure. There are many purposes for writing, and they all have different frameworks. However, there are commonalities that students can learn to effectively organize their writing so it makes sense to the reader. Students learn to invite the reader into their work with an effective introduction. They are taught how to create thoughtful transitions between ideas and key points in their writing and how to create logical and purposeful sequencing of ideas. Finally, students are taught how to create a powerful conclusion to their piece that summarizes the information but leaves the reader with something to think about. Many students are inclined to jump into their writing without a clear direction for where it is going. The organization trait teaches them to plan and purpose their writing toward excellence.

The Voice Trait

This is the trait that gives the writing a sense of individuality and connection to the author. It shows that the writing is meaningful and that the author cares about it. It is what makes the writing uniquely the author's own. It is how the reader begins to know the author and what she or he "sounds like." Students learn to recognize "voice" in some writing samples and find their own "voice" to apply to their work. Students are taught to speak on an emotional level directly to their readers. Students experiment with matching their style to the audience and the purpose of the writing. Students are taught to enjoy taking risks and putting their personal touch into their work.

The Word Choice Trait

This trait gives writing a sense of functional communication through precise language that is rich and enlightening. If the work is narrative, the words create images in the mind's eye; if the work is descriptive, the words clarify and expand thoughts and ideas. If the work is persuasive, the words give new perspective and invite thought. Students learn not only to choose exceptional vocabulary, but also to hone their skills for using ordinary words well. Students are taught to describe things using striking language. They learn to use exact language that is accurate, concise, precise, and lively.

The Sentence Fluency Trait

When sentences are built to fit together and move with one another to create writing that is easy to read aloud, the author has written with fluency. Students learn to eliminate awkward word patterns that otherwise would encumber the reader. Sentences and paragraphs start and stop in precisely the right places so that the writing moves well. Students are taught to establish a flow, develop a rhythm, and give cadence to their work. They edit their sentences to vary the structure and length. Educators can teach fluency through reading aloud beautifully written examples and contrasting them with less fluent work.

The Conventions Trait

Here the focus changes from creation of the piece to preparation for the reader. Instead of revision that the first five traits teach, this trait teaches editing skills. The students learn to make their writing clear and understandable through the use of proper grammar, spelling, capitalization, and punctuation. Students are taught the differences between revision and editing. They learn basic editing marks and symbols. Teachers can assist students to learn conventions through guided editing and regular practice. Expectations for correctness need to be kept developmentally appropriate. If immediate correctness is expected, students may shy away from experimenting and taking risks.

The Presentation Trait

This trait focuses on the final appearance of the work. Presentation is not a concern during the process of the other six traits, nor must perfect presentation be expected for every work a student does. Students are taught to make their work inviting and accessible to the reader of the end product. They learn to show they care about their writing when it is neat and readable. Students are taught about uniform spacing, legible handwriting, appropriate use of fonts and sizes, and how to use bullets, numbers, headings, charts, graphs, and pictures to help make the work visually appealing. Students are taught about the publishing process and are given opportunities to showcase their finished products.

Purposeful Writing

Purposeful writing practices have a significant effect on writing development. **Purposeful writing** refers to intentional writing practices for the purpose of communicating. Through learning to write well, students can begin to use writing as a method of thinking through issues and solving problems. They become more adept with questioning and investigation. Students learn to accurately convey and critique information. They can more readily express real or imagined experiences to others. Through the varied writing purposes, students learn to focus on what the audience understands, while at other times, they focus on the topic and what information they are trying to impart. Other situations call for focus on their own thinking and feelings. Writing as a whole becomes more effective and accessible as students glean skills for writing with purpose. Some of the writing purposes are as follows:

- Letter writing
- Poetry and Songs
- Creative and Narrative writing
- Informative writing
- Opinion writing
- Persuasive writing
- Compare and Contrast writing
- Explanatory/Expository writing
- Problem and Solution writing

Using Resource Materials and Digital Tools

Resource Materials and Digital Tools

Teachers are learning to adapt their writing instruction to integrate today's technology standards and to enhance engagement in the writing process. The key is to still build a strong foundation of the fundamentals of writing while using current technology. Gone are the days when writing relied solely on handwritten pieces and when the tools of the trade were pencils, paper, hardback dictionaries, and encyclopedias. Online resources are now the backbone of the writing experience. It is now possible to integrate photo, video, and other interactive components into a completed project to provide a well-rounded engagement with media. In order to have an education conducive to college and career readiness and success, students need online research and digital media writing skills.

There are many compelling reasons to teach students to be digitally aware and prudent users of technology when it comes to their writing. With current digital technology, the writing process has become a much more collaborative experience. In higher education and in career settings, collaborative skills are essential. Publishing and presenting are now simplified such that completed work is often read by a wide variety of audiences. Writing can be instantly shared with parents, peers, educators, and the general public, including experts in the field. Students are more apt to take an interest in the writing process when they know that others are reading their writing. Feedback is also simplified because so many platforms allow comments from readers. Teachers can be interactive with the students throughout the process, allowing formative assessment and integration of personalized instruction. Technology is simply a new vehicle for human connection and interactivity.

A student may be exposed to a plethora of technology, but this does not mean that she or he necessarily knows how to use it for learning. The teacher is still responsible for guiding, monitoring, and scaffolding the students toward learning objectives. It is critical that educators teach students how to locate credible information and to reliably cite their sources using bibliographies. Platforms and apps for online learning are varied and plentiful. Here are some ideas for how to use technology for writing instruction in the classroom:

- Use a projector with a tablet to display notes and classwork for the group to see. This increases instructional time because notes are already available rather than having to be written in real-time. This also provides the ability to save, email, and post classwork and notes for students and parents to access on their own time. A student can work at his or her own pace and still keep up with instruction. Student screens can be displayed for peer-led teaching and sharing of class work.

- More technology in class means less paperwork. Digital drop-boxes can be used for students to turn in assignments. Teachers can save paper, keep track of student revisions of work, and give feedback electronically.

- Digital media can be used to differentiate instruction for multiple learning styles and multiple skill levels. Instead of using standardized textbook learning for everyone, teachers can create and collect resources for individualizing course content.

- Inquiry- and problem-based learning is easier with increased collaborative capabilities provided by digital tools.

- Digital textbooks and e-readers can replace hardback versions of text that are prone to damage and loss. Students can instantly access definitions for new words, as well as annotate and highlight useful information without ruining a hardbound book.

- Library databases can be used to locate reliable research information and resources. There are digital tools for tracking citation information, allowing annotations for internet content, and for storing internet content.

- Mobile devices may be used in the classroom to encourage reading and writing when students use them to text, post, blog, and tweet.

- PowerPoint and other presentation software can be used to model writing for students and to provide a platform for presenting their work.

- Students can create a classroom blog, review various blog sites, and use blogs as they would diaries or journals. They can even write from the perspective of the character in a book or a famous historical person.

- Web quests can be used to help guide students on research projects. They can get relevant information on specific topics and decide what pieces to include in their writing.

- Students can write about technology as a topic. They can "teach" someone how to use various forms of technology, specific learning platforms, or apps.

- Students can create webpages, make a class webpage, and then use it to help with home-school communication.

- Online feedback and grading systems can be used. There are many to choose from. This may allow students to see the grading rubric and ask questions or receive suggestions from the teacher.

- Students and teachers can use email to exchange ideas with other schools or experts on certain topics that are being studied in the classroom.

- Game show-style reviews can be created for units of study to use on computers or on an overhead projector.

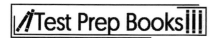

- A wiki website can be created that allows students to collaborate, expand on each other's work, and do peer editing and revision.

- Publishing tools can be used to publish student work on the web or in class newspapers or social media sites.

Obj 4

Speaking, Listening, and Presenting

A **Fostering Students' Participation in Collaborative Conversations with Diverse Partners**

Effective and Responsible Practices in Communication with Children

The foundation of a child's academic, social, and emotional success in any classroom lies directly in the educator's ability to use effective communicative interactions. **DAP**, or **Developmentally Appropriate Practice**, was designed by researchers who took into consideration what is known about how children develop, as well as what is known about effective early education instruction. Classrooms with effective communication techniques will generally see enthusiastic, engaged children. DAP focuses on these 10 basic principles that aim to help educators build an effective foundation of communication:

- Acknowledgement
- Encouragement
- Immediate and beneficial feedback
- Modeling
- Demonstrating
- Challenging
- Questioning
- Providing effective assistance
- Providing valuable information
- Giving appropriate directions

Acknowledgement

Students are not simply little subjects for educators to enlighten. They are intellectual, social, and emotional beings worthy of recognition and appreciation. Acknowledgement of students begins with understanding where they are coming from and the experiences they bring with them. When a teacher considers prior knowledge before beginning instruction, they are being considerate of the student's time and intellect. They are acknowledging that the student already has the capacity for learning and brings valid experiences and aptitudes that are useful for assimilating new information. The teacher doesn't waste time re-teaching what students have already mastered. Review is necessary, of course, but not to the extent that there is a risk of losing student engagement and interest.

Students come to learn at various stages of intellectual development. In the early stages, there is a duplicity of black-and-white thinking. Multiplicity should come next, where there is some understanding of opinion and perspective. Finally, learning to value evidence and validity helps students understand topics at various levels of complexity. When teachers take this into account, they are acknowledging the students' individuality and honoring their learning needs.

Significant differences exist in the way teaching and learning is conceptualized for various cultures. Values for particular types of learning, the beliefs about best practices, and the role of the teacher/student relationship may be strikingly different from culture to culture. The value of learning itself is a bridge for multicultural connection. When teachers recognize and celebrate cultural differences, they are acknowledging the students at the level of their individual identity.

The social trends and expectations of students and teachers grow and change over generations. The topics and ways that students are learning and teachers are teaching are likely quite different from what they were even a decade ago. Educators cannot expect students to learn the same way from generation to generation. Awareness of generational differences acknowledges the student and his or her perception of the world.

Encouragement

Ideally, students come into classrooms hopeful and willing to take risks. With this in mind, teachers have to develop the kind of classroom that fosters participation and motivation. Here are some ways that teachers can encourage classroom participation:

- Students should be praised. This helps them know they are at the center of learning. They need to feel cared for and valued. Positive behavior should be rewarded and progress acknowledged.

- Students should be allowed to have some control in their lives. Choices should be offered and mistakes forgiven.

- Excellence should be expected from students. High but realistic expectations should be held for them. The effort they put forth should be respected. The learning process, over the end product, should be valued.

- Children should be allowed to be children. There should be much activity and collaboration.

- The fun of learning should be shown to students. They should be encouraged by taking part in the planning of field trips, guest speakers, and other extraordinary activities.

- Students should be made aware of how learning relates to their lives. Teachers should teach to the interests of the students and understand where they are coming from.

- Clear and simple lessons should be presented at a pace they can all follow. Teachers should communicate clearly and enunciate understandably so students do not have to struggle to follow along. Teachers should regularly check on the students' level of understanding.

- A pleasant and comfortable environment free from obvious distractions should be created.

Immediate and Beneficial Feedback

Students need to know what they are doing well and what needs improvement. There should be no mystery about the learning targets. They need a positive self-image fostered by repeated success. Feedback should be positive and specific. Giving clear and effective feedback communicates to the student that her or his work is worthwhile, and that someone cares enough to review and consider it.

Informal feedback is part of formative assessment and should let students know where they are in the learning process and what they should do next. They should be able to formulate a plan for improvement and a vision of the next success they can achieve. Informal feedback is often oral and interactive.

Formal feedback is driven by objectives and rubrics that students should be given prior to a learning task. This gives them a clear goal for the activity and outlines expectations. Formal feedback should be presented in writing or another tangible format. Formal feedback is often summative in nature and may or may not be tied to grades and final assessments.

Feedback strategies are variable. Individualized adjustments can be made regarding timing, amount, mode, and audience. The timing may be immediate or delayed and given frequently or infrequently. Feedback might describe progress on many points or just a few, and it may go into great detail or be generalized. It may be oral, written, or demonstrative. It might be addressed to the individual, a small group, or the entire class. Feedback content is also infinitely variable. Feedback might focus on the work itself, the process, or the student's self-regulation but never on the student personally. Feedback comparisons might be criterion-, norm-, or self-referenced. It may function as a description of the work or an evaluation of the work but should not be judgmental. It can be both positive and negative, but any negative comments should be accompanied by suggestions for improvement. Feedback should be understandable to the student and developmentally appropriate. In some cases, feedback can be too specific so that it becomes difficult for a student to apply it to other situations. It can also be overly general, which does not give the student enough information to help with correction. Finally, feedback should communicate respect, activate motivation, and inspire thought.

Modeling, Explaining, and Demonstrating

In order to learn to read and write well, all children need effective modeling and demonstration. Educators often are content to assign reading and writing tasks and ask students to answer questions about the task in lieu of quality direct interactive instruction.

Modeling is when teachers engage in the activity of reading or writing and the children observe and imitate the procedures and strategies. Children can pick up many skills by simply watching and attempting to copy adult behaviors. Reading aloud is one of the most powerful strategies for teaching in the classroom. When being read to, students are given a model for how reading should sound and how stories are constructed. Talking about the reading selection during and after reading models an appropriate response to text. It also fosters comprehension strategies that children need in order to become effective readers. Writing down main points of the reading selection and taking notes models a function of writing. Designating a time each day for reading aloud highlights the importance of reading. High-quality literature with rich text and content should be chosen to read in the classroom. This models the evaluation of literature and the selection of quality reading material. Response groups should be formed so children have a model for collaboratively comprehending text. Modeling is an essential component of any classroom. However, modeling is not sufficient to give children enough information about how to accomplish the tasks that readers and writers actually need to be proficient.

Explanation is also a key component of classroom instruction. Adults in classrooms spend much time explaining reading and writing methods to students. Unfortunately, students often miss key messages because their attention span isn't long enough to follow wordy explanations. Explanations often involve specialized vocabulary that students may not be able to use to comprehend the instruction. Giving excellent explanations is an essential skill for teachers. Seeing teachers and other children model reading and writing and being told how to read and write is still not sufficient for teaching literacy to many struggling learners. This is where *demonstration* comes into play.

Demonstration is when a teacher not only models and explains how to do a task but also engages in thinking through the task with the students. Effective teachers narrate their thinking processes when modeling a strategy. An effective demonstration includes opportunities for the student to try the strategy with immediate feedback from the teacher. Demonstration is teaching and learning in real-time. Effective demonstration occurs in four steps: preparation, presentation, application, and evaluation.

During **preparation,** a teacher puts the students at ease with the impending learning task. He or she assesses students for prior knowledge of the information. Explaining the importance of the learning task is essential. This step may include an attention-getter or motivational strategy. Finally, preparation includes getting the students ready to observe, ensuring they can see and hear well and have appropriate note-taking supplies.

During **presentation,** the teacher tells, shows, illustrates, explains, questions, and models the task. By carefully and patiently narrating the process step-by-step, stressing key points and learning goals, the teacher presents all information and models all skills needed.

Application is guided practice. It includes students attempting the task and then having the teacher give them immediate feedback. Repetition is often used to solidify the skills. The teacher's job is to narrate the steps taken, to ask questions for a measure of understanding, and to prevent errors.

Evaluation is following up with the learning that occurred during the demonstration. The teacher reviews the objectives and evaluates whether they were covered effectively. Checking for readiness and making sure the students know how to get help if they need it are parts of this step.

Challenging and Questioning

Educators are constantly asking questions. This is because questioning serves a wide range of functions in the classroom. Teachers ask questions to involve and engage students in a lesson. Questions increase interest and motivation. A teacher asks questions to assess prior knowledge and readiness for learning. Questioning can help check for completion of learning tasks. It is key for developing critical thinking skills. Questions might be asked to review or assess mastery of learning goals. Asking questions stimulates independent and collaborative learning and invites insight and forethought.

When questioning, it is important to consider how many questions to ask. During the lesson, it is vital to know when the questions are the most appropriate. Will the questions lend meaning to the instruction? Will the questions cause students to focus on all the information presented or only on the parts that help them answer the question? Will the questions lead away from the topic? It is also important to consider how much wait-time to give students to answer the question before the teacher elaborates or asks a new question. Typically, students need to be afforded at least three seconds to formulate an answer to a question. The way a teacher responds to answers is just as important as the questions themselves. The teacher can affirm a correct response, probe the student for more information, or redirect him if the answer is wrong or misinterpreted.

It can be difficult for teachers to give lessons at the appropriate level of difficulty in a classroom of students who are at varying levels of academic readiness. How does a teacher reach a student who is struggling and one who is above grade level in the same lesson? Knowing the appropriate challenge level is essential for learning in the classroom. If a lesson is too challenging, some students will give up. Conversely, if a lesson is not challenging enough, some students will get bored. There are many strategies that teachers can use to differentiate lessons for varying challenge levels including:

- Allowing choices
- Integrating technology

- Allowing collaboration
- Accommodating pace
- Assessing prior knowledge
- Encouraging goal setting
- Providing creative teaching
- Allowing independent learning
- Allowing students to explore their interests
- Using self-assessment

Providing Effective Assistance and Valuable Information

Students need assistance and guidance in a classroom; however, knowing how much help to offer is always a balancing act. If teachers give too much assistance, they end up doing the work for students, who then do not learn. If teachers do not offer enough assistance, students become lost, overwhelmed, and do not learn. What does the right amount of help look like for each student? Giving effective assistance to students is a foundational teaching strategy. The goal is to help students become as self-motivated and autonomous as possible.

Autonomy in the classroom begins with establishing clear and consistent classroom procedures. Students should be taught how the classroom runs and how to manage themselves. If a student knows what to do to solve simple problems such as sharpening pencils, teachers do not need to waste valuable teaching time with disruptions. Educators can continue to build autonomy by allowing freedom of choice and giving students some power.

Related to autonomy is the concept of self-motivation. Teachers can help students become self-motivated learners by making learning individualized and accessible to all. Instruction should be differentiated for levels of readiness, for personal interests and aptitudes, and for varied learning styles and multiple intelligences. Offering students choices of learning activities and methods of assessment helps individualize education. Educators should have knowledge of the Universal Design for Learning, which promotes differentiation through considering the following three premises:

1. Content should be presented in multiple ways: visual, oral, kinesthetic, etc.

2. Students should be able to show their learning in multiple ways: writing, speaking, drawing, acting, etc.

3. Engaging students should occur in multiple formats: videos, technology, group work, etc.

Teachers can also foster self-motivation by holding high expectations of students and giving them a sense of competence. When adults expect excellence from students, the students often rise to the occasion. Care must be taken that expectations are developmentally appropriate and attainable, but they should always stretch students to the top of their capabilities. Giving students a sense of competence means learning effective praise techniques. It is best to praise effort (something students can control) over intelligence (something out of their control). Students will gain a sense that they learn through their own hard work.

Giving Appropriate Directions

One of the biggest obstacles to learning is when students do not understand or cannot remember the directions they are given. Present directions in auditory and visual formats and assess for understanding

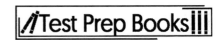

by having students retell them to each other or to the teacher. Some tips for teachers to give good directions include:

- Providing directions in story form. Students can often remember stories, since they are typically more interesting and therefore, better than other forms of communication for multi-step directions.

- Starting with *"when I say go,"* which gets them to listen for all the directions before moving, then telling students what they're *"going to"* do for each step of the process. Students create pictures of themselves doing the steps in their mind's eye and assume they can do it without help.

- Being silly! Throwing in some funny character voices, different facial expressions, or random silly instructions for things they should do between steps of the real task adds interest and increases the desire of students to listen more closely.

- Asking students to speak up if they don't understand all the steps. Teachers should inform students that they want to know of any questions before the students begin the task, rather than find out in the middle of the activity that the students didn't hear or understand all the instructions at the beginning. This makes students responsible for knowing what to do.

- Begin with requiring students to only do a few things at a time. However, as they get used to working with provided instructions, they will be able to take on much more lengthy activities and remember more directions.

The Abecedarian Approach

The **Abecedarian Approach** is primarily concerned with a child's behavioral and intellectual successes from birth to adulthood. There are four main components of the Abecedarian Approach: 1) learning games; 2) conversational reading; 3) language priority; and 4) enriched caregiving. Two areas explicitly involve literacy development: conversational reading and language priority. They both involve playful, responsive approaches to rich language instruction.

The Abecedarian Approach to Conversational Reading

The Abecedarian Approach to conversational reading has been demonstrated to have significant benefits in the areas of reading fluency and comprehension. **Conversational reading** involves a conversational-style of reading instruction in which the educator plays an active role by partnering in shared reading activities. Conversational reading gets its name from being a back-and-forth reading conversation. During the reading process, educators prompt the children to "see, show, and say" what they are reading. This is referred to as the **3S Strategy**. Children may be encouraged to identify the words they know on a given page, look for rhyming words, or draw pictures that correspond to the reading. Educators take an active role in the reading process by running their fingers along the words, asking questions about the reading, prompting conversations, and strengthening comprehension, as well as pointing out interesting ideas about the reading to encourage a dialogue.

The Abecedarian Approach to Language Priority

The Abecedarian Approach uses language priority to focus on rich language stimulation. By emphasizing language throughout the day, the language priority strategy creates endless occasions for meaningful conversations. Educators work to extend conversations from a variety of different angles, promoting higher cognitive thinking and engagement. Educators will also use the **3N Approach** by *noticing* the student's current reading level, *nudging* or encouraging the student to go one step beyond this level, and *narrating* the student's activities.

Developing Skills Necessary for Speaking, Listening, and Presenting

<u>Instructing Children to Enhance Their English Language Literacy Development</u>
Speaking, listening, reading, and writing are all intimately connected as essential elements of literacy development. As social beings, children begin to recognize that with effective literacy skills, their social, emotional, and physical needs can be met, and their curiosity can be satisfied. They also begin to learn that they can develop communication skills to answer questions that others pose. This can be an exciting and self-affirming realization for young children. In order to encourage literacy development, educators should ensure that all activities in the classroom involve meaningful language and literacy experiences. Each child learns at a unique pace and in a unique way. With this sensitivity in place, classroom activities should be as differentiated as possible.

Developing Listening Skills
Actively teaching good listening skills is essential in the classroom. Behaviors should not be expected that have not been taught. Students need to learn the difference between what an excellent listener does and what poor listening behaviors are. Good listening skills that should be taught include:

- Focusing on the speaker, looking them in the eye, and choosing not to interrupt.

- Looking at the speaker to indicate that the student is ready to hear what the speaker has to say and to pick up body language cues and facial expressions.

- Giving nonverbal signals that the student is listening (e.g., nods, smiles).

- Giving verbal signals that indicate interest in the speaker (e.g., repeating back what is heard to indicate understanding).

- Subtly matching the energy and emotional level of the speaker to indicate understanding.

- Choosing not to make side comments or to focus on other things occurring in the room.

Some strategies for teaching these skills in the classroom include, but are not limited to:

- Providing pre-listening activities, such as teaching new vocabulary words, outlining what students will be hearing, distributing study guides or pre-listening questions, and teaching students the objectives of the listening activity beforehand.

- Avoiding repeating directions multiple times. Teachers are often inclined to repeat steps and directions several times before allowing students to begin working. This is counterproductive because it teaches students that they do not have to listen the first time. Students should be taught that the teacher will say things only once and they are expected to listen, but they may ask for clarification. Students should also be taught to seek other sources of finding the instructions.

- Modeling good listening and speaking skills in the classroom because students learn by watching and emulating others. Teachers need to consistently model choosing not to interrupt and focusing their full attention on the speaker. They also need to model speaking clearly with proper grammar and foster an environment in the classroom of good peer modeling as well.

- Teaching students to take notes, write down questions, and report on or paraphrase what they have heard the speaker say. Students should be given active listening activities to complete during and after the listening task.

- Giving students multiple methods to contribute to conversations. Some students are not inclined to speak in front of others. In such cases, it may be helpful to allow them to give other signals of understanding such as "thumbs up," "thumbs sideways," "thumbs down," or sign language for "yes" and "no" answers.

- Encouraging the use of technology in the classroom to allow students to blog, tweet, or use quiz show-style games to indicate understanding of what they heard.

Developing Speaking Skills

Similar to listening skills, students also need to be taught speaking and presenting skills. Students need to learn such skills as:

- How to introduce themselves effectively
- How to make appropriate eye contact with listeners
- How to begin a conversation and keep it going
- How to interact with various types of audiences
- How to answer questions in an interview
- How to stand and deliver a speech with confidence
- How to ask for and answer questions during a presentation

The following strategies can help teach conversational and speaking skills:

- Students can be taught to use "conversation enhancers" when working with others. Some examples are: "Really?" "Wow!" "That's interesting" "Tell me more about …" "Can you say that in another way?" "Tell me what you are thinking …" and "Can you add to my idea?"

- Good conversational skills can be modeled as frequently as possible in one- to two-minute one-on-one dialogues with students. This is especially important for the introverted and shy students.

- A safe speaking environment can be fostered by teaching good manners to listeners, and by challenging students who are disrespectful listeners to act in a different way.

- Students should be asked open-ended questions that have no right or wrong answer and that invite lengthy answers instead of just "yes" or "no" responses.

- "I don't know" should not be accepted for an answer. Students should be taught that their thinking is valued rather than whether they *know* something.

- Students should be taught how to take turns in the classroom fairly and to not interrupt one another.

- Students should be instructed not to read their presentations word for word, and to speak toward the audience instead of toward the project or PowerPoint slide.

- Videos of good and poor presentations can be shown as models for students to critique.

- Students should be taught to build in humor and good non-verbal communication into their presentations.

- Students should be shown how to curb involuntary habits such as repeating themselves or saying "um" or "like" too much.

Task, Purpose, and Audience

Teaching students to present and speak to an audience involves teaching them how to structure a presentation so that it is appropriate for the task, purpose, and audience. **Task** is what the students are required to do with their presentation. **Purpose** is the reason for the presentation and how it will achieve the outcome of the task. **Audience** is whom the presentation is for, the population it is trying to reach, and why it is specifically for that group. Some presentation tips that teachers should impart to students are as follows:

- During student preparation, students should ask themselves: "Why am I giving this presentation?" "What do I want people to take away from the presentation?" and "How much does my audience already know about the topic?"

- Presentations should be structured with an effective introduction, covering each item on their agenda succinctly, and wrapping up with a memorable conclusion.

- Presentations should be given with clarity and impact. The audience won't remember everything a student presents, so he or she needs to highlight the key points clearly and concisely and then expand and illustrate as needed.

- Visual aids should be used to enhance the presentation without causing distractions—such as useless images and animated transitions between slides—from the information.

- Presentations should be given without memorization. Students should be charged with becoming more familiar with their content and to "test drive" the presentation beforehand.

- Appropriate pauses should be used during presentations to help the audience better absorb the information.

- Various techniques can be employed if there is a "stumbling point" or a piece of information is forgotten during the presentation.

Obj 5 English-Language Grammar and Vocabulary Development

A Conventions of Standard English Grammar, Punctuation, and Spelling

Conventions of Standard English

Educators must first be masters of the English language in order to teach it. Teachers serve several key roles in the classroom that all require that they know the conventions of grammar, punctuation, and spelling. Teachers are communicators. They must know how to structure their own language for clarity.

They must also be able to interpret what the students are saying to accurately either affirm or revise it for correctness. Teachers are educators of language. They are the agents of change from poor-quality conventions to mastery of the concepts. Teachers are responsible for differentiating instruction so that students at all levels and aptitudes can succeed with language learning. Teachers need to be able to isolate gaps in skill sets and decide which skills need intervention in the classroom. Teachers are evaluators. They are responsible for making key decisions about a student's educational trajectory based on their assessment of the student's capabilities. Teachers also have great impact on how students view themselves as learners. Teachers are models. They must be superb examples of educated individuals. Just like with any other subject, people need a strong grasp of the basics of language. They will not be able to learn these things unless the teachers themselves have mastered it. Teachers foster socialization; socialization to cultural norms and to the everyday practices of the community in which they live is of utmost importance to students' lives. These processes begin at home but continue early in a child's life at school. Teachers play a key role in guiding and scaffolding students' socialization skills. If teachers are to excel in this role, they need to be adept with the use of the English language.

Teachers need to have mastery of the conventions of English. The following sections, though not exhaustive, provide information about parts of speech, spelling and punctuation conventions, and other grammatic rules that should be followed.

Nouns
A **noun** is a person, place, thing, or idea. All nouns fit into one of two types, common or proper.

A **common noun** is a word that identifies any of a class of people, places, or things. Examples include numbers, objects, animals, feelings, concepts, qualities, and actions. *A, an,* or *the* usually precedes the common noun. These parts of speech are called *articles*. Here are some examples of sentences using nouns preceded by articles.

> *A* building is under construction.
> *The* girl would like to move to *the* city.

A **proper noun** (also called a **proper name**) is used for the specific name of an individual person, place, or organization. The first letter in a proper noun is capitalized. "My name is *Mary.*" "I work for *Walmart.*"

Nouns sometimes serve as **adjectives** (which themselves describe nouns), such as "hockey player" and "state government."

Pronouns
A word used in place of a noun is known as a **pronoun**. Pronouns are words like *I, mine, hers,* and *us.*

Pronouns can be split into different classifications (as shown below) which make them easier to learn; however, it's not important to memorize the classifications.

- **Personal pronouns:** refer to people

- **First person pronouns:** we, I, our, mine

- **Second person pronouns:** you, yours

- **Third person pronouns:** he, she, they, them, it

- **Possessive pronouns:** demonstrate ownership (mine, his, hers, its, ours, theirs, yours)

- **Interrogative pronouns:** ask questions (what, which, who, whom, whose)

- **Relative pronouns:** include the five interrogative pronouns and others that are relative (whoever, whomever, that, when, where)

- **Demonstrative pronouns:** replace something specific (this, that, those, these)

- **Reciprocal pronouns:** indicate something was done or given in return (each other, one another)

- **Indefinite pronouns:** have a nonspecific status (anybody, whoever, someone, everybody, somebody)

Indefinite pronouns such as *anybody, whoever, someone, everybody*, and *somebody* command a singular verb form, but others such as *all, none,* and *some* could require a singular or plural verb form.

Antecedents

An **antecedent** is the noun to which a pronoun refers; it needs to be written or spoken before the pronoun is used. For many pronouns, antecedents are imperative for clarity. In particular, a lot of the personal, possessive, and demonstrative pronouns need antecedents. Otherwise, it would be unclear who or what someone is referring to when they use a pronoun like *he* or *this*.

Pronoun reference means that the pronoun should refer clearly to one, clear, unmistakable noun (the antecedent).

Pronoun-antecedent agreement refers to the need for the antecedent and the corresponding pronoun to agree in gender, person, and number. Here are some examples:

The *kidneys* (plural antecedent) are part of the urinary system. *They* (plural pronoun) serve several roles.

The kidneys are part of the *urinary system* (singular antecedent). *It* (singular pronoun) is also known as the renal system.

Pronoun Cases

The **subjective pronouns** —*I, you, he/she/it, we, they,* and *who*—are the subjects of the sentence.

Example: *They* have a new house.

The **objective pronouns**—*me, you* (*singular*)*, him/her, us, them,* and *whom*—are used when something is being done for or given to someone; they are objects of the action.

Example: The teacher has an apple for *us*.

The **possessive pronouns**—*mine, my, your, yours, his, hers, its, their, theirs, our,* and *ours*—are used to denote that something (or someone) belongs to someone (or something).

Example: It's *their* chocolate cake.

Even Better Example: It's *my* chocolate cake!

One of the greatest challenges and worst abuses of pronouns concerns *who* and *whom*. Just knowing the following rule can eliminate confusion. *Who* is a subjective-case pronoun used only as a subject or subject complement. *Whom* is only objective-case and, therefore, the object of the verb or preposition.

> *Who* is going to the concert?

> You are going to the concert with *whom*?

Hint: When using *who* or *whom*, think of whether someone would say *he* or *him*. If the answer is *he*, use *who*. If the answer is *him*, use *whom*. This trick is easy to remember because *he* and *who* both end in vowels, and *him* and *whom* both end in the letter *M*.

Many possessive pronouns sound like contractions. For example, many people get *it's* and *its* confused. The word *it's* is the contraction for *it is*. The word *its* without an apostrophe is the possessive form of *it*.

> I love that wooden desk. It's beautiful. (contraction)

> I love that wooden desk. Its glossy finish is beautiful. (possessive)

If you are not sure which version to use, replace *it's/its* with *it is* and see if that sounds correct. If so, use the contraction (*it's*). That trick also works for *who's/whose*, *you're/your*, and *they're/their*.

Adjectives

"The *extraordinary* brain is the *main* organ of the central nervous system." The adjective *extraordinary* describes the brain in a way that causes one to realize it is more exceptional than some of the other organs while the adjective *main* defines the brain's importance in its system.

An **adjective** is a word or phrase that names an attribute that describes or clarifies a noun or pronoun. This helps the reader visualize and understand the characteristics—size, shape, age, color, origin, etc.—of a person, place, or thing that otherwise might not be known. Adjectives breathe life, color, and depth into the subjects they define. Life would be *drab* and *colorless* without adjectives!

Adjectives often precede the nouns they describe.

> *She drove her <u>new</u> car.*

However, adjectives can also come later in the sentence.

> *Her car is <u>new</u>.*

Adjectives using the prefix *a*– can only be used after a verb.

> Correct: The dog was alive until the car ran up on the curb and hit him.

> Incorrect: The alive dog was hit by a car that ran up on the curb.

Other examples of this rule include *awake, ablaze, ajar, alike,* and *asleep.*

Other adjectives used after verbs concern states of health.

> The girl was finally *well* after a long bout of pneumonia.

> The boy was *fine* after the accident.

An adjective phrase is not a bunch of adjectives strung together, but a group of words that describes a noun or pronoun and, thus, functions as an adjective. *Very happy* is an adjective phrase; so are *way too hungry* and *passionate about traveling*.

Possessives

In grammar, **possessive nouns** show ownership, which was seen in previous examples like *mine, yours,* and *theirs*.

Singular nouns are generally made possessive with an apostrophe and an *s* (*'s*).

My *uncle's* new car is silver.

The *dog's* bowl is empty.

James's ties are becoming outdated.

Plural nouns ending in *s* are generally made possessive by just adding an apostrophe (*'*):

The pistachio *nuts'* saltiness is added during roasting. (The saltiness of pistachio nuts is added during roasting.)

The *students'* achievement tests are difficult. (The achievement tests of the students are difficult.)

If the plural noun does not end in an *s* such as *women,* then it is made possessive by adding an *apostrophe s* (*'s*)—*women's*.

Indefinite possessive pronouns such as *nobody* or *someone* become possessive by adding an *apostrophe s— nobody's* or *someone's*.

Verbs

A verb is the part of speech that describes an action, state of being, or occurrence.

A verb forms the main part of a predicate of a sentence. This means that the verb explains what the noun (which will be discussed shortly) is doing. A simple example is *time flies*. The verb *flies* explains what the action of the noun, *time,* is doing. This example is a *main* verb.

Helping (auxiliary) verbs are words like *have, do, be, can, may, should, must,* and *will*. "I *should* go to the store." Helping verbs assist main verbs in expressing tense, ability, possibility, permission, or obligation.

Particles are minor function words like *not, in, out, up,* or *down* that become part of the verb itself. "I might *not*."

Participles are words formed from verbs that are often used to modify a noun, noun phrase, verb, or verb phrase.

The *running* teenager collided with the cyclist.

Participles can also create compound verb forms.

He is *speaking*.

Verbs have five basic forms: the **base** form, the **-s** form, the **-ing** form, the **past** form, and the **past participle** form.

The past forms are either **regular** (*love/loved; hate/hated*) or **irregular** because they don't end by adding the common past tense suffix "-ed" (*go/went; fall/fell; set/set*).

Adverbs

Adverbs have more functions than adjectives because they modify or qualify verbs, adjectives, or other adverbs as well as word groups that express a relation of place, time, circumstance, or cause. Therefore, adverbs answer any of the following questions: *How, when, where, why, in what way, how often, how much, in what condition,* and/or *to what degree. How good looking is he? He is <u>very</u> handsome.*

Here are some examples of adverbs for different situations:

- how: quickly
- when: daily
- where: there
- in what way: easily
- how often: often
- how much: much
- in what condition: badly
- what degree: hardly

As one can see, for some reason, many adverbs end in *-ly.*

Adverbs do things like emphasize (*really, simply,* and *so*), amplify (*heartily, completely,* and *positively*), and tone down (*almost, somewhat,* and *mildly*).

Adverbs also come in phrases.

> The dog ran as <u>though his life depended on it.</u>

Prepositions

Prepositions are connecting words and, while there are only about 150 of them, they are used more often than any other individual groups of words. They describe relationships between other words. They are placed before a noun or pronoun, forming a phrase that modifies another word in the sentence. **Prepositional phrases** begin with a preposition and end with a noun or pronoun, the **object of the preposition.** *A pristine lake is <u>near the store</u> and <u>behind the bank.</u>*

Some commonly used prepositions are *about, after, anti, around, as, at, behind, beside, by, for, from, in, into, of, off, on, to,* and *with.*

Complex prepositions, which also come before a noun or pronoun, consist of two or three words such as *according to, in regards to,* and *because of.*

Interjections

Interjections are words used to express emotion. Examples include *wow, ouch,* and *hooray.* Interjections are often separate from sentences; in those cases, the interjection is directly followed by an exclamation point. In other cases, the interjection is included in a sentence and followed by a comma. The punctuation plays a big role in the intensity of the emotion that the interjection is expressing. Using a comma or semicolon indicates less excitement than using an exclamation mark.

Conjunctions

Conjunctions are vital words that connect words, phrases, thoughts, and ideas. Conjunctions show relationships between components. There are two types:

Coordinating conjunctions are the primary class of conjunctions placed between words, phrases, clauses, and sentences that are of equal grammatical rank; the coordinating conjunctions are *for*, *and*, *nor*, *but*, *or*, *yet*, and *so*. A useful memorization trick is to remember that all the first letters of these conjunctions collectively spell the word fanboys.

> I need to go shopping, *but* I must be careful to leave enough money in the bank.

> She wore a black, red, *and* white shirt.

Subordinating conjunctions are the secondary class of conjunctions. They connect two unequal parts, one **main** (or **independent**) and the other **subordinate** (or **dependent**). I must go to the store *even though* I do not have enough money in the bank.

> *Because* I read the review, I do not want to go to the movie.

Notice that the presence of subordinating conjunctions makes clauses dependent. *I read the review* is an independent clause, but *because* makes the clause dependent. Thus, it needs an independent clause to complete the sentence.

Subject-Verb Agreement

The subject of a sentence and its verb must agree. The cornerstone rule of subject-verb agreement is that subject and verb must agree in number. Whether the subject is singular or plural, the verb must follow suit.

> Incorrect: The houses is new.
> Correct: The houses are new.
> Also Correct: The house is new.

In other words, a singular subject requires a singular verb; a plural subject requires a plural verb. The words or phrases that come between the subject and verb do not alter this rule.

> Incorrect: The houses built of brick is new.
> Correct: The houses built of brick are new.

> Incorrect: The houses with the sturdy porches is new.
> Correct: The houses with the sturdy porches are new.

The subject will always follow the verb when a sentence begins with *here* or *there*. Identify these with care.

> Incorrect: Here *is* the *houses* with sturdy porches.
> Correct: Here *are* the *houses* with sturdy porches.

The subject in the sentences above is not *here*, it is *houses*. Remember, *here* and *there* are never subjects. Be careful that contractions such as *here's* or *there're* do not cause confusion!

Two subjects joined by *and* require a plural verb form, except when the two combine to make one thing:

> Incorrect: Garrett and Jonathan is over there.
> Correct: Garrett and Jonathan are over there.

> Incorrect: Spaghetti and meatballs are a delicious meal!
> Correct: Spaghetti and meatballs is a delicious meal!

In the example above, *spaghetti and meatballs* is a compound noun. However, *Garrett and Jonathan* is not a compound noun.

Two singular subjects joined by *or, either/or,* or *neither/nor* call for a singular verb form.

> Incorrect: Butter or syrup are acceptable.
> Correct: Butter or syrup is acceptable.

Plural subjects joined by *or, either/or*, or *neither/nor* are, indeed, plural.

> The chairs or the boxes are being moved next.

If one subject is singular and the other is plural, the verb should agree with the closest noun.

> Correct: The chair or the boxes are being moved next.
> Correct: The chairs or the box is being moved next.

Some plurals of money, distance, and time call for a singular verb.

> Incorrect: Three dollars *are* enough to buy that.
> Correct: Three dollars *is* enough to buy that.

For words declaring degrees of quantity such as *many of, some of,* or *most of,* let the noun that follows *of* be the guide:

> Incorrect: Many of the books is in the shelf.
> Correct: Many of the books are in the shelf.

> Incorrect: Most of the pie *are* on the table.
> Correct: Most of the pie *is* on the table.

For indefinite pronouns like anybody or everybody, use singular verbs.

> Everybody *is* going to the store.

However, the pronouns *few, many, several, all, some,* and *both* have their own rules and use plural forms.

> Some *are* ready.

Some nouns like *crowd* and *congress* are called *collective nouns* and they require a singular verb form.

> Congress *is* in session.
> The news *is* over.

Books and movie titles, though, including plural nouns such as *Great Expectations*, also require a singular verb. Remember that only the subject affects the verb. While writing tricky subject-verb arrangements, say them aloud. Listen to them. Once the rules have been learned, one's ear will become sensitive to them, making it easier to pick out what's right and what's wrong.

Independent and Dependent Clauses

Independent and **dependent clauses** are strings of words that contain both a subject and a verb. An independent clause *can* stand alone as complete thought, but a dependent clause *cannot*. A dependent clause relies on other words to be a complete sentence.

> Independent clause: The keys are on the counter.
> Dependent clause: If the keys are on the counter

Notice that both clauses have a subject (*keys*) and a verb (*are*). The independent clause expresses a complete thought, but the word *if* at the beginning of the dependent clause makes it *dependent* on other words to be a complete thought.

> Independent clause: If the keys are on the counter, please give them to me.

This example constitutes a complete sentence since it includes at least one verb and one subject and is a complete thought. In this case, the independent clause has two subjects (*keys* & an implied *you*) and two verbs (*are* & *give*).

> Independent clause: I went to the store.
> Dependent clause: Because we are out of milk,
>
> Complete Sentence: Because we are out of milk, I went to the store.
> Complete Sentence: I went to the store because we are out of milk.

A **phrase** is a group of words that does not contain both a subject and a verb.

Active and Passive Voice

Active voice is a sentence structure in which the subject performs the action of the sentence. The verbs of these sentences are called *active verbs*.

> The deer jumped over the fence.

In the example above, the deer is the one jumping. **Passive voice** is a sentence structure in which the object performs the action of the sentence. The verbs of these sentences are called **passive verbs**.

> The fence was jumped by the deer.

In this example, the fence is the subject, but it is not jumping over anything. The deer is still the one performing the action, but it is now the object of the sentence.

Passive voice is helpful when it's unclear who performed an action.

The chair was moved.

While passive voice can add variety to writing, active voice is the generally preferred sentence structure.

Irregular Plurals

Irregular plurals are words that aren't made plural the usual way.

- Most nouns are made plural by adding *–s* (book*s*, television*s*, skyscraper*s*).

- Most nouns ending in *ch, sh, s, x,* or *z* are made plural by adding *–es* (church*es*, marsh*es*).

- Most nouns ending in a vowel + *y* are made plural by adding *–s* (day*s*, toy*s*).

- Most nouns ending in a consonant + *y*, are made plural by the *-y* becoming *-ies* (baby becomes *babies*).

- Most nouns ending in an *o* are made plural by adding *–s* (piano*s*, photo*s*).

- Some nouns ending in an *o*, though, may be made plural by adding *–es* (example: potato*es*, volcano*es*), and, of note, there is no known rhyme or reason for this!

- Most nouns ending in an *f* or *fe* are made plural by the *-f* or *-fe* becoming *-ves*! (example: wolf becomes *wolves*).

- Some words function as both the singular and plural form of the word (fish, deer).

- Other exceptions include *man* becomes *men, mouse* becomes *mice, goose* becomes *geese,* and *foot* becomes *feet.*

Contractions

The basic rule for making **contractions** is one area of spelling that is pretty straightforward: combine the two words by inserting an apostrophe (') in the space where a letter is omitted. For example, to combine *you* and *are*, drop the *a* and put the apostrophe in its place: *you're*.

> he + is = he's
> you + all = y'all (informal but often misspelled)

Note that *it's*, when spelled with an apostrophe, is always the contraction for *it is*. The possessive form of the word is written without an apostrophe as *its*.

Capitalization

Here's a non-exhaustive list of things that should be capitalized.

- The first word of every sentence
- The first word of every line of poetry
- The first letter of proper nouns (World War II)
- Holidays (Valentine's Day)
- The days of the week and months of the year (Tuesday, March)

- The first word, last word, and all major words in the titles of books, movies, songs, and other creative works (In the novel, *To Kill a Mockingbird*, note that *a* is lowercase since it's not a major word, but *to* is capitalized since it's the first word of the title.)
- Titles when preceding a proper noun (President Roberto Gonzales, Aunt Judy)

When simply using a word such as president or secretary, though, the word is not capitalized.

> Officers of the new business must include a *president* and *treasurer*.

Seasons—spring, fall, etc.—are not capitalized.

North, *south*, *east*, and *west* are capitalized when referring to regions but are not when being used for directions. In general, if it's preceded by *the* it should be capitalized.

> I'm from the South.
> I drove south.

Ellipses

An **ellipsis** (…) consists of three handy little dots that can speak volumes on behalf of irrelevant material. Writers use them in place of words, lines, phrases, list content, or paragraphs that might just as easily have been omitted from a passage of writing. This can be done to save space or to focus only on the specifically relevant material.

> Exercise is good for some unexpected reasons. Watkins writes, "Exercise has many benefits such as…reducing cancer risk."

In the example above, the ellipsis takes the place of the other benefits of exercise that are more expected.

The ellipsis may also be used to show a pause in sentence flow.

> "I'm wondering...how this could happen," Dylan said in a soft voice.

Commas

A **comma** (,) is the punctuation mark that signifies a pause—breath—between parts of a sentence. It denotes a break of flow. As with so many aspects of writing structure, authors will benefit by reading their writing aloud or mouthing the words. This can be particularly helpful if one is uncertain about whether the comma is needed.

In a complex sentence—one that contains a **subordinate (dependent)** clause or clauses—the use of a comma is dictated by where the subordinate clause is located. If the subordinate clause is located before the main clause, a comma is needed between the two clauses.

> I will not pay for the steak, *because I don't have that much money.*

Generally, if the subordinate clause is placed after the main clause, no punctuation is needed.

> I did well on my exam because I studied two hours the night before.

Notice how the last clause is dependent because it requires the earlier independent clauses to make sense.

Use a comma on both sides of an interrupting phrase.

I will pay for the ice cream, *chocolate and vanilla*, and then will eat it all myself.

The words forming the phrase in italics are nonessential (extra) information. To determine if a phrase is nonessential, try reading the sentence without the phrase and see if it's still coherent.

A comma is not necessary in this next sentence because no interruption—nonessential or extra information—has occurred. Read sentences aloud when uncertain.

I will pay for his chocolate and vanilla ice cream and then will eat it all myself.

If the nonessential phrase comes at the beginning of a sentence, a comma should only go at the end of the phrase. If the phrase comes at the end of a sentence, a comma should only go at the beginning of the phrase.

Other types of interruptions include the following:

- interjections: Oh no, I am not going.
- abbreviations: Barry Potter, M.D., specializes in heart disorders.
- direct addresses: Yes, Claudia, I am tired and going to bed.
- parenthetical phrases: His wife, lovely as she was, was not helpful.
- transitional phrases: Also, it is not possible.

The second comma in the following sentence is called an Oxford comma.

I will pay for ice cream, syrup, and pop.

It is a comma used after the second-to-last item in a series of three or more items. It comes before the word *or* or *and*. Not everyone uses the Oxford comma; it is optional, but many believe it is needed. The comma functions as a tool to reduce confusion in writing. So, if omitting the Oxford comma would cause confusion, then it's best to include it.

Commas are used in math to mark the place of thousands in numerals, breaking them up so they are easier to read. Other uses for commas are in dates (*March 19, 2016*), letter greetings (*Dear Sally,*), and in between cities and states (*Louisville, KY*).

Semicolons

The **semicolon** (;) might be described as a heavy-handed comma. Take a look at these two examples:

I will pay for the ice cream, but I will not pay for the steak.
I will pay for the ice cream; I will not pay for the steak.

What's the difference? The first example has a comma and a conjunction separating the two independent clauses. The second example does not have a conjunction, but there are two independent clauses in the sentence, so something more than a comma is required. In this case, a semicolon is used.

Two independent clauses can only be joined in a sentence by either a comma and conjunction or a semicolon. If one of those tools is not used, the sentence will be a run-on. Remember that while the clauses are independent, they need to be closely related in order to be contained in one sentence.

Another use for the semicolon is to separate items in a list when the items themselves require commas.

> The family lived in Phoenix, Arizona; Oklahoma City, Oklahoma; and Raleigh, North Carolina.

Colons

Colons (:) have many miscellaneous functions. Colons can be used to precede further information or a list. In these cases, a colon should only follow an independent clause.

> Humans take in sensory information through five basic senses: sight, hearing, smell, touch, and taste.

The meal includes the following components:

- Caesar salad
- spaghetti
- garlic bread
- cake

The family got what they needed: a reliable vehicle.

While a comma is more common, a colon can also proceed a formal quotation.

> He said to the crowd: "Let's begin!"

The colon is used after the greeting in a formal letter.

> Dear Sir:
> To Whom It May Concern:

In the writing of time, the colon separates the minutes from the hour (*4:45 p.m.*). The colon can also be used to indicate a ratio between two numbers (*50:1*).

Hyphens

The **hyphen** (-) is a little hash mark that can be used to join words to show that they are linked.

Hyphenate two words that work together as a single adjective (a compound adjective).

> honey-covered biscuits

Some words always require hyphens, even if not serving as an adjective.

> merry-go-round

Hyphens always go after certain prefixes like *anti-* & *all-*.

Hyphens should also be used when the absence of the hyphen would cause a strange vowel combination (*semi-engineer*) or confusion. For example, *re-collect* should be used to describe something being gathered twice rather than being written as *recollect*, which means to remember.

Parentheses and Dashes

Parentheses are half-round brackets that look like this: ( ). They set off a word, phrase, or sentence that is an afterthought, explanation, or side note relevant to the surrounding text but not essential. A pair of commas is often used to set off this sort of information, but parentheses are generally used for information that would not fit well within a sentence or that the writer deems not important enough to be structurally part of the sentence.

> The picture of the heart (see above) shows the major parts you should memorize.
> Mount Everest is one of three mountains in the world that are over 28,000 feet high (K2 and Kanchenjunga are the other two).

See how the sentences above are complete without the parenthetical statements? In the first example, *see above* would not have fit well within the flow of the sentence. The second parenthetical statement could have been a separate sentence, but the writer deemed the information not pertinent to the topic.

The **em-dash** (—) is a mark longer than a hyphen used as a punctuation mark in sentences and to set apart a relevant thought. Even after plucking out the line separated by the dash marks, the sentence will be intact and make sense.

> Looking out the airplane window at the landmarks—Lake Clarke, Thompson Community College, and the bridge—she couldn't help but feel excited to be home.

The dashes use is similar to that of parentheses or a pair of commas. So, what's the difference? Many believe that using dashes makes the clause within them stand out while using parentheses is subtler. It's advised to not use dashes when commas could be used instead.

Quotation Marks
Quotation marks are best known for their use in offsetting dialogue. Other uses include:

- around titles of songs, short stories, essays, and chapter in books
- to emphasize a certain word
- to refer to a word as the word itself

> Example: What's the meaning of "indubitably"?

Apostrophes
This punctuation mark, the **apostrophe** (') is a versatile little mark. It has a few different functions:

- Quotes: Apostrophes are used when a second quote is needed within a quote.

    - In my letter to my friend, I wrote, "The girl had to get a new purse, and guess what Mary did? She said, 'I'd like to go with you to the store.' I knew Mary would buy it for her."

- Contractions: Another use for an apostrophe in the quote above is a contraction. *I'd* is used for *I would*.

- Possession: An apostrophe followed by the letter s shows possession (*Mary's* purse). If the possessive word is plural, the apostrophe generally just follows the word.

    - The trees' leaves are all over the ground.

Sentences

A **sentence** is a set of words that make up a grammatical unit. The words must have certain elements and be spoken or written in a specific order to constitute a complete sentence that makes sense.

1. A sentence must have a **subject** (a noun or noun phrase). The subject tells whom or what the sentence is addressing (i.e. what it is about).

2. A sentence must have an **action** or **state of being** (*a* verb). To reiterate: A verb forms the main part of the predicate of a sentence. This means that it explains what the noun is doing.

3. A sentence must convey a complete thought.

When examining writing, be mindful of grammar, structure, spelling, and patterns. Sentences can come in varying sizes and shapes; so, the point of grammatical correctness is not to stamp out creativity or diversity in writing. Rather, grammatical correctness ensures that writing will be enjoyable and clear. One of the most common methods for catching errors is to mouth the words as you read them. Many typos are fixed automatically by our brain, but mouthing the words often circumvents this instinct and helps one read what's actually on the page. Often, grammar errors are caught not by memorization of grammar rules but by the training of one's mind to know whether something *sounds* right or not.

Types of Sentences

There isn't an overabundance of absolutes in grammar, but here is one: every sentence in the English language falls into one of four categories.

- Declarative: a simple statement that ends with a period

  The price of milk per gallon is the same as the price of gasoline.

- Imperative: a command, instruction, or request that ends with a period

  Buy milk when you stop to fill up your car with gas.

- Interrogative: a question that ends with a question mark

  Will you buy the milk?

- Exclamatory: a statement or command that expresses emotions like anger, urgency, or surprise and ends with an exclamation mark

  Buy the milk now!

Declarative sentences are the most common type, probably because they are comprised of the most general content, without any of the bells and whistles that the other three types contain. They are, simply, declarations or statements of any degree of seriousness, importance, or information.

Imperative sentences often seem to be missing a subject. The subject is there, though; it is just not visible or audible because it is *implied*. Look at the imperative example sentence.

  Buy the milk when you fill up your car with gas.

You is the implied subject, the one to whom the command is issued. This is sometimes called *the understood you* because it is understood that *you* is the subject of the sentence.

Interrogative sentences—those that ask questions—are defined as such from the idea of the word *interrogation*, the action of questions being asked of suspects by investigators. Although that is serious business, interrogative sentences apply to all kinds of questions.

To exclaim is at the root of **exclamatory sentences**. These are made with strong emotions behind them. The only technical difference between a declarative or imperative sentence and an exclamatory one is the exclamation mark at the end. The example declarative and imperative sentences can both become an exclamatory one simply by putting an exclamation mark at the end of the sentences.

> The price of milk per gallon is the same as the price of gasoline!
> Buy milk when you stop to fill up your car with gas!

After all, someone might be really excited by the price of gas or milk, or they could be mad at the person that will be buying the milk! However, as stated before, exclamation marks in abundance defeat their own purpose! After a while, they begin to cause fatigue! When used only for their intended purpose, they can have their expected and desired effect.

Parallel Structure in a Sentence

Parallel structure, also known as **parallelism**, refers to using the same grammatical form within a sentence. This is important in lists and for other components of sentences.

> Incorrect: At the recital, the boys and girls were dancing, singing, and played musical instruments.
> Correct: At the recital, the boys and girls were dancing, singing, and playing musical instruments.

Notice that in the second example, *played* is not in the same verb tense as the other verbs, nor is it compatible with the helping verb *were*. To test for parallel structure in lists, try reading each item as if it were the only item in the list.

> The boys and girls were dancing.
> The boys and girls were singing.
> The boys and girls were played musical instruments.

Suddenly, the error in the sentence becomes very clear. Here's another example:

> Incorrect: After the accident, I informed the police *that Mrs. Holmes backed* into my car, *that Mrs. Holmes got out* of her car to look at the damage, and *she was driving* off without leaving a note.

> Correct: After the accident, I informed the police *that Mrs. Holmes backed* into my car, *that Mrs. Holmes got out* of her car to look at the damage, and *that Mrs. Holmes drove off* without leaving a note.

> Correct: After the accident, I informed the police that Mrs. Holmes *backed* into my car, *got out* of her car to look at the damage, and *drove off* without leaving a note.

Note that there are two ways to fix the nonparallel structure of the first sentence. The key to parallelism is consistent structure.

Test Prep Books!!!

Basic Components of Vocabulary

Vocabulary

Vocabulary consists of the bank of words that children can understand and apply fluently in order to communicate effectively. A strong vocabulary and word recognition base enables children to access prior knowledge and experiences in order to make connections in written texts. A strong vocabulary also allows children to express ideas, learn new concepts, and decode the meanings of unfamiliar words by using context clues. Conversely, if a child's vocabulary knowledge is limited and does not steadily increase, reading comprehension will be negatively affected. If children become frustrated with their lack of understanding of written texts, they will likely choose to only read texts at their comfort level or refuse to read altogether. With direct instruction, educators introduce specific words to pre-teach before reading, or examine word roots, prefixes, and suffixes. Through indirect instruction, educators ensure that students are regularly exposed to new words. This engages students in high-quality conversations and social interactions and provides access to a wide variety of challenging and enjoyable reading material.

Morphology

The study of **morphology** generally deals with the structure and formation of words. A **phoneme** is the smallest unit of sound that does not necessarily carry meaning. Essentially, phonemes are combined to form words, and words are combined to form sentences. Morphology looks at the smallest meaningful part of a word, known as a **morpheme**. In contrast to a phoneme, a morpheme must carry a sound and a meaning. Free morphemes are those that can stand alone, carrying both sound and meaning, as in the following words: *girl, boy, man*, and *lady*. Just as the name suggests, bound morphemes are bound to other morphemes in order to carry meaning. Examples of bound morphemes include: *ish, ness, ly*, and *dis*.

Semantics

Semantics is the branch of linguistics that addresses meanings. Morphemes, words, phrases, and sentences all carry distinct meanings. The way these individual parts are arranged can have a significant effect on meaning. In order to construct language, children must be able to use semantics to arrange and rearrange words to achieve the particular meaning they are striving for. Activities that teach semantics revolve around teaching the arrangement of word parts (morphology) and root words, and then the teaching of vocabulary. Moving from vocabulary words into studying sentences and sentence structure leads children to learn how to use context clues to determine meaning and to understand anomalies such as metaphors, idioms, and allusions. There are five types of semantic relationships that are critical to understand:

- **Hyponyms** refer to a relationship between words where general words have multiple more-specific words (hyponyms) that fall into the same category (e.g., horse: mare, stallion, foal, Appaloosa, Clydesdale).

- **Meronyms** refer to a relationship between words where a whole word has multiple parts (meronyms) that comprise it (e.g., horse: tail, mane, hooves, ears).

- **Synonyms** refer to words that have the same meaning as another word (e.g., instructor/teacher/educator, canine/dog, feline/cat, herbivore/vegetarian).

- **Antonyms** refer to words that have the opposite meaning as another word (e.g., true/false, up/down, in/out, right/wrong).

- **Homonyms** refer to words that are spelled the same (homographs) or sound the same (homophones) but mean different things (e.g., there/their/they're, two/too/to, principal/principle, plain/plane, (kitchen) sink/ sink (down as in water)).

Syntax

With its origins from the Greek word, "syntaxis," which means arrangement, **syntax** is the study of phrase and sentence formation. The study of syntax focuses on the ways in which specific words can be combined to create coherent meaning. For example: the simple rearrangement of the words, "I can run," is different from the question, "Can I run?" which is also different from the meaningless "Run I can."

The following methods can be used to teach syntax:

- Proper Syntax Modeling: Students don't need to be corrected for improper syntax. Instead, they should be shown ways to rephrase what they said with proper syntax. If a student says, "Run I can," then the teacher should say, "Oh, you can run how fast?" This puts syntax in place with conversational skills.

- Open-Ended Sentences: Students can complete open-ended sentences with proper syntax both orally and in written format, or they can correct sentences that have improper syntax so that they make sense.

- Listening for Syntax: Syntax is auditory. Students can often hear a syntax error before they can see it in writing. Teachers should have students use word cards or word magnets to arrange and rearrange simple sentences and read them aloud to check for syntax.

- Repetition: Syntax can be practiced by using songs, poems, and rhymes for repetitive automation.

Pragmatics

Pragmatics is the study of what words mean in certain situations. It helps to understand the intentions and interpretations of intentions through words used in human interaction. Different listeners and different situations call for different language and intonations of language. When people engage in a conversation, it is usually to convey a certain message, and the message (even using the same words) can change depending on the setting and the audience. The more fluent the speaker, the more success she or he will have in conveying the intended message.

The following methods can be used to teach pragmatics:

- When students state something incorrectly, a response can be given to what they intended to say in the first place. For instance, if a student says, "That's how it didn't happen." Then the teacher might say, "Of course, that's not how it happened." Instead of putting students on defense by being corrected, this method puts them at ease and helps them learn.

- Role-playing conversations with different people in different situations can help teach pragmatics. For example, pretend playing can be used where a situation remains the same but the audience changes, or the audience stays the same but the situations change. This can be followed with a discussion about how language and intonations change too.

- Different ways to convey a message can be used, such as asking vs. persuading, or giving direct vs. indirect requests and polite vs. impolite messages.

- Various non-verbal signals can be used to see how they change pragmatics. For example, students can be encouraged to use mismatched words and facial expressions, such as angry words while smiling or happy words while pretending to cry.

Strategies to Help Read New and/or Difficult Words

Children who are developing reading fluency and comprehension skills can become frustrated when presented with unfamiliar words in a given text. With direct phonics instruction, educators can teach children to decode words and then use context clues to define the words while reading. If children have a strong enough understanding of language structures, including nouns and verbs, educators can ask them to consider what part of speech the unknown word might be based on and where it might fit into the sentence. Other useful strategies involve **self-monitoring**, in which children are asked to think as they read and ask themselves if what they have just read makes sense. Focusing on visual clues, such as drawings and photographs, may give children valuable insight into deciphering unknown words. Looking for the word in another section of the text to see how it relates to the overall meaning could give a clue to the new vocabulary word. Spelling the word out loud or looking for word chunks, prefixes, and suffixes, as well as demonstrating how to segment the unknown word into its individual syllables, may also be effective strategies to employ.

One of the most valuable strategies, however, for helping children to read and understand new words is pre-teaching. In this strategy, educators select what they evaluate to be the unfamiliar words in the text and then introduce them to the class before reading. Educators using this method should be careful not to simply ask the children to read the text and then spell the new words correctly. They should also provide clear definitions and give the children the opportunity to read these words in various sentences to decipher word meaning. This method can dramatically reduce how often children stop reading in order to reflect on unknown words. Educators are often unsure as to whether to correct every mispronounced word a child makes when reading. If the mispronounced word still makes sense, it is sometimes better to allow the child to continue to read, since the more the child stops, the more the child's reading comprehension and fluency are negatively affected.

Practice Questions

1. When children begin to negotiate the sounds that make up words in their language independently, what skill/s are they demonstrating?
    a. Phonological awareness
    b. Phonemes
    c. Phoneme substitution
    d. Blending skills

2. What is phonics?
    a. The study of syllabication
    b. The study of onsets and rimes
    c. The study of sound-letter relationships
    d. The study of graphemes

3. The author's purpose, major ideas, supporting details, visual aids, and vocabulary are the five key elements of what type of text?
    a. Fictional texts
    b. Narratives
    c. Persuasive texts
    d. Informational texts

4. When students use inference, what are they able to do?
    a. Make logical assumptions based on contextual clues
    b. Independently navigate various types of text
    c. Summarize a text's main idea
    d. Paraphrase a text's main idea

5. Context clues assist vocabulary development by providing:
    a. A knowledge of roots, prefixes, and suffixes are used to determine the meaning a word
    b. Information within the sentence that surrounds an unknown word is used to determine the word's meaning
    c. Content learned in previous grades that serves as a bridge to the new term
    d. Background knowledge to fill in a missing word within a sentence

Answer Explanations

1. A: Phonological Awareness refers to a child's ability to understand and use familiar sounds in his or her social environment in order to form coherent words. Phonemes are defined as distinct sound units in any given language. Phonemic substitution is part of phonological awareness—a child's ability to substitute specific phonemes for others. Blending skills refers to the ability to construct or build words from individual phonemes by blending the sounds together in a unique sequence.

2. C: When children begin to recognize and apply sound-letter relationships independently and accurately, they are demonstrating a growing mastery of phonics. Phonics is the most commonly used method for teaching people to read and write by associating sounds with their corresponding letters or groups of letters, using a language's alphabetic writing system. Syllabication refers to the ability to break down words into their individual syllables. The study of onsets and rimes strives to help students recognize and separate a word's beginning consonant or consonant-cluster sound—the onset—from the word's rime—the vowel and/or consonants that follow the onset. A grapheme is a letter or a group of letters in a language that represent a sound.

3. D: Informational texts generally contain five key elements in order to be considered informative. These five elements include the author's purpose, the major ideas, supporting details, visual aids, and key vocabulary. Narratives are accounts—either spoken or written—of an event or a story. Persuasive texts, such as advertisements, use persuasive language to try to convince the reader to act or feel a certain way. Informational texts strive to share factual information about a given subject in order to advance a reader's knowledge.

4. A: When a person infers something, he or she is demonstrating the ability to extract key information and make logical assumptions based on that information. The information provided is not direct, but implied. Being able to navigate a variety of texts independently has nothing to do with inference; it demonstrates a student's reading comprehension and fluency. Successfully summarizing and paraphrasing texts are advanced literacy skills that demonstrate a student's reading comprehension and writing proficiency.

5. B: When using contextual strategies, students are indirectly introduced to new words within a sentence or paragraph. Contextual strategies require students to infer the meaning(s) of new words. Word meaning is developed by utilizing semantic and contextual clues of the reading in which the word is located.

Social Studies

Information Processing Skills

A **Helping Students Locate, Analyze, and Synthesize Information Related to Social Studies Topics**

An early education social studies curriculum should offer content that is comprehensive and thematic, introducing a variety of viewpoints on historical events and highlighting the relevance of connecting the past with the present. Teachers must know how to guide students in obtaining, evaluating, and processing the information associated with these topics. Although the school's textbook is a ready resource, teachers should suggest and encourage alternate sources of information, such as the library, field trips, maps, and other visual material, interviews, and discussions of current events. These opportunities allow students to analyze information and increase their societal understanding. Classroom activities can help students apply previously acquired learning through problem solving, such as performing their own mock election in order to gain a better grasp of the election process. Encouraging students to investigate social studies topics that interest them and involve real-world projects helps them to become objective observers and develop a sense of public duty. When students can interpret, organize, and present what they have learned through a variety of methods, it promotes a deeper understanding and application of wider social studies themes.

Historical Understandings and History Processes

A **Important People, Events, and Symbols of the United States and Georgia**

There have been hundreds of men and women whose influence has shaped the United States throughout its history, including:

- George Washington
- Thomas Jefferson
- Benjamin Franklin
- Abraham Lincoln
- Susan B. Anthony
- Harriet Tubman
- Franklin D. Roosevelt
- Martin Luther King, Jr.

The state of Georgia has also been influenced by many important historical figures, including:

- Hernando de Soto
- James Edward Oglethorpe
- Mary Musgrove
- Andrew Jackson
- William T. Sherman
- Booker T. Washington
- Martin Luther King, Jr.
- Jimmy Carter

A number of momentous events have affected the United States throughout its history, including various land discoveries and purchases, wars, and political and economic actions, such as:

- The founding of Jamestown, Virginia in 1607
- The Signing of the Declaration of Independence on July 4, 1776
- The Civil War from 1861-1865
- The Great Depression of 1929
- The bombing of Pearl Harbor on December 7, 1941
- The moon landing in 1969
- The attacks on the World Trade Center on September 11, 2001

[handwritten margin note: Emancipation Proclamation when freed slaves in the states/parts of states in rebellion]

[handwritten margin note: Trail of Tears]

Many historical events have also impacted Georgia, including:

- The exploration of the region in 1540 by Spanish explorer Hernando de Soto
- The founding of the colony of Georgia in 1733
- The invention of the cotton gin in 1793 by Eli Whitney
- General William Sherman's march on Atlanta and its subsequent burning during the Civil War in 1864
- The organization of the first Girl Scout Troop in America by Juliette Low of Savannah in 1912
- The Southern Christian Leadership Conference (SCLC) formed in Atlanta in 1957 by Martin Luther King, Jr.

Symbols are specific objects that stand for a country or region's unique beliefs, values, traditions, or other ideals. Their recognizable and nostalgic qualities can help unite its residents by evoking historical events or periods and important values. Important U.S. symbols include:

- Independence Hall in Philadelphia
- The U.S. flag
- The bald eagle
- The U.S. National Anthem ("The Star-Spangled Banner")
- The White House
- The Washington Monument
- The Statue of Liberty

Important Georgia symbols include:

- The state flag
- The state fruit (peach)
- The state flower (Cherokee Rose)
- The state crop (peanut)

Chronology and Important Figures and Cultures in the History of Georgia

Chronology is the ordering of dates and events in the correct sequence, from oldest to most recent, in order to show an historical progression. Using a timeline to illustrate and designate these occurrences is a useful tool for those studying the subject of history.

First Settlers

Beginning around 10,000 BC, the first people to settle Georgia were Native American Indian groups. The Paleo Indians were the first settlers, followed by the Archaic Indians, Woodland Indians, and finally the Mississippian Indians. The Spanish and French began exploring and colonizing the area that is now Georgia in the 1500s. The British began to claim southern regions of the American coast in the 1600s, including land that is within the boundaries of present-day Georgia. Since all three countries laid claim to this region, it was referred to as the **debatable land**. This area was sandwiched between Florida, which was under Spanish rule, and North Carolina and South Carolina, which Britain controlled. In 1732, British parliament member James Oglethorpe convinced King George II to colonize this area with individuals from Britain's overflowing debtor prisons. It was named Georgia in honor of the king. Led by Oglethorpe, the new settlers arrived on February 1, 1733, establishing Georgia as an official colony and naming Savannah as the first settlement.

Colonization

When American patriots began to openly oppose British rule in the 1770s, Georgia citizens were still divided in their views. As a result, Georgia was the only colony that did not send delegates to Philadelphia for the First Continental Congress in 1774. Opposition to the British Crown continued to build in Georgia, and when Georgia's first provincial congress was held the following year, they agreed to send delegates to the Second Continental Congress. Three Georgians were signers of the Declaration of Independence in 1776—Button Gwinnett, Lyman Hall, and George Walton. In 1838, U.S. soldiers forced Cherokee Indians to leave their homes and relocate to the western region, which is now Oklahoma. Many died during the difficult journey, leading the Cherokees to refer to this horrific experience as the **Trail of Tears**.

Secession and Civil War

In 1793, Georgia resident Eli Whitney patented the cotton gin, a device that mechanically removes seeds from cotton fiber. This transformed cotton production and caused Georgia to cling tightly to the practice of slavery in order to maintain its many profitable plantations. The Georgia Secession Convention of 1861 voted to secede from the Union and create a new constitution. In 1864, Union Major General William T. Sherman conducted his **March to the Sea**, leading over 60,000 soldiers through Georgia, burning much of Atlanta and forcing Savannah to surrender. Segregation continued in Georgia and other Southern states long after slavery was abolished at the end of the Civil War.

Civil Rights Movement

In the 1960s, the practice of segregation and racial tension led to the Civil Rights Movement, which included many protests and demonstrations. Not only did these protests capture the national spotlight, but they also eventually led to the passing of the Civil Rights Act of 1964. Chief activist Martin Luther King, Jr., who was assassinated in 1968, led many of these demonstrations.

Political Roots of Democracy in the United States

The path to democracy in the United States began when Europeans colonized the region in the 1500s. It culminated in the mid-1700s when British colonists began to rebel against British rule and its restrictions. Colonists particularly rebelled against the burden of taxation without representation in Parliament. These **Patriots** decided to fight for their freedom, defeated Great Britain in the Revolutionary War, and established a new country they called the United States of America. The U.S. Constitution was drafted in 1787 at the Constitutional Convention in Philadelphia. The goal was to create a government with checks and balances, and by dividing it into three branches, no single branch had ultimate governmental control. They designated the two legislative bodies—the House and Senate—as the Congress. This document is recognized as the world's first formal plan for a modern democracy and the oldest working constitution in existence.

Many people made significant contributions toward expanding the rights and freedoms of Americans by fighting in the Revolutionary War, signing the Declaration of Independence, and serving as delegates to the Constitutional Convention. The men who shaped the democracy of the United States are often referred to as America's **Founding Fathers**.

This prestigious group includes:

- George Washington
- Alexander Hamilton
- James Madison
- John Adams
- Thomas Jefferson
- James Monroe
- Benjamin Franklin

Washington, Adams, Jefferson, Madison, and Monroe became U.S. Presidents, and Washington, Hamilton, and Madison were instrumental in leading the charge for discussion at the Constitutional Convention.

Development of Native American Cultures in North America

The first people arrived in North America at least 15,000 years ago by crossing the land bridge from Asia to present-day Alaska. Their descendants are referred to as **Native Americans** or **American Indians**. They gradually made their way through North and South America, adapting to the climate and landscape of the varied regions and splitting off into numerous tribes. There was a great deal of diversity among these tribes with each possessing its own culture and language. Although the different tribes did lay claim to their own specific territories, land within a tribe was considered communal. The concept of individual land ownership was not recognized. This sense of equality was also evident in the way women were generally viewed and treated. They were given some degree of political power and worked in the fields while the men fought wars, hunted, and cleared the land for planting crops.

Indians in the East, upper Midwest, and Northwest sections of North America survived by hunting, gathering, and fishing. Some of them also farmed the land. Their dwellings were wood longhouses, plank houses, or wigwams, which are round, wood-framed, domed huts. Plains Indians hunted buffalo, often following them across the open prairies and living in teepees that were easily moved from place to place to suit their nomadic lifestyle. Indians in the Southwest relied on farming for much of their food and built adobes, which are houses made of dried clay or earth.

European Exploration in North America and Factors that Shaped British Colonial America

Early Exploration
European exploration in North America dates back to around 1000 AD when Scandinavian Vikings, led by Leif Eriksson, first made their way to Greenland and then journeyed on to modern-day Newfoundland. They settled briefly in an area now known as **L'Anse Meadows**. However, clashes with the Native

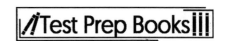

American people living nearby caused them to return to Greenland a few years later. The first permanent settlements in North America began after Italian sailor Christopher Columbus landed in the Caribbean in 1492. This was a significant breakthrough since most Europeans did not know that this huge landmass even existed. It initiated a period of discovery, conquest, and colonization of the Americas by the Europeans. Often referred to as the **Columbian Exchange**, this period allowed people who had been cut off from each other for 15,000 years to share knowledge, ideas, culture, food, plants and animals, technology, and religion; this led to significant changes and enhancements for both regions.

European Expansion and Influence

Other European cultures quickly followed, sending sailors across the Atlantic to find new passages to the East and lay claim to new lands. Explorers typically hailed from countries with a seafaring reputation. Spain, France, and England were the major forces, whereas Portugal, Holland, Russia, and Sweden played lesser roles. This merging of cultures had an unfortunate effect on the Native American people who were not immune to the diseases the new arrivals brought with them. Millions died from deadly diseases; others were killed or enslaved in territorial encounters when some Europeans sought to conquer the Indians. Over the next few centuries, this led to a 90 percent population decline among the Native Americans.

England and Spain waged the biggest struggle to claim the most land in North America. Spain took the initial lead in the early 1500s, exploring or establishing settlements in the southern portion of what is now the United States. Spain settled in present-day Florida, Texas, California, Arizona, New Mexico, Mexico, and a good portion of Central America and South America. Up until the 1840s, Spain, and later Mexico, controlled large expanses of the area now known as the southwestern United States.

Colonization

The British first established a presence in 1585 when Sir Walter Raleigh founded the Roanoke colony in what was then called Virginia, but later became North Carolina. It is now known as the **Lost Colony** because John White, the colony's leader, went back to England for supplies in 1587 and later returned to find that all of the colonists had mysteriously disappeared. In 1607, the British established their first permanent settlement in Jamestown, Virginia. In 1620, a group of approximately one hundred people sailed from England on the ***Mayflower*** and landed at a site they named Plymouth. Many were Pilgrims seeking religious freedom. They founded the first permanent European settlement in New England. Within seventy-five years, England had established thirteen British colonies along the east coast of North America, laying the foundation for the future United States of America.

French Influence

The French gained a stronghold in Canada in 1534 when Jacques Cartier sailed up the St. Lawrence River and claimed the territory for France. In 1608, French explorer Samuel de Champlain further explored the region and later founded Quebec. By 1673, France expanded their claim from Canada to the Gulf of Mexico when Father Jacques Marquette and Louis Joliet journeyed down the Mississippi River, naming the territory Louisiana after King Louis XIV.

The American Revolution and the Challenges that Faced the New Nation

The English and French, and their various allies, fought a series of wars between 1689 and 1763. The fourth war was **The French and Indian War** (1754-1763), which ended with the British controlling a good portion of North America—the region east of the Mississippi from the Hudson Bay to the Florida Keys. This made England the leading world power, but it also caused the country to go deeply into debt. In order to subsidize this deficit and finance the thousands of British soldiers that were stationed in North America, the British imposed a series of controls on American colonists. These included: the **Sugar Act** of 1764, which placed import duties on items such as molasses, sugar, coffee, and wine; the **Stamp Act** of 1765, which taxed printed items, including playing cards and newspapers printed in the colonies; and the **Currency Act**, which banned the issuing of paper money in the colonies and mandated the use of gold in business dealings. This control infuriated many colonists and led them to protest that **taxation without representation** was a violation of their rights as English citizens. A group who called themselves the **Sons of Liberty** began to start riots and encourage boycotting.

Taxation

Although the British repealed the Stamp Act in 1766, they continued to impose taxes on imported items and issued the **Townsend Act** in 1767, which taxed imported lead, glass, paints, paper, and tea. This increased the colonists' anger and further strained the relationship between England and the colonies. The colonies began to unite in opposition to British rule, which prompted a series of incidents. These incidents included: the **Boston Massacre** in 1770, during which British troops killed five protesting colonists, and the **Boston Tea Party**, during which colonists dumped 342 chests of expensive tea into the Boston Harbor in defiance of the tea tax. As punishment, the British issued a series of **Coercive Acts**, which the colonists referred to as the **Intolerable Acts** of 1774.

First Continental Congress

The **Intolerable Acts** incited the colonists to band together and hold the First Continental Congress in Philadelphia in 1774. It included fifty-six delegates from twelve colonies. Although Georgia did not attend, the colony's leaders did pledge their support to the meeting. The **First Continental Congress** issued the Declaration and Resolves of colonists' rights and petitioned England's King George to hear their objections. The Congress also agreed to ban the import of British goods, as well as the export of American goods to Britain. They agreed to meet the following May if the situation did not improve. The English government brought their plan of resolution to Parliament in 1775, but the House of Lords rejected it, considering Massachusetts to be in rebellion.

American Revolution

In anticipation of British hostility, Massachusetts's residents began to stockpile arms and organize militia groups. These groups were known as the **Minutemen** since they were reportedly ready to pick up their guns on a minute's notice. The British heard about the colonists' activities and sent troops to Concord to seize the weapons. However, their plan was thwarted when Paul Revere and William Dawes rode out from Boston to warn the men. A group of approximately seventy Minutemen confronted the British soldiers on Lexington green. A scuffle ensued, and the first shot of the **American Revolution** occurred on April 19, 1775. The side that fired the first shot has never been determined.

Declaration of Independence

The **Second Continental Congress** met on May 10, 1775 and appointed George Washington as chief of the **Continental Army**. Although skirmishes began to occur, the Continental Congress made one more attempt to reconcile with the British by sending them the Olive Branch Petition. The petition was refused, and this rejection, combined with a pamphlet written by Thomas Paine in early 1776 called *Common Sense*, pushed the colonists to seek independence in earnest. A committee was chosen to draft a **Declaration of Independence**, which was written by Thomas Jefferson and approved on July 4, 1776. Another committee was appointed to create an organized government, which was adopted by Congress in November 1777 as the **Articles of Confederation**. However, this was not approved by all the states until March 1781; therefore, throughout much of the Revolutionary War, there was no official form of government.

The Revolutionary War

The first major American victory occurred on December 25, 1776 when Washington led his troops across the Delaware River to wage a surprise attack on British and Hessian soldiers stationed in Trenton. European countries began to help fund the American cause after General John Burgoyne had a major victory at Saratoga, New York in October 1777. While stationed in Valley Forge, Pennsylvania during the winter of 1777, Washington's troops suffered major losses as a result of starvation, disease, and exposure to the cold. The following year, the Americans signed the Treaty of Alliance with France. In 1779, American Captain John Paul Jones captured the British warship *Serapis* off the coast of England— the only major naval battle of the war. In the war's final battle on October 19, 1781, British General Lord Cornwallis surrendered to Washington's troops at Yorktown, Virginia. The two sides began negotiations, and the **Treaty of Paris** was signed in 1783, which officially ended the war and recognized the independence of the United States of America.

A New Nation

The new nation was faced with many challenges, including instituting a solid government and leadership. Although the **Articles of Confederation** was approved in 1781, the country's leaders recognized it was not effective and set to revise it. The **Constitutional Convention** was held in Philadelphia in 1787 to debate the issues and subsequently elect George Washington as president. The men decided to separate the government into three branches: the **legislative**, to create the laws (containing two houses of Congress); the **executive** branch, headed by the president to carry out the laws; and the **judicial** branch, controlled by the Supreme Court to ensure enforcement of the laws as stated in the Constitution. This division was to prevent any one governmental group from having too much power and ensure checks and balances between them. George Washington took the oath of office as America's first president on April 30, 1789.

The Three Branches of the U.S. Government

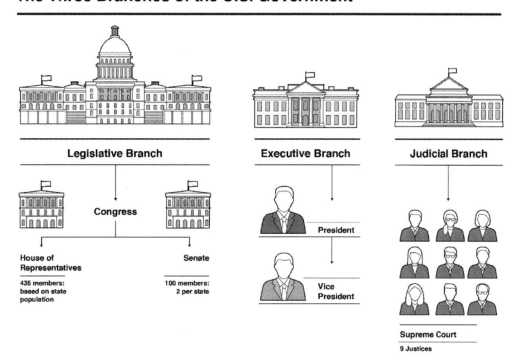

This new democracy was greatly tested in the years following the Revolution as Americans began to forge their way west and leaders acquired more land. One such acquisition was the **Louisiana Purchase** in 1803, which was purchased from France for $15 million during Thomas Jefferson's presidency. Tensions also continued to build between the United States and Britain and culminated in the **War of 1812** (1812-1815). Although the British managed to burn much of Washington, D.C.—including the White House—neither side won. However, it did stop British intimidation against the U.S. It also caused many Native Americans to align with the British to fight against the Americans who were trying to drive them further west and force them to assimilate.

Key People, Events, and Developments in the History of the United States between 1860 and 1945

Slavery

Slavery was an issue for America from its early days when Africans were brought to Virginia to work in the tobacco fields. In the 1800s, the Underground Railroad was a secret network of tunnels and safe houses that helped slaves escape slavery in the South and gain freedom in the North. Escaped slave Harriet Tubman was its most famous "conductor." Slave owners and abolitionists bitterly debated slavery, and southern leaders began to threaten secession. Slavery became the major focus of the 1860 presidential election, particularly since the South was convinced that Abraham Lincoln would abolish slavery if elected. Lincoln won the election, which only further increased tensions. Southern states began to secede in late 1860. By February 1861, they had formed the new nation of the **Confederate States of America**, electing Jefferson Davis as their president in November of that year.

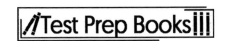

Civil War

In April 1861, Confederate soldiers fired upon a Union-held ship seeking to reinforce Fort Sumter in Charleston, South Carolina. This signaled the beginning of the Civil War and divided the U.S. into the North (**Union**) and South (**Confederates**). The two sides battled for four years, and the smaller Confederate Army surprised the Union Army with their tenacity. The Confederate Army claimed various victories throughout Virginia from 1861-1863 under the leadership of General Robert E. Lee. These victories included the Battle of Bull Run, Fredericksburg, and Chancellorsville. The turning point was the **Battle of Gettysburg** in Pennsylvania, which resulted in 51,000 troops on both sides being killed, wounded, or declared missing. The Confederate Army suffered a loss of one-third of its soldiers. In 1864, Union General William T. Sherman marched through Georgia, burning Atlanta and devastating much of the landscape. In 1865, he then moved through the Carolinas to Richmond, Virginia where General Lee, who was facing the determined assaults of future president Ulysses S. Grant, surrendered. Five days later, John Wilkes Booth shot President Lincoln who was watching a play at Ford's Theatre in Washington, D.C.; Lincoln died the next morning.

Reconstruction

During the **Reconstruction** period following the Civil War, the North and South continued to wage power and economic struggles. Many African Americans from the South moved north and west to seek more fair treatment. The American frontier provided opportunities for immigrants and others seeking new prospects. Many people made their way west, farming the land and finding jobs in industries such as mining, forestry, and oil. This forced Native Americans to fight for their land or pick up and move to reservations. In the 1876 conflict known as **Custer's Last Stand**, Colonel George Custer's troops were killed by a group of Sioux Indians led by Chiefs Crazy Horse and Sitting Bull. This defeat angered the U.S. government and caused them to increase their efforts against the Indians, which put an end to the Indian Wars. The introduction of the railroad in the mid-nineteenth century provided many jobs and allowed people and goods to travel the vast landscape of North America at a much quicker pace.

Industrial Revolution

Author Mark Twain deemed the period of business and industrial growth from 1876 through the turn of the twentieth century as the **Gilded Age** since it appeared shiny and golden on the surface, but was fueled by undercurrents of corruption led by big businessmen known as robber barons. They controlled many of America's booming new industries, including steel (Andrew Carnegie), steamships and railroads (Cornelius Vanderbilt), oil (John D. Rockefeller), and banking (J.P. Morgan). None of the U.S. Presidents during this period were particularly strong leaders and practiced a hands-off approach to business. High tariffs were another issue supported by businesses and Congress. In 1890, Congress passed the **McKinley Tariff**, named after future President and then Representative William McKinley. This tariff raised duties over 48 percent on average.

U.S. Expansion

The U.S. continued to seek out and acquire new lands, a tactic often referred to as **Manifest Destiny**. This practice led to the purchase of Alaska from Russia in 1867 and the annexation of Hawaii in 1898. The Spanish-American War in 1898 lasted just a few weeks, but helped Cuba gain its independence from Spain and helped the U.S. gain a strategic foothold in many distant locales that were formerly Spanish territories. These included Guam and the Philippines. Future president Theodore Roosevelt became a hero when his troops defeated the Spanish fleet at the Battle of San Juan Hill.

World War I

World War I began in 1914 when a Serbian assassin killed Archduke Franz Ferdinand of Austria, which prompted Austria-Hungary to declare war on Serbia. Due to protective alliances they had forged, other European countries soon joined the war. If one country was attacked, the country's allies were obliged to defend it.

Most Americans supported the Allies, particularly after German submarines sank the passenger ship *Lusitania* in 1915, killing 128 Americans. In 1917, news leaked that Germany was trying to turn Mexico against the U.S. As a result, President Woodrow Wilson declared war on Germany. American troops helped defeat the German army in September 1918. Fighting ended in November of that year after Germany signed a peace agreement. President Woodrow Wilson's plan for peace was the League of Nations, which was adopted as part of the **Treaty of Versailles** in 1919, but then rejected by the U.S. Senate.

Prohibition and The Great Depression

Prohibition (the 18th Amendment to the U.S. Constitution) was passed in 1919 and prohibited the production and sale of alcoholic beverages. This amendment fueled corruption since people made, sold, and transported liquor illegally. The 21st Amendment repealed it in 1933. Women had been campaigning for the right to vote since the 1840s, and these **suffragettes** used the outbreak of World War I to leverage their fight, stating they would help support the war if they were granted the right to vote. The 19th Amendment, which guaranteed women the right to vote in federal elections, was finally passed by Congress in 1919 and ratified the following year. On October 29, 1929 (referred to as **Black Tuesday**) the stock market crashed, marking the beginning of the Great Depression that lasted through the 1930s. President Franklin Delano Roosevelt's solution was the **New Deal**—a variety of new programs and laws to provide government funding to help rebuild America's economy.

World War II

In 1939, after Adolf Hitler began to invade and occupy several European nations, World War II broke out in Europe and many countries declared war on Germany. Germany aligned with Italy and Japan in 1940 to form the **Axis Alliance**. Their goal was to establish a German empire in Europe and place Japan in control over Asia. When Germany invaded the Soviet Union in June 1941, the Soviets immediately allied with Britain. The U.S. entered the war when Japan bombed Pearl Harbor in Hawaii on December 7, 1941. Battles raged in Europe and the Pacific, and the Allied forces won an important victory in June 1942 at the Battle of Midway. At this battle, the U.S. stopped the Japanese from advancing and prevented the invasion of Australia. In 1943, Axis troops in North Africa surrendered to the Allies, who then began to invade Italy, and finally France on June 6, 1944 (known as **D-Day**), which resulted in severe losses on both sides. In early 1945, President Roosevelt met with British Prime Minister Winston Churchill and Soviet director Joseph Stalin in Yalta, Crimea to plan their final assault on Germany and discuss postwar strategies. The Allies continued their attack, liberating Nazi death camps. This forced Hitler to commit suicide, and Germany surrendered in May. However, Japan did not yield, even after the capture of Okinawa in June. As a result, the U.S. dropped an atomic bomb on the Japanese cities of Hiroshima and then Nagasaki, forcing Japan to surrender in early September.

Key People, Events, and Developments in the United States between 1950 and the Present

In the years following World War II, the U.S. and Soviet Union arose as the two dominant world forces. But because the countries had very different political systems—democracy (the U.S.) and Communism (the Soviet Union)—a feeling of mistrust developed between the two. This was heightened by the fact that both countries had developed nuclear weapons. This became known as the Cold War. The Soviet Union introduced Communism into Eastern Europe, which it had occupied since World War II. This led to the formation of the **North Atlantic Treaty Organization (NATO)** between Western Europe, Canada, and the U.S. in defense of Soviet hostility. The Soviet Union countered by creating the **Warsaw Pact**.

United Nations

Toward the end of World War II, a group of fifty nations (including the U.S. and the Soviet Union) formed the **United Nations** as a peacekeeping group. However, Communism still continued to spread throughout the world, including to Latin America, Africa, and Asia. When Communist North Korea invaded South Korea in June 1950, the U.N. sent a group of troops led by the U.S. to help South Korea. This action led to a three-year conflict that ended in a cease-fire in 1953. Although war was never officially declared and neither side won, the fighting showcased President Truman's hard stance against Communism.

Baby Boom

The 1950s were generally a prosperous time for Americans. Many Americans took advantage of college loan programs and the G.I. Bill, which gave military veterans a free education. Mortgage programs provided more affordable housing, which enabled many people to move to the suburbs. The population surged during this **baby boom**, labor unions helped workers increase their wages, and people were able to afford more expensive items, such as cars and television sets.

Civil Rights Movement

During this time, African Americans were still repressed, particularly in the southern U.S., and segregation was rampant in many public places. When the Supreme Court ruled that school segregation was illegal in 1954 in the revolutionary case **Brown vs. the Board of Education**, the **Civil Rights Movement** was set in motion. This movement continued throughout the 1950s and 1960s and included dozens of nonviolent protests, such as the Montgomery bus boycott in Alabama. The boycott was organized after Rosa Parks was arrested because she refused to give up her seat on the bus to a white man. The Southern Christian Leadership Conference (SCLC) was soon formed as a way to bring African Americans together to help fight segregation in a peaceful way. The Reverend Dr. Martin Luther King, Jr. was its first president. Dr. King and his supporters kept up the fight throughout the 1960s, staging sit-ins at segregated lunch counters, **Freedom Rides** on segregated buses, and marches and protests in segregated cities, such as Birmingham, Alabama. The demonstrations often ended in violence and police brutality, which served to aid the cause and led to the passage of the **Civil Rights Act** in 1964.

U.S. Conflicts

The Cold War between the U.S. and Soviets continued as both countries tried to assert their dominance through technological and military advances. This spawned events such as the creation of the Berlin Wall by the Russians in 1961, which was devised to separate the sector of Berlin they occupied from the area controlled by the **Western allies** (France, Britain, and the U.S.). The **Cuban Missile Crisis** in 1962 was sparked by the failed invasion of Cuba by the U.S. a year earlier. After the invasion, the Soviets placed nuclear missiles aimed at the U.S. in Cuba. However, when U.S. spy planes spotted them, President John F. Kennedy demanded the dismantling and removal of the missile sites, and as a concession agreed to go forward with the planned removal of U.S. missile sites in Turkey. A year later on November 22, 1963, President Kennedy was assassinated in Dallas by Lee Harvey Oswald.

Space Race

The Cold War prompted the *space race* between the U.S. and Soviets, each attempting to outdo the other with different space exploration milestones. In 1957, the Russians launched **Sputnik**, the first satellite, into space. This prompted President Eisenhower to establish the National Aeronautics and Space Administration (NASA) in 1958. Although the Soviets were also the first nation to send a human into space in 1961, the U.S. quickly caught up. President Kennedy vowed to land an American on the moon by 1969—a feat that was accomplished by astronaut Neil Armstrong on July 20, 1969.

Vietnam War

In 1954, rebels seized control of Vietnam from France. The country was split into two regimes with the northern part under Communist leadership. As the threat of communism continued to loom, the U.S. sent advisors and weapons to South Vietnam beginning in 1955. The U.S. got more directly involved in the 1960s during the presidency of Lyndon B. Johnson, who sent troops in great numbers to help South Vietnam win the fight. Many Americans opposed the war, which caused anti-war protests and unrest. A cease-fire was signed in 1973, and the last U.S. forces pulled out in 1975.

Women's Rights Movement

Women gained the right to vote in 1920, but still were not on equal terms with men in many areas. Suffragist leader Alice Paul had introduced the **Equal Rights Amendment (ERA)** in 1923 to help bridge this gap. Congress finally passed the ERA in 1972 and sent it to the states for ratification. However, not all states ratified the amendment, and to date only a total of thirty-five have ratified it, which is three less than the thirty-eight required to pass. In the controversial 1973 court case **Roe vs. Wade**, the Supreme Court gave women the right to legally obtain abortions within the first three months of pregnancy.

1970s and Watergate

U.S. diplomatic relations with the Communist nations of China and the Soviet Union improved a bit in the 1970s. President Richard Nixon paid visits to both countries in 1972. The **Strategic Arms Limitation Talks (SALT I and II)**, negotiated between 1972 and 1979, resulted in limits on nuclear weapons for both the U.S. and Russia. In 1974, Nixon became the first and only U.S. president to resign from office as a result of the **Watergate** scandal. The scandal erupted when five of his staff members were caught stealing information from the Democratic Party headquarters in Washington, D.C. In 1973, a group of Arab nations tried to regain land seized by Israel in the 1967 Six-Day War. The U.S. was a main Israeli ally, and the Arab-controlled Organization of Petroleum Countries (OPEC) cut off oil shipments to the U.S. Because the U.S. was highly dependent on imports of oil from the Middle East, this energy crisis resulted in a huge surge in gas prices and long lines at the pumps.

The Reagan Years

In his role as U.S. president from 1980-1988, Ronald Reagan was against big government and supported industry deregulation, fewer social programs, lower taxes, and bigger military spending. A scandal referred to as the **Iran-Contra Affair** emerged during Reagan's presidency, involving the secret sale of weapons to Iran in exchange for American hostages. Profits from the sale were then sent to aid Nicaraguan Contras in their cause to overthrow the communist Sandinista government. Reagan opposed Communism and advocated **peace through strength**, building up the U.S. military and launching the Strategic Defense Initiative (SDI), also called **Star Wars**, designed to shield the U.S. from nuclear attack. Reagan worked with Soviet President Gorbachev to put controls on nuclear weapons after Gorbachev launched the policies of **glasnost** (political openness) and **perestroika** (economic restructuring). This led to the breakup of the Soviet Union, and the end of the Cold War.

Desert Storm

In 1990, Iraqi dictator Saddam Hussein invaded Kuwait in order to take possession of the tiny country's huge oil fields. A few months later, U.S. President George H.W. Bush launched **Operation Desert Storm** with a coalition of several Middle Eastern and European countries. This **Gulf War** started with air bombings and ended in a five-day ground war that drove Hussein out.

The Clinton Years

Democratic President William (Bill) Clinton was elected in 1992. Unlike Reagan, he supported social programs, although his plan for a national health care system never passed through Congress. He negotiated the North American Free Trade Agreement (NAFTA) with Canada and Mexico in 1993. In 1996, he was impeached for lying under oath about his relationship with a young White House intern, Monica Lewinsky, but the Senate did not think his crimes were severe enough to remove him from office.

1990s and Technology Boom

IBM had introduced personal computers in 1981, and the early 1990s marked the public adoption of the **Internet**, an interconnected communications network that changed the way people accessed information. The 1990s were also a time of violence. This violence included bombings on New York's World Trade Center in 1993 by an Islamic Fundamentalist group, the bombing of the Murrah Federal Building in Oklahoma City in 1995 by antigovernment extremists, race riots, and school shootings.

September 11th Terrorist Attacks

On September 11, 2001, terrorists led by Islamic fundamentalist Osama bin Laden hijacked four airplanes. Terrorists flew two planes into the World Trade Center in New York City, bringing down both buildings, and flew one plane into the Pentagon in Washington, D.C. The other plane crashed into a Pennsylvania field when passengers tried to overthrow the terrorists. The terrorist attack killed over three thousand people. This led President George W. Bush to wage a **war on terror** and resulted in bombing raids on various locations in Afghanistan where bin Laden and his al-Qaeda network were purportedly hiding. When Iraqi dictator Saddam Hussein defied terms of the truce agreed upon in 1991 after the Gulf War, Bush was convinced that the country possessed **weapons of mass destruction (WMDs)** and invaded Iraq in 2003.

Obama's Presidency

Barack Obama, America's first African American President, was elected in 2008. Fighting in the Iraq region continued between groups with differing political and religious views. Obama pulled U.S. troops from the region in 2011, but many have been trickling back into the country in efforts to help maintain order. In 2011, Obama gave the order to launch a raid on bin Laden's compound in Pakistan, which resulted in a group of Navy SEALs finding and killing the al-Qaeda leader. In December 2010, a revolution in Tunisia kicked off a series of democratic uprisings and protests throughout the Middle East. These uprisings are often referred to as the **Arab Spring**. The U.S. pledged support and military aid, but tensions continue to escalate particularly in Syria. The militant group **Islamic State of Iraq and al-Sham (ISIS)** has taken advantage of the Syrian civil war by launching a series of terrorist attacks there and in areas outside the Middle East. Domestically, one of Obama's pledges was to launch a health care reform plan providing affordable and accessible health care for all Americans. He signed the **Affordable Care Act**, sometimes referred to as **Obamacare**, into law in 2010.

Obj 3 *Geography Concepts and Processes*

A **Influence of United States Culture and Geographic Systems on Physical and Human Systems**

<u>Geography</u>

The study of Earth's natural features is referred to as **physical geography**. As the world's third largest country, the United States encompasses an area of approximately 3.8 million square miles. The continental U.S. stretches approximately 2800 miles across North America from the Atlantic Ocean to the Pacific Ocean. This large area is often split into various geographical regions or sub-regions for categorization purposes, such as weather forecasting or determining U.S. census figures. However, five main regions are most typically used to describe the U.S.: Northeast, Southeast, Midwest, Southwest, and West, which includes Alaska and Hawaii, although these two states are separated from the contiguous United States. The unique features of each region help shape and define that area, as well as the United States as a country.

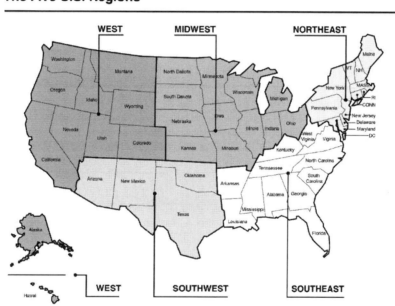

The Five U.S. Regions

<u>U.S. Landforms</u>

The U.S. contains a wide range of landforms with areas of forests, deserts, mountains, large flat plains, and coastal lowlands. Climate variations include: humid continental, arid, semi-arid, Mediterranean (in parts of California), humid subtropical, subarctic (Alaska), and tropical (Hawaii). Major mountain ranges include the Rocky Mountains and Pacific Mountain System in the West and the Appalachian Mountains in the East. The nation's two largest rivers—the Mississippi River and the Missouri River—cut through the Great Plains in the center of the country. The five Great Lakes—Superior, Erie, Ontario, Huron and Michigan—border Canada to the north. The varied landscape also includes a vast number of natural resources, such as lumber, coal, oil, and natural gas, and minerals including iron, uranium, zinc, gold, silver, and copper.

Human Geography

The study of the way that humans populate and interact with Earth is called **human geography**. The first inhabitants of the area now known as the U.S. traveled across a land bridge over the Bering Strait from Asia. Their descendants are the various Native American cultures we know today. Rather than create large cities or agricultural centers, they tracked weather patterns, farmed according to seasonal cycles, and followed animal migrations. After Europeans started coming to America in great numbers, these immigrants built larger population centers on the East Coast, which evolved into big cities including Boston, Philadelphia, New York, and Washington, D.C. However, much of the rugged landscape in the U.S. proved challenging to navigate, particularly for early colonists attempting to migrate to the western part of the country. This rugged landscape included the Appalachian Mountain range, the Mississippi River, and the Rocky Mountains. However, the colonists persevered. Eventually, large cities were built throughout the nation and were interconnected by a transportation system of roads and railroads.

B Using Maps and Globes

The study and making of maps is known as **cartography**. The ability to read a map is a very important skill. Unlike a globe, which represents the Earth's circular shape, maps are flat and two-dimensional. Since maps cannot offer an exact depiction of the coverage area, scale is used to show the relationship between the map measurements and the equivalent distance on the world's surface. Latitude and longitude are used to pinpoint location on a map. **Latitude:** imaginary lines covering the globe from east to west—is always measured north and south of the equator and divides the world into Northern and Southern hemispheres. **Longitude:** imaginary lines running north to south – is measured east or west of the prime meridian and runs through Greenwich, England to divide the Earth into the Eastern and Western hemispheres.

There are many different types of maps and each type is used for various purposes. **Physical maps** show a region's physical landscape and water features. Different color shades are usually used to show vegetation and climate variations. On these maps, green depicts land, brown depicts mountains, and blue depicts water. **Topographical maps** are like physical maps, but are designed to highlight a region's particular surface features by using contour lines to depict detailed elevation. **Thematic maps** emphasize a specific theme, such as social, political, or economic aspects, in tandem with geographical information, which is very useful in studying an area's cultural distribution.

Obj 4 *Government, Civics, Economics, and Their Processes*

A Government and Good Citizenship

A **government** is a system put in place by a country, state, city, or region to institute rules and guidelines for its people to follow. It is typically made up of groups of people, offices, or departments and can be classified into several types, including democracy, republic, monarchy, aristocracy, dictatorship, theocracy, and totalitarian government. The United States is a **democracy**, which literally means *rule by the people*. This means that the people have the power to make changes and decisions. America's Founding Fathers realized that forming a democratic government would be difficult in the U.S. due to the country's sizeable and varied population spread over a vast area. Therefore, they established an **indirect** or **representative democracy** in which the people choose representatives to make decisions for the whole country. This is also referred to as a **democratic republic**.

Native-born and naturalized members of a society who pledge loyalty to its government and are thus protected by its laws are its **citizens**. The status of being a citizen is called **citizenship** and embodies the characteristics that a person is expected to uphold as a responsible member of a community. The term **citizen** originated from the Latin word for city and dates back to government's early days when people aligned with cities rather than countries. Under America's democratic form of government, citizens have the right to keep themselves informed about issues affecting the country, to have a say in government decisions by voting in elections, and to hold public office. They must also obey the law, pay taxes, serve on a jury if asked to do so, and defend the country if necessary (unless it is against their religious beliefs). In order to completely participate in society and understand what it means to be a citizen, it is crucial for students to develop an awareness of civic principles and systems.

Protection of Citizens' Rights Under the United States Constitution

The **U.S. Constitution** is a series of written rules defining the power of the U.S. government and the rights of U.S. citizens. Written in 1787 to create a stronger national government, it is the world's oldest working constitution. It gave Americans more rights than any other country had previously given its people. Collectively referred to as the Bill of Rights, the first ten amendments to the Constitution were added to protect the individual rights of U.S. citizens and to keep the federal government from wielding too much control. These are rights such as freedom of speech, freedom of religion, freedom of the press, and right to a fair trial. The Constitution has been amended twenty-seven times in order to accommodate changes and updates. Some of these amendments were made to be more inclusive to the wide range of American citizens. For example, the 14th Amendment, adopted in 1868, abolished slavery and stated that all citizens must be treated equally under Constitutional law and allowed the same protection within each state.

Foundation of a Republican Form of Government

America's Founding Fathers wanted to break away from the monarchy style of rule they had fled from in England. There, equality and freedoms were suppressed or non-existent. They decided to form a democratic style of government and preserving liberties was the core ideal. They realized that this style of government must have checks and balances in order to run smoothly and ensure the rights and freedoms of its citizens. Therefore, they devised a system of three separate branches—legislative, judicial, and executive. Although each has different responsibilities, the three branches work together to ensure that no one section of the government exerts too much power, and the rights of U.S. citizens are not overlooked or disregarded. Realizing the U.S. was such a huge landmass with many citizens spread out over a large area, they decided on a type of democracy referred to as a **democratic republic**—governed by the people in the form of elected representatives.

Basic Economic Concepts and their Effect on Historic Events

The term **economy** is used to describe and calculate the supply and demand of goods and services. **Economics** is the study of how people decide which resources to use in order to fulfill their needs and the outcome of these choices. It is a multi-tiered dynamic; people need to make personal choices about their own individual spending, while governments must make judgments that shape a whole society. There are two types of economics: micro and macro. **Microeconomics** looks at the interplay of consumers, households, and companies within individual markets and the relationships between them. **Macroeconomics** is the study of entire economies, such as a specific region (the U.S. Northeast, for example); an entire country (the U.S., for example); or a group of countries that share economic traits

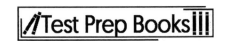

(the European Union, for example). It also includes the analysis of the influence economies have on each another.

Economic activity is cyclical with periods of booms and busts, which are typically prompted by extreme changes in the economy. **Booms** are cycles of increased activity resulting in new businesses, technologies, and jobs. However, these are often followed by periods of economic slowdowns, or **busts**, which can lead to recessions and even depressions. For example, the Wall Street Crash of 1929 triggered the Great Depression of the 1930s. During the Great Depression, New York Stock Market share prices dropped dramatically, causing the world's economic output to decrease by one-third and prompting a spike in unemployment levels of 25 percent or greater among global economies.

Types of Productive Resources and the Role of Money as a Resource

Productive resources are the means used by a society to succeed and survive. The four types are:

1. **Natural resources**—the raw materials taken from the land, such as corn, beef, lumber, water, oil, and iron.

2. **Human resources**—the human labor, both mental and physical, that are required to produce goods.

3. **Capital resources**—the man-made physical resources used to create products, such as machinery, tools, buildings, and equipment.

4. **Entrepreneurship**—the capability and motivation to cultivate, organize, and oversee the other three resources into a business venture.

Money functions as a method of exchange to obtain goods or services. It replaced the barter system, which was often considered inefficient and disorganized. Economists referred to the barter system as a double coincidence of wants since trades between parties were not always considered equal. Prices of goods are determined by supply and demand. **Inflation** occurs when people have money to spend, but not enough goods can be produced or imported to meet their demand for a product, which causes prices to rise. The amount of money issued by government-controlled central banks and the prices of leading commodities, such as oil, can also affect inflation. **Deflation** is when people save their money and spend less, leaving stores with surplus goods, which causes prices to drop.

Major Sectors of the United States Economy and the Interactions Between Businesses and Consumers

Economies consist of the following four business sectors, or parts, that share similar products or services:

- **Primary sector**—gathers natural resources, including industries such as farming, fishing, and oil and gas drilling.

- **Secondary sector**—develops raw materials from the primary sector into finished goods through enhancement, manufacture, or construction, including industries such as car manufacturing, food processing, and steelworks.

- **Tertiary sector**—provides consumer or business services, including industries such as entertainment, travel and tourism, and banking.

- **Quaternary sector**—provides informational and knowledge services, including industries such as universities, consultancies, and research and development companies.

These sectors function like interconnected links in a chain, with each one passing its production along to the next sector. Service industries typically increase as a country develops and constitute the largest sector of both the U.S. and global economies. The U.S. is the leading global economy in terms of size and significance providing twenty percent of the world's total production of goods and services. About eighty percent of this output comes from its innovative, technically advanced services sector, and fifteen percent comes from manufacturing.

Economists often use the **circular flow model** to describe the movement of supply, demand, and payment between businesses and consumers (also referred to as **sectors**). Functioning as an interdependent continuous loop, consumers obtain income, goods, and services from business producers. These producers then receive profits and the ability to buy necessary supplies. Money flows one way, and the goods and productive resources flow in the opposite direction. Each sector relies on the other.

Here's an illustration of that:

Circular Flow Model

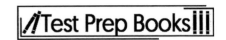

Costs and Benefits of Personal Spending and Savings Choices

Individuals earn an income by trading their labor – both mental and physical – for pay. They then budget their money through spending or saving it. As consumers, every choice has an opportunity cost since they must choose which goods and services they want to buy with a limited income. By purchasing one good or service, they give up the chance to purchase another.

Additionally, consumers have the choice to save money when they don't have enough money to purchase what they want, or when they want to utilize a savings account to use during emergencies or periods of economic difficulty. People also choose to save for **retirement**, a time when they will no longer be working and drawing a salary. Saving money by putting it in a bank is considered low-risk—the bank will pay the saver a low interest rate to keep it safe, but it will not increase much in value. A riskier path is investing money through the purchase of valuable items (or **assets**) in the hopes that they will increase in worth over time and yield returns (or **profits**). Assets can include shares in companies, real estate or land investments, or capital such as money, equipment, and structures used to create wealth.

Practice Questions

1. Which of the following civilizations developed the first democratic form of government?
    a. Roman Empire
    b. Ancient Greece
    c. Achaemenid Empire
    d. Zhou dynasty

2. What are the two main parts of the federal legislative branch?
    a. President and vice president
    b. Federal and state
    c. District court and court of appeals
    d. Senate and House of Representatives

3. What was a concern that George Washington warned of in his Farewell Address?
    a. The danger of political parties
    b. To be prepared to intervene in Europe's affairs
    c. The abolition of slavery
    d. To protect states' rights through sectionalism

4. What is NOT a responsibility for citizens of democracy?
    a. To stay aware of current issues and history
    b. To avoid political action
    c. To actively vote in elections
    d. To understand and obey laws

5. Which of the following statements is true?
    a. Times zones are defined by their latitude.
    b. Eastern and Western hemispheres are defined by the prime meridian.
    c. A place is constant, while a location is changeable with the movement of people.
    d. A continent is one of six especially large landmasses in the world.

Answer Explanations

1. B: Ancient Greeks created many of the cultural and political institutions that form the basis of modern western civilization. Athens was an important Greek democracy, and all adult men could participate in politics after they had completed their military service. The Roman Empire, Choice *A*, evolved from the Roman Republic, but it was not democratic. The Achaemenid Empire and Zhou Dynasty, Choices *C* and *D*, were imperial monarchies that did not allow citizens to have much, if any, political voice.

2. D: The president and vice president are part of the executive branch, not the legislative branch. The question focuses specifically on the federal level, so state government should be excluded from consideration. As for the district court and the court of appeals, they are part of the judicial branch. The legislative branch is made up of Congress, which consists of the House of Representatives and the Senate.

3. A: George Washington was a slave owner himself in life, so he did not make abolition a theme in his Farewell Address. On the other hand, he was concerned that sectionalism could potentially destroy the United States, and he warned against it. Furthermore, he believed that Americans should avoid getting involved in European affairs. However, one issue that he felt was especially problematic was the formation of political parties, and he urged against it in his farewell.

4. B: To avoid involvement in political processes such as voting is antithetical to the principles of a democracy. Therefore, the principal responsibility of citizens is the opposite, and they should be steadily engaged in the political processes that determine the course of government.

5. B: Time zones are determined by longitude, not latitude. Locations are defined in absolute terms, while places are in part defined by the population, which is subject to movement. There are seven continents in the world, not six. On the other hand, it is true that the prime meridian determines the border for the Eastern and Western hemispheres.

Analysis

Incorporating Appropriate Teaching Approaches into Classroom Instruction for English Language Arts

Applying and Using Developmentally-Appropriate Pedagogical Practices for Planning Curriculum, Designing Instruction, and Evaluating Student Progress in Reading and Language Arts

Visual Instructional Techniques

Studies continue to show a strong correlation between language development and the use of visual aids. From the primary years of education through the post-secondary years, the use of visual aids as a way to enhance reading comprehension has proven to be very effective. In the primary grades, picture books provide students with visual cues that help them to decode unknown words and strengthen reading comprehension. Visual aids support and clarify meaning, helping to make the learning and reading process more enjoyable and more interactive. When educators engage the students in a **picture walk**, skimming through picture books prior to reading, children become more motivated to read. Even reluctant readers, struggling readers, and English language learners are more apt to pick up a picture book and attempt to read it from cover to cover, enjoying the graphics and using them as powerful clues to the text's overall meaning.

Graphic novels are also becoming a popular addition to classroom and school libraries. With a structural approach that is similar to comic books, graphic novels have a strong appeal to children in the middle school years, teen years, and beyond. The visual images within graphic novels help children to make immediate connections to a story's plot and help them to understand potentially more challenging information.

As a universal learning tool, visual aids help all learners to comprehend the meaning behind the words and strengthen their ability to retain information over a longer period of time.

Oral Instructional Techniques

When children are just learning to read, they benefit greatly from shared reading and oral reading experiences. Having a teacher or a classmate read a book aloud helps emergent readers connect their phonemic awareness skills to a growing understanding and application of print awareness. This will begin to form the foundation for more advanced reading skills in later years.

Oral reading also helps children strengthen their use of vocabulary and advances their vocabulary inventory. Educators and more advanced readers who model oral reading fluency—including rate, accuracy, and prosody—demonstrate to young readers that the process of reading is highly interactive and meaningful. Educators who spend significant time engaging in classroom discussions and asking and answering questions help children develop social interaction skills, listening comprehension skills, and oral communication skills. When early and intensive instruction focuses on oral language development, educators set the groundwork for future reading success.

Oral and Visual Instructional Techniques

Multimedia presentations, such as PowerPoint or SlideShare, have been traditionally most effective at the higher education levels. However, as young children are more and more exposed to a world of technology, educators at the primary years are beginning to employ multimedia presentations in the classroom.

If carefully planned out, multimedia presentations can be used to enhance comprehension on virtually any subject. Using powerful graphic imagery that is directly relevant to the topic—coupled with effective textual language or audio—has been particularly effective in a growing number of classrooms.

Presenting students with the challenge of creating their own multimedia presentations can also be very rewarding for educators and students alike. Either independently, in pairs, or in groups, children take the learning process into their own hands with the opportunity to demonstrate the knowledge of a given subject by employing relevant written text and graphics.

Phonics and Word Analysis

As mentioned, **phonics** is the study of sound-letter relationships in alphabetic writing systems, such as the English language, and it is paramount to a child's future ability to read and write. Phonics helps children recognize and identify letter symbols and translate these symbols into their corresponding sound units, phonemes. The study of phonics concerns itself with the **Alphabetic Principle**—the systematic relationships that exist between letters and sounds—as well as with **Phonemic Awareness**—the understanding that letters correspond with distinct sounds and that there are specific rules governing the placement of letters in the English language.

As children become more familiar with recognizing the names and shapes of each letter, called **graphemes**, they begin to verbally practice their corresponding sounds—the **phonemes**. Although this sounds straightforward, it can pose significant challenges to both the children and teachers.

For example, when children learn that the letter *y* is pronounced /wigh/, but that it can make other various sounds, including /ee/, /i/, and /igh/—depending on letter placement—it may take repeated practice in order for children to pronounce and read this one letter accurately. Some examples would be the words, *happy, gym,* and *cry*. Although each word contains the same vowel, *y*, the placement of the *y* in each word differs, which affects the letter's pronunciation.

For this reason, there is an ongoing debate in literacy circles regarding the appropriate instructional approach for teaching phonics. Should educators teach letter shapes with their corresponding names or letter shapes with their corresponding sound or sounds? Is it possible to combine instruction to include shapes, names, and sounds, or should each of these skills be taught in isolation with a cumulative approach—shape, sound/s, and name? Some experts believe that when children are introduced to letter names and shapes in isolation of their corresponding sounds, children can become quickly confused, which can delay reading acquisition. Therefore, the answer to what approach to take lies with a keen understanding of a student's background knowledge in English and each child's specific needs. In order to create effective phonics instruction and help students strengthen literacy development, it is strongly suggested that educators are sensitive and aware of these unique challenges to English language acquisition.

It is widely accepted that letter-sound relationships are best taught systematically, introducing one relationship at a time and gradually increasing in complexity. Effective instruction in the initial stages of phonics awareness involves explicit introduction of the most important and the most frequently used letter-sound relationships. For instance, short vowels should be introduced and practiced ahead of long vowels, and lowercase letters should be introduced ahead of uppercase as they occur the most often. Letters that frequently appear in simple words, such as /a/, /m/, and /t/ would be logical starting points.

The following guide offers an introduction of phonics instruction:

Introduction	Examples
Initial consonants	s, t, m, n, p
Short vowel and consonant	-it, -in, -at, -an
Consonant blends	-st, -bl, -dr
Digraphs	-th, -ph, -sh, -ch
Long vowels	ear, eat, oar, oat
Final (silent) e	site, mine, lane
Variant vowels and diphthongs	-au, -oo, -ow, -ou, -oi
Silent letters and inflectional endings	-kn, -gn, -wr, es, s

Effective phonics instruction begins with focusing on the overall literacy experiences of the students and connecting these experiences to further their literacy development. Best practices in teaching will work to establish a student's prior phonics knowledge, if there is any at all. Educators can differentiate their instruction based on their students' unique needs and background knowledge of phonics. Creating phonics activities that ensure students are actively engaged and motivated is key to overall success in literacy development.

Once children have mastered the relationship that exists between the names, shapes, sounds of letters, and letter combinations, educators may begin a more implicit instructional approach by incorporating the children's current phonics awareness with simple basal readers that focus on basic monosyllabic words. Grouping monosyllabic words according to their initial sounds continues to be an effective approach to instruction as the students advance in their understanding and application of phonics. When educators combine or further this practice with that of identifying the names of the initial letters in the words, children are likely to have more success with overall literacy development. A **word wall** with simple consonant-vowel-consonant words in alphabetical order acts as a visual reference to help strengthen a child's literacy development:

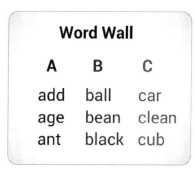

At this stage, educators begin laying the foundation for reading readiness. Children begin listening to others read and start to recognize familiar sounds within the words being read. They independently practice sounding out words and will soon learn how to independently segment, blend, and manipulate the individual sounds in each newly acquired word.

When a child demonstrates phonological awareness and a clear understanding of how phonics works, they are ready to further their literacy development with **word analysis**. Word analysis is an effective study that helps students acquire new vocabulary. **Morpheme**s are when words are broken down into their smallest units of meaning. Each morpheme within words carry specific meanings, therefore adding to children's understanding of entire words. When children begin to recognize key morphemes—especially prefixes and suffixes—they are beginning to demonstrate word analysis skills, which is a critical foundation in literacy development.

Word analysis helps children to read and comprehend complex reading materials, including informational texts. It is essential for vocabulary development. Word analysis skills also help children clarify the meaning of unknown words, figurative language, word relationships, and nuances in word meaning with the use of context clues.

Some effective instructional strategies to teach word analysis skills include Universal Design for Learning (UDL), studying words according to a subject theme, using diagrams and graphic organizers, and pre-teaching and reviewing new vocabulary on a regular basis. UDL involves the modeling of how to analyze new words by breaking them down into their individual morphemes and studying each morpheme separately. Once each morpheme in a given word has been identified and defined, students put the morphemes back together in order to understand the word in its entirety. The following is a word analysis study of the word *astronaut*:

Word	Morpheme 1	Morpheme 2	Word Meaning
astronaut	astro—Greek origin, roughly translates to anything relating to the stars and outer space	naut—Greek origin, roughly translates to "sailor"	a sailor of outer space

Studying words according to a shared theme is another effective word analysis strategy. For instance, when studying mathematics, educators may focus on words that contain the same prefix, such as *kilometer*, *kilogram*, and *kilowatt*. Common suffixes in science include *microscope*, *telescope*, and *macroscope*.

Diagrams and graphic organizers provide students with visual clues to contrast and compare word meanings. From organizational charts and mind maps to Venn diagrams and more, visual aids help students readily see and analyze the similarities and differences in various word meanings.

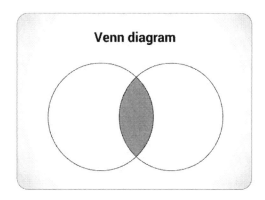

With the introduction to new topics of discussion or a new theme to any subject area, it is likely that there will also be an introduction to new, unfamiliar words. Both educators and students will benefit from a formal introduction to these new words prior to the lesson. Pre-teaching new vocabulary increases vocabulary acquisition and allows children to become comfortable and familiar with new terms ahead of the lesson. Pre-teaching new vocabulary has also been shown to reduce unnecessary stress and time that would otherwise be taken to stop lessons in order to explain unfamiliar words.

Letter-Sound Correspondences

When children begin to learn the various letter-sound correspondences, their phonemic awareness begins to overlap with their awareness of orthography and reading. One of the widely accepted strategies to employ when introducing children to letter-sound correspondences is to begin with those correspondences that occur the most frequently in simple English words. In an effort to help build confidence in young learners, educators are encouraged to introduce only a few letter-sound combinations at a time and provide ample opportunities for practice and review before introducing new combinations. Although there is no formally established order for the introduction of letter-sound correspondences, educators are encouraged to consider the following general guidelines, but they should also keep in mind the needs, experiences, and current literacy levels of the students. The following is intended as a general guide only:

1. a	6. n	11. g	16. l	21. x
2. m	7. c	12. h	17. e	22. v
3. t	8. d	13. i	18. r	23. y
4. p	9. u	14. f	19. w	24. z
5. o	10. s	15. b	20. k	25. j
				26. q

As a generally accepted rule, short vowels should be introduced ahead of long vowels, and uppercase letters should be mastered before the introduction of their lowercase counterparts.

Spelling conventions in the English language are primarily concerned with three areas: mechanics, usage, and sentence formation.

Mechanics

For primary students who are just beginning to master the alphabetic principle, educators should first concentrate on proper letter formation, the spelling of high-frequency words and sight words, and offer classroom discussions to promote the sharing of ideas. When children begin to write in sentences to share their thoughts and feelings in print, educators may consider the introduction of an author's chair, in which students read their writing out loud to their classmates.

Although the phonetic spelling or invented spelling that primary students employ in these early stages may not be the conventional spelling of certain words, it allows primary students to practice the art and flow of writing. It works to build their confidence in the writing process. This is not the time for educators to correct spelling, punctuation, or capitalization errors as young learners may quickly lose interest in writing and may lose self-confidence.

One strategy to employ early on to help students with proper spelling is to ensure there is an easily accessible and updated word wall that employs high-frequency words and sight words. Students should be encouraged to refer to the word wall while they write.

Usage

Usage concerns itself with word order, verb tense, and subject-verb agreement among other areas. As primary children often have a basic knowledge of how to use oral language effectively in order to communicate, this area of spelling conventions may require less initial attention than the mechanics of spelling. During read-aloud and shared reading activities, educators may wish to point out punctuation marks found in print, model how to read these punctuation marks, and periodically discuss their importance in the reading and writing process.

When children begin to engage in writing exercises, educators may wish to prompt self-editing skills by asking if each sentence begins with a capital and ends with a period, question mark, or exclamation point.

Sentence Formation

Verbs, nouns, adverbs, and adjectives all play significant roles in the writing process. However, for primary students, these concepts are fairly complex to understand. One instruction approach that may prove effective is to categorize a number of simple verbs, nouns, adverbs, and adjectives on index cards by color coordination. Educators can then ask one child to choose a noun card and another student to choose a verb card. The children can then face the class and read their words starting with the noun and then the verb. The students can even try reading the verb first followed by the noun. A class discussion can follow, analyzing whether or not the sentences made sense and what words might need to be added to give the sentence more meaning.

Distinguishing High-Frequency Sight Words from Decodable Words

Beginning readers enter primary school years with many challenges involving literacy development. Tackling the alphabetic principle and phonemic awareness helps children to recognize that specific sounds are usually comprised of specific letters, or a combination thereof, and that each letter or combination of letters carries a specific sound. However, these young readers are also faced with the challenge of sight word mastery. **Sight words** do not necessarily follow the alphabetic principle and appear quite often in primary reading material. Some sight words are decodable, but many are not, which requires the additional challenge of memorizing correct spelling. Some of these non-decodable sight words include words such as *who, the, he, does,* and so on. There are approximately one hundred sight words that appear throughout primary texts.

The goal for primary teachers is to help emergent readers to recognize these sight words automatically, in order to help strengthen reading fluency. One effective instructional approach is to provide children daily opportunities to practice sight words in meaningful contexts and to establish a clearly visible, large print word wall that children can freely access throughout the day. Dr. Edward William Dolch was a well-known and respected children's author and professor who, in the late 1940s, published a list of sight words he believed appeared most frequently in children's literature for grades kindergarten through second grade. Now known as the Dolch Word List, these sight words are still widely used in primary classrooms throughout the United States. Organized by grade and frequency, the Dolch Word List consists of 220 words in total, with the first one hundred known as the "Dolch 100 List." Dr. Edward Fry, a university professor, author, and expert in the field of reading, published another commonly used high-frequency word list approximately a decade later. Although similar in many ways to the Dolch List, the Fry Word List primarily focuses on sight words that appear most frequently in reading material for third to ninth grade. Other high-frequency word lists now exist, but the Dolch and Fry word lists are still widely used in today's elementary classrooms. The debate, however, is whether to teach high-frequency sight words in isolation or as part of the integrated phonics program.

Unlike many sight words, **decodable words** follow the rules of phonics and are spelled phonetically. They are spelled precisely the way they sound—as in words like *dad* and *sit*. When a child has mastered his or her phonics skills, these decodable words can also be easily mastered with continued opportunities to practice reading. Activities involving segmenting and blending decodable words also help to strengthen a child's decoding skills. Some educators will find that it is beneficial to integrate lessons involving decodable words and high-frequency sight words, while others may see a need to keep these lessons separate until children have demonstrated mastery or near mastery of phonemic awareness. Some activities that encourage the memorization of sight words and strengthen decoding skills involve the use of flash cards, phonemic awareness games, air writing, and card games, such as *Bingo* and *Go Fish*.

Both Dolch and Fry word lists are organized according to frequency and grade level. It is widely accepted that educators follow a cumulative approach to reading instruction, introducing high-frequency sight words that are also phonetically decodable. Should words appear in the lesson that are not phonetically decodable, educators may wish to use this as an opportunity to evaluate the children's phonemic awareness skills and determine whether or not students are ready for lessons that integrate non-decodable sight words. For instance, an educator might challenge a student to study the parts of the non-decodable sight word by asking whether or not there are parts of the word that are phonetically decodable and parts that are not. This approach gives students the opportunity for guided word study and acts as a bridge between phonemic awareness skills and sight word memorization.

Determining what lists of words to introduce to students varies greatly and depends on an initial and ongoing spelling assessment of each child to determine his or her current spelling and reading levels. Effective instructional approaches also involve the intentional selection of words that demonstrate a specific spelling pattern, followed by multiple opportunities to read, spell, segment, and blend these word families. Students will benefit the greatest with ongoing formative and summative assessments of their decoding skills as well as their ability to apply their word knowledge to and memorize non-decodable sight words.

With the reinforcement of high-frequency word walls, daily opportunities to read, write, and engage in meaningful word games and activities, children will gradually begin to develop their reading and spelling skills and learn to become more fluent and capable readers.

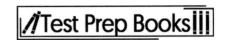

When students are invited to become word detectives, the study of root words and affixes is of prime importance. There are several instructional approaches to the study of root words and affixes, including a multi-sensory guided approach in which children can physically pull apart the affixes to be left with the root word and then manipulate the root word by playing with a variety of suffixes and prefixes. The following table begins with the original word containing both a prefix and suffix. The word is pulled apart into its individual components—root, prefix, and suffix. Then, it is given a new prefix and suffix to form a new word, carrying a completely new meaning:

Original Word	Root Word	Prefix	Suffix	New Prefix	New Suffix	New Word
inactive	act	in	ive	De	ate	deactivate
disbelieving	believe	dis	ing	Un	able	unbelievable
unbearable	bear	un	able	For	ing	forbearing

Effective instruction for root, prefix, and suffix study should involve the active exploration of words, with ample opportunity for children to read the words in meaningful context. Typically, a formal study of root words and affixes is introduced by the 4th grade, but it may be introduced earlier, depending on the students' understanding of basic phonics and spelling patterns. It is important for educators to keep in mind that new vocabulary terms, verb forms, plurals, and compound words may present a challenge for some students.

A formal study of root words, prefixes, and suffixes strengthens a child's knowledge of word meanings, expands vocabulary knowledge, and advances his or her understanding and application of various spelling patterns. Children will learn more about how affixes affect the spelling of the root word and can completely alter its meaning, which ultimately strengthens their ability to read, write, and spell accurately and effectively. As children become familiar with various affixes, they will begin to decipher the meaning of unfamiliar words that share the same affixes and roots.

Inferences Made from Text Supported with Appropriate Evidence

Although related to predictions and the finding of factual information, **inferences** refer to the ability to make logical assumptions based on contextual clues. People of all ages make inferences about the world around them on a daily basis but may not be aware of what they are doing. Even young children may infer that it is likely cold outside if they wake up and their bedroom is chilly or the floor is cold. While being driven somewhere on the highway and a child notices a person at the side of the road with a parked car, that child will likely infer that the individual is having car problems and is awaiting some assistance. Therefore, the challenge for educators is not necessarily teaching children how to infer, but rather demonstrating how this skill they already use can be transferred into the study of various texts.

One effective introductory strategy may be to set up scenarios within the classroom and challenge the children to infer what is happening. For instance, the educator may arrive at school pretending to have a cold without saying anything. By placing a personal box of tissues on the desk along with a nasal spray and frequently sneezing, the teacher is challenging the students to infer that he or she not feeling well. Once the children begin to understand that making inferences is indeed similar to detective work by collecting key evidence, the educator can now introduce more inanimate objects like photographs, pictures, or diagrams void of explanatory language. The children's task would be to study the visual aids to try to infer what the subject is about. Educators can assist the children initially by asking questions aloud, modeling how to arrive at a logical inference. For example, the teacher might hold up a picture of a school in which all children are gathered in the playground and grouped according to their classes. Upon closer examination, the children might spot a fire truck parked at the side of the road and may infer that the school had a fire drill or an actual fire.

As the children progress in their ability to infer based on picture clues, it is time to transfer their new skill to texts. Educators may wish to begin with inference challenges in which students are prompted to write short stories about specific events—without directly mentioning the event. For instance, if a child is interested in swimming, they may write about the ideal temperature of the water, backstroke, freestyle, full laps, and so on without ever mentioning the word *swimming*. Other children in the class will then be prompted to read the short story and infer what the text is about. The children must examine the clues in the text, make an inference, and support the inference with evidence from the text:

> In the second paragraph, it says that the water was relatively warm, so it was easy to finish a full lap. This must mean that the person was swimming in the water.

The more initial practice children receive before moving into more complicated texts, the most success they will have in making accurate inferences and, in turn, the more fun they will have acting as text detectives.

Summarization of Information

Summarizing should be explicitly taught beginning in the primary school years with continual reinforcement and gradual introduction to more complex texts as students progress. In order to summarize effectively, children need to demonstrate the following abilities:

- Text comprehension
- Identification of main idea
- Elimination of inconsequential information
- Ability to condense
- Ability to paraphrase
- Ability to organize writing in a logical order

Personal Summaries

Educators are encouraged to first assist children in summarizing texts as a means to strengthen personal comprehension. For instance, when children are able to identify a text's main idea, state that idea in their own words, and back up that main idea with supporting evidence, they are learning to summarize, and their comprehension undoubtedly strengthens.

Summarizing for oneself is also an invaluable tool for studying and memorizing, which children will use throughout their academic careers. When students summarize for themselves, the goal is to strengthen overall comprehension of the text, arrive at the author's point of view, and isolate the main idea. Since the summary is intended to be only for the student, there is no need to pay particular attention to spelling, grammar, or sentence structure. Students are learning to make personal notes for the purpose of comprehension strengthening and, possibly, memorization for upcoming tests.

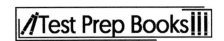

Summaries for Others

Once children have demonstrated a clear ability to summarize a variety of texts for their own understanding, educators may begin to introduce them to the skill of **summarizing for others**. This involves a more complex approach to summarization. Now that students have ownership of the given text, they inherit the challenge of explaining the text's meaning to an audience. In addition to extracting the main idea, eliminating unimportant text elements, reorganizing and condensing the text, and paraphrasing, students must now pay close attention to the summary's length, the mechanics of writing, and the audience. For example, are students writing to classmates to help them better understand the text? Are they writing the summary for their teacher, in an effort to demonstrate their ability to summarize? Since this type of summarization involves a polished finish, children must also employ proofreading and revision skills.

Educators who are introducing summarization for the first time should focus on less complex texts that involve familiar subject matter, and the texts should be well organized, with titles, possible subtitles, and easily identifiable main ideas. Allowing children to refer to the text as often as possible while learning to summarize is also an important teaching strategy. Children at the early stages of summarizing should not be expected to have memorized and clearly understood what they have read. Sometimes children need to reread the same text several times before beginning a summarization. By explicitly teaching children how to recognize signaling devices, educators help them summarize and isolate a text's main idea. Some signaling devices may be found in an introductory or summary statement or specific words or phrases that have been placed in italics, bold print, or are underlined.

The more advanced students become with summarizing texts, the greater their comprehension and ability to apply what they learn will be.

Key Claims from Textual Evidence

The ability to identify significant claims made by the author and to support those claims with evidence found within the text is integral to the development of reading comprehension and critical thinking skills. Educators need to introduce key vocabulary words and phrases that authors use when stating and supporting claims. These vocabulary terms can be added to an ever-changing and expanding classroom word wall, incorporated into personal dictionaries and captured on charts to further classroom discussions. Once children begin to identify key words and phrases as indicators of claims and claim evidence, they are ready to begin the more complex task of evaluating these claims.

When children can identify claims and show evidence that supports the claims, educators may wish to initiate a class discussion on whether or not these claims are valid. For instance, prompting a reader's background knowledge and personal experiences on the topic, examining the author's expertise on the subject, weighing any possible cultural or personal bias the author may have, and comparing/contrasting the author's claims to claims made by other authors on the same subject will help children develop objectivity as they read.

Key Details, Moral, and/or Theme of a Literary Text

Literary analysis of a text involves the study of character development, setting, mood, plot, point(s) of view, figurative language, and other literary elements. The **study of informational text** involves nonfictional elements, such as the author's purpose, major ideas or concepts, and more. All of these individual components in a text often interrelate and form the text's overall theme or message. Some common universal themes found in literature include disappointment, courage, overcoming obstacles, loneliness, and good triumphing over evil. In informational texts, the themes or messages vary greatly, but they usually involve subjects that pertain to the natural or social world. When children reach the stage in their literacy development that allows them to begin literary analysis exercises, they are beginning to take their reading comprehension beyond the surface details to arrive at an even deeper understanding of the text by studying these individual themes and messages.

When first introducing literary analysis, it is important for educators to select texts that carry themes children can relate to. Educators are encouraged to consider themes that depict similar life experiences or interests. Although many themes in texts are universal in nature, the younger the students are, the more important it is to choose texts that have themes with which they can identify, that appeal to their interests, and that inspire discussion and debate. As children progress and strengthen their literacy skills, they will be able to apply these skills to a wider variety of themes.

An ideal strategy to introduce literary analysis is to hold class discussions at the beginning and ending of texts, as well as periodically throughout the reading of a given text. Educators may prompt these class discussions with key questions that help students to make connections between the events and characters in a fictional text and the students' life experiences. Class discussions allow children to hear multiple ideas, which works to strengthen overall comprehension and build an appreciation of alternate points of view. These key questions also prompt children to consider their own feelings as they read the text, helping them to connect on a personal or emotional level, which strengthens overall comprehension. Class discussions should also challenge children a little further by asking them to explain why they feel a certain way about a message in the text. Once children have had ample opportunity to practice and master this skill, the next step is to teach children how to support their thoughts, feelings, and ideas by finding textual evidence that supports their views.

Learning to find supporting evidence within a text is a very complex skill that can initially cause some confusion and frustration. One strategy to employ that may assist children in learning how to find key information is the introduction of graphic organizers. The following is an example of a graphic organizer that is split into three sections:

Student Answer	Text Evidence (quotation and page number)	Explanation

Searching for supportive evidence involves more than merely finding a quotation. The above graphic organizer guides students to connect the specific quotation(s) to their interpretation and further provides students the opportunity to explain, in their own words, how their answers and the quotations are connected. Forming credible and logical responses to questions and supporting those responses with appropriate quotations from the text are considered very advanced literary skills, which take students to a much deeper understanding of literature.

In order for students to become independent readers and draw their own conclusions about what they read, it is critical that they learn to discern the **author's purpose**. One obvious approach to teaching children how to reveal an author's purpose is to simply ask children why they think the author wrote this information. These types of open-ended class discussions allow children to express their ideas, explore

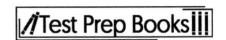

theories, and consider what others have to say on the subject. Educators can record various answers and then ask the children to return to the text as detectives, looking for clues that support each theory.

Another approach to uncovering the author's purpose is for students to take a closer look at the written structure of the text and the vocabulary usage. For example, is the text's structure written in chronological order, simply listing events as they occurred? Does the text open up with a problem that is then resolved? Is the author using cause/effect or compare/contrast vocabulary? Learning about the structure of the text gives great insight into the author's purpose.

When children develop reading fluency, they are able to read a text with minimal to no errors, with consistent speed, and with appropriate expression, and they learn to connect with what they are reading on a personal level. As children read through an informational text, educators may ask how the students are feeling. Did they begin feeling one way and end up feeling another by the end of the text? When children examine their own personal feelings with regard to what they have read, they will be in a better position to explore the author's purpose.

Once children have had several opportunities to explore the author's purpose using a variety of informational texts, prompting them to write their own informational texts will help them to develop and strengthen a better understanding about writing with a purpose. Perhaps they can write a procedural text that lists the steps in how to ride a bike, or they can write a persuasive paper to try to convince their teacher that extra free time during the school day stimulates learning.

Learning to identify an author's purpose connects children with their reading on a deeper level. Instead of believing everything they read, they will begin to understand that there are many reasons why authors write, and they will further understand that they possess the ability to draw their own conclusions and make their own decisions on any given topic.

Some children struggle with identifying the main idea of an informational text. Before prompting students to locate the main idea of a given text or passage, educators must first explain what the main idea actually is. Here are some guidelines, tips, and tricks to follow that will help children identify the main idea:

Identifying the Main Idea
The most important part of the text
Text title and pictures may reveal clues
Opening sentences and final sentences may reveal clues
Key vocabulary words that are repeatedly used may reveal clues

Providing students with simple lists of related vocabulary may be a logical starting point when teaching how to recognize a main idea. For instance, on a large chart, educators may list several fruits, vegetables, snacks, and meals, and then prompt the children to explain what they have in common. This also works well with a set of images, pictures, or photographs that all represent the same idea. After repeated practice, children will begin to strengthen their ability to center in on the main idea that connects all the elements on the list.

Once children begin to identify and demonstrate a clear understanding of the main idea in simple lists, educators may wish to introduce simple texts that gradually increase in complexity.

Once the main idea, the apple, is accurately identified, educators can now ask children to locate words that describe or support this main idea and highlight/circle each supporting word:

The *apple* is hard, red, and juicy.

Simple sentence exercises will gradually become simple paragraphs and, eventually, full texts in which children are challenged with the task of locating the main idea and the supporting details. Children must learn to differentiate between trivial and supporting details by evaluating whether or not the detail in question further quantifies or qualifies the main idea. If the detail does neither, it is likely not important enough to be considered a supporting detail and can be left alone.

Graphic organizers can also be a helpful tool when working with main ideas and supporting details. There are many graphic organizers that help students to organize their analysis into clear and visible representations. The following are examples of graphic organizers that are commonly used when teaching the main idea and supporting details.

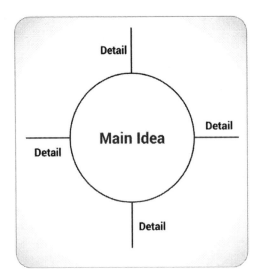

Children who demonstrate the ability to accurately identify a text's main idea and supporting details can further strengthen these skills by attempting to write their own texts with a main idea and supporting details. Likewise, graphic organizers can be used as tools that help children to organize their thoughts and ideas before they begin this writing process.

Visual or Graphic Aids

Authors of informational texts will often employ the use of visual or graphic aids in strategic locations throughout the text in order to strengthen the reader's understanding of the topic at hand. Visual aids can provide an overview of key information, illustrate relationships among important text elements, and summarize the main idea. Visual aids are generally colorful and catch students' attention; they help to simplify what could be potentially complicated information. There are a multitude of visual aids that are frequently used in informational texts, including models, graphs, charts, tables, maps, drawings, photographs, and time lines. Some visual aids also involve a side bar, which defines key vocabulary necessary to understand the topic.

In most instances, children merely need to look at the visual aid to make an instant connection. The implementation of graphic aids in writing reduces instructional time and strengthens comprehension. During read alouds and guided reading sessions, educators may wish to model how to extract meaning from visual aids by connecting the graphic to specific elements in the text. Before reading begins, educators have students skim through the pages to find the visual aids and predict what the text may be about based on the text's graphics. Therefore, visual aids may often help students to identify the text's main idea.

The time it requires to read and process the written text is considerably longer than the time it takes to derive meaning from the graph. Helping students to identify and derive meaning from visual aids will help to strengthen their reading comprehension skills and overall literacy development.

Vocabulary

Vocabulary used throughout informational texts is generally quite different than vocabulary found in fictional print. For this reason, it is imperative that educators help children strengthen and increase their vocabulary inventory so that they can eventually become successful at reading and understanding informational text.

For instance, educators can point out **signal words** throughout texts to help children more readily and accurately identify the author's purpose. There are specific vocabulary words that authors employ that spotlight the author's intent. For instance, if authors wish to list examples to support a main idea, they may use vocabulary such as *for example*, *such as*, or *as illustrated*. When displaying the chronological order of events, authors may use *first*, *lastly*, *before*, and *finally*. Some common compare and contrast vocabulary words include *but*, *same as*, *similar to*, *as opposed to*, and *however*. There are several key phrases that signal cause and effect relationships, including *because of*, *as a result of*, and *in order to*.

Using word walls and personal dictionaries, sorting vocabulary words according to theme, introducing text maps, and teaching children to become familiar with sidebars and glossaries in informational texts, educators will help expand their students' vocabulary and strengthen their ability to read and comprehend informational texts successfully.

Determining Point of View

To help students develop an awareness of which point of view the author is applying, educators may wish to model the thinking process required to locate point of view evidence. Beginning with a character analysis in chart form, for instance, educators and students can list all characters within a story and discuss the character traits of each one. Teachers may then ask the students why they believe characters possess certain traits and may then facilitate this understanding by referring to specific areas in the story that reveal these traits.

Using various excerpts from familiar stories to develop a character analysis also helps children strengthen point of view awareness. Working as literary detectives, students should be prompted to look for the pronouns *he, she,* and *I* and then focus on the key vocabulary surrounding these pronouns. The ability to identify key vocabulary used to evoke emotion, as well as vocabulary used to simply state facts, will be very useful in developing a student's ability to recognize points of view within a story:

Emotional Vocabulary	Factual Vocabulary
Fear: apprehensive, cautious, concerned, hesitant, uneasy, watchful	Facts: details, knowledge, information, proof
Anger: annoyed, cranky, critical, frustrated, irritated	Data: as evidenced by statistics
Sadness: disappointed, heartbroken, gloomy, depressed	Historical Information: recorded, an account of
Happy: amused, inspired, joyful, pleased	Quotations: testimony, witness, verification, affidavit

Educators should consider using a variety of instructional approaches when comparing and contrasting points of view. One strategy educators can implement is a class debate or partner debate. A debate brings students to center stage as they learn to defend the point of view of various characters within a story while listening to classmates defend the points of view of other characters. Friendly debating has been proven to strengthen a student's ability to reason, apply logic, communicate with self-expression, listen to others, and organize thoughts and opinions. Debating also helps children develop an appreciation for opposing points of view and, therefore, works to build stronger bonds both in and out of the classroom. By taking on the point of view of a character in a story with the added responsibility of defending that point of view with evidence, students broaden their own thought processes and challenge the world around them in more depth.

Visual aids are another strategy that educators use when comparing and contrasting points of views, especially when examining characters in stories. Venn diagrams are especially effective as they provide a clear space for unique perspectives, with a common overlapping section for similarities. There are several visual aids available for use in the classroom depending on the age and ability of the students. From the earliest of primary education to the upper level high school grades, visual aids continue to be a powerful instructional tool.

The visual aid below demonstrates opposing and shared characteristics of characters:

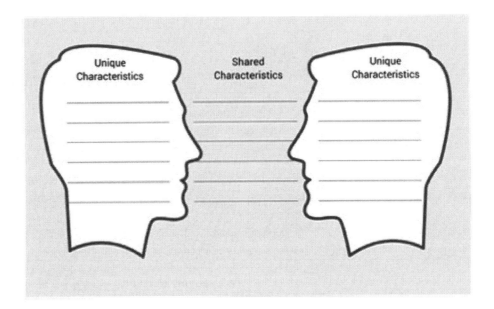

Engaging Oral Presentations

Oral presentations can cause panic in a classroom as children scramble to figure out how, when, where, why, and what to speak about. However, if given proper guidance, appropriate time, and constructive feedback, the panic will soon fade, and in turn, students will learn how to give powerful oral presentations.

In order to be effective, educators should follow best practices, including sharing a well-designed rubric with the class, discussing the importance of each skill listed, answering any questions the children might have, and providing ongoing and constructive feedback while children develop their presentations.

Key areas to develop oral presentations:

Volume

Children should consider where the presentation would be held. Will it be indoors, outdoors, in an auditorium, or in the classroom? Learning to match the volume of the presentation with the location and size of the audience will greatly improve the presentation.

Articulation

Pronouncing words clearly is another aspect of effective communication, especially during an oral presentation. Slurred words, rushed words, mumbling, or leaving out the beginning or ending of sentences will have a negative impact on the message, and the presenter risks losing the interest of the audience.

Awareness of Audience

Facing the audience at all times is paramount to the success of an oral presentation. If possible, walking around the room and maintaining eye contact with the audience have proven to be effective techniques. Welcoming questions from the audience, restating questions for everyone to hear, and providing honest and thoughtful responses, also play a key role in ensuring a successful oral presentation.

Evaluation of a Piece of Writing

Traditionally, evaluating a student's writing has been a one-sided affair performed by the educator at the end of the writing process. This is no longer the customary practice since research has clearly shown the importance of formative assessments, as well as the importance of including the students as welcomed and respected self-evaluators. However, no evaluation or assessment should take place unless the instructions given for a particular writing assignment have been made clear, and the students have received quality, comprehensive writing instruction, in general. Assuming these requirements have been met, assessment and evaluation can take on many forms.

Formative assessments help keep the students focused and on task, and they also help to drive instruction. For example, educators are able to determine a child's individual needs, as well as common errors made by many students in the class. During formative assessments, children receive constructive feedback, and educators focus on the individual needs of each student. Formative assessments may also require students to perform self-evaluation using a guided rubric, which helps advance writing skills and develop autonomy. Summative assessments are equally important and also come in many forms. Some summative assessments are curriculum-based to ensure the appropriate standards are being met. Others may be anecdotal, wherein educators write endnotes that highlight areas that require improvement, praise the student's effort and progress, and provide next-step instructions.

Regardless of the type of assessments used, it is critical to a student's continued success that each assessment be personal, meaningful, well understood, and constructive, providing a clear pathway for his or her continued advancement in the writing process.

Planning, Revising, and Editing

Planning is the precursor to writing. This brainstorming stage is when writers consider their purpose and think of ideas that they can use in their writing. Graphic organizers are excellent tools to use during the planning stage. Graphic organizers can help students connect the writing purpose to supporting details, and they can help begin the process of structuring the writing piece. Brainstorming can be done independently, in partners, or as a whole-class activity.

As students begin writing their first draft of a writing piece, they need to continuously revise and edit their work. **Revisions** take place during and after the writing process. As students revise their writing, they are encouraged to frequently refer back to the planning stage. This helps ensure that they are staying focused and are remaining on topic. During the revising and editing stage, educators prompt students to reread their work several times and to focus on one aspect of their writing each time.

For example, the first review may be to examine the writing content, while the second review may focus on spelling, grammar, and punctuation. Another helpful strategy during this stage is to have students display the graphic organizers they used during the planning stage and read their work aloud to the class, in small groups, or with a partner to receive constructive feedback and to welcome other perspectives and ideas. Students are able to refer to the planning stage as the classmate reads and can make connections as to whether or not the writer has stayed on topic.

Correction of Errors

Usage and mechanics are often mistakenly used as interchangeable terms in the educational field. In writing, **usage** refers to a student's ability to choose appropriate words that clearly express an idea, thought, or opinion, or accurately summarize information. Therefore, usage is a very important component of learning to be an effective writer. **Mechanics** involve the writer's ability to use capitalization, ending punctuation, apostrophes, and commas properly. For writing to be both coherent and fluent, mechanics play an important role. **Spelling** is a little less complicated to understand, as it refers to the student's ability to spell decodable and non-decodable words accurately. Learning how and when to correct errors in usage, mechanics, and spelling can be a source of frustration for educators, but it need not be. By creating a logical balance and manageable plan for correcting student writing, educators will help children to be more effective, lifelong writers. The key is balance.

Traditionally, English language educators have focused a great deal of evaluation and feedback on correcting mistakes in usage, mechanics, and spelling alone. Although it is widely accepted that these components are necessary in order to write fluent and coherent sentences, too much focus on correcting these areas—and not enough attention paid to the creative side of writing—may have a negative impact on the writing process.

For example, instead of emphasizing or highlighting every spelling error, educators should ensure that their corrections reflect the task. In other words, if children are given a writing assignment that must incorporate their spelling words, they will undoubtedly expect the educator to correct and evaluate how well they spelled these key words. However, since the assignment also asked the children to use a creative approach to this writing assignment, educators would be doing students a disservice if they did not also offer praise and feedback on the children's writing creativity.

Developing a writing checklist with well-defined goals and sharing this checklist with the class helps educators keep the correction process clear and specific, and it provides children with the opportunity to self-correct and edit their work prior to submission. Using a standardized system of symbols that helps children focus on spelling, capitalization, or word choice is also an effective strategy. Displaying these symbols in a readily-accessible place in the classroom will allow them to self-correct and help their peers with the correction process.

For writing to be meaningful and for students to advance in their writing skills, educators should follow a balanced approach to correcting student work with frequent, timely, and appropriate feedback that reflects the task.

Incorporating Appropriate Teaching Approaches into Classroom Instruction for Social Studies

Applying and Using Developmentally-Appropriate Pedagogical Practices for Planning Curriculum, Designing Instruction, and Evaluating Student Progress in Social Studies

Social studies curriculum should offer content that is comprehensive and thematic, introducing a variety of viewpoints on historical events and highlighting the relevance of connecting the past with the present. Teachers must know how to guide students in obtaining, evaluating, and processing the information associated with these topics. Although the school's textbook is a ready resource, teachers should suggest and encourage alternate sources of information, such as the library, field trips, maps, and other visual material, interviews, and discussions of current events. These opportunities allow students to analyze information and increase their societal understanding. Classroom activities can help students apply previously acquired learning through problem solving, such as performing their own mock election in order to gain a better grasp of the election process. Encouraging students to investigate social studies topics that interest them and involve real-world projects helps them to become objective observers and develop a sense of public duty. When students can interpret, organize, and present what they have learned through a variety of methods, it promotes a deeper understanding and application of wider social studies themes.

Constructed-Response Questions

The GACE constructed-response questions include one English Language Arts question and one Social Studies question. These questions describe a specific teaching scenario and ask the test-taker to explain how they would react in the situation given the tools they have learned through their teaching education. Each question is graded on a scale from zero (lowest possible score) to three (highest possible score). Test takers should spend about ten to fifteen minutes for each question.

Brainstorming

In order to write an effective paragraph, it is essential to put the most valuable ideas onto paper before you begin writing. For example, if a response prompt asked the test-taker to describe a scenario where they employed a strategy to help students understand the theme of exploration in the book *The Little Prince*, the test-taker might write down the following points while they brainstorm:

1. Have students write down any time they see the Little Prince exploring his environment, his own feelings, etc.

2. Break students up into groups after so that they can talk about what they wrote down to each other

3. Go around to each group and have them share their ideas with the class

You should not spend too much time on brainstorming because you're limited on time. However, getting the main ideas out of the mind and onto paper will help with organization before the actual writing begins.

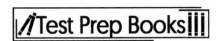

Paragraph Writing

Usually, effective paragraphs provide an introduction, body, and a conclusion. This **three-part structure** is the foundation for the basic understanding of a body of writing. However, because the constructed-response question is time-sensitive and asks the test-taker for a straightforward series of descriptions, it might be helpful to jump right into answering the question in a direct way. For example, if we were asked to put our brainstorming above into a paragraph answering the constructed-response question, we might begin like this:

> First, I would have the students begin reading *The Little Prince* at their own pace while also writing down any instance where they see the theme of exploration.

This avoids any kind of conceptual fluff (i.e. "Recognizing theme is extremely important to third graders . . .") and tells the reader that we have a clear, straightforward plan for our students. Moving forward with this paragraph, we would finish listing our plan for the theme recognition for the students.

> Next, I would break the students up into groups and have them share their written responses with each other. Finally, we would go around the room and have each group share their ideas with the class. While they shared, I would write down their responses on the board so the whole class can see.

After the test-taker writes out a clear plan of action, it's important to address the *why*. Why will this plan work? Here are some possible reasons why we've chosen this plan:

> Having the students read individually will allow every student to go at their own pace, as some students might have anxiety over reading slower than others. This will allow them to write down their own ideas without feeling rushed. Breaking up students into their own groups without the teacher interfering allows them to share their ideas freely and aids in their own experience of the exploration of knowledge. Finally, listing their ideas on the board will allow the students to visually see how their ideas have contributed to group discussion. This plan works for visual, auditory, and verbal learning students and will foster a sense of independence of ideas.

After test-takers have written out the plan, it helps to show the reader why they've selected it. This gives test-takers a chance to display their theoretical knowledge of the teacher-student relationship and the different ways in which students learn and explore various concepts. Remember this two-part structure when answering the constructed-response question; here, it might help to go into more depth about what the plan is and why.

Two Example Prompts

Sample English Language Arts Question

A third-grade class is examining the theme of exploration in language arts. The class is reading *James and the Giant Peach*, a book about an orphan who sets out on an adventure to New York on a giant peach, away from a greedy aunt.

I.   Write about an instructional strategy you would use to help the class understand the theme of exploration in the book *James and the Giant Peach*.

II.   Explain how you would evaluate the effectiveness of the class.

Sample Social Studies Question

Scenario: A first-grade teacher gives the students the following assignment:

1. Write down a list of people in your community who do good things.

2. Put these people in a web chart with your name in the middle.

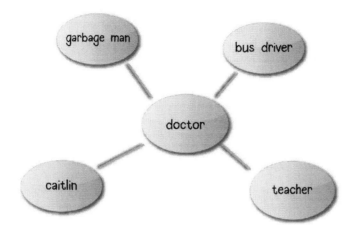

Tasks:

I.   Evaluate the student's work and list the strengths and errors.

II.   Explain how you would help the student correct the errors.

Grading System

The grading system for the constructed-response questions are on a scale from zero to three. A score of "3" means that the test-taker answered the question in its entirety and demonstrated a thorough understanding of the content as well as the content-specific pedagogy they have written down. A score of "2" means that the test-taker demonstrated a basic understanding of the content and the content-specific pedagogy, and their explanations were adequately supported by details. A score of "1" means that the test taker demonstrated a limited understanding of the question and failed to answer most parts of the question. In addition, they demonstrated a limited knowledge of the content and pedagogy or used explanations that were weak that had limited details. Finally, a "0" means that the teat taker displayed little to no understanding of the content or pedagogy, failed to respond to any part of the question, and provided an unintelligible response to the question.

Two Sample Responses

The first sample below is English-Language, and the second sample is Social Studies. These samples demonstrate a score of "3" for the constructed-response questions, which means the test-taker demonstrates a strong understanding of the content as well as the content-specific pedagogy and provides the explanation with detailed examples. These responses answer the scenarios in the previous section.

English-Language Response

a) The students will have already read a specific section in *James and the Giant Peach* for their homework. I will have written questions on the board about the theme of exploration in the novel. Then, I will break them up into groups and have them answer the questions as a group, using the book to find specific examples of inner and outer exploration. When they are done, we will go around and have each group share their ideas on exploration. I will make sure all students get a chance to voice their ideas. Assigning the majority of the reading at home will free up time in class to work together and answer questions. Allowing the students to work in groups will give them the opportunity to share their ideas in an open environment with their peers, with minimal teacher interference. The students will use visual, auditory, and verbal learning skills in order to complete the assignment.

b) I would evaluate the effectiveness of the class by having the students write their own story about inner or outer exploration. This fosters creativity, connects reading with writing, and allows students to further develop their writing skills. This would also allow me to gauge whether or not the students understand how exploration can be used as a tool of learning more about oneself and the world around oneself.

Social Studies Response

a) Strengths: The student demonstrates a basic understanding of what a web chart visually looks like. They have drawn a circle in the middle with lines connecting outer circles. They have also spelled all the words correctly.

Errors: One error I see is that their name is not in the center of the web chart as requested. Instead, the word "doctor" is at the center of the web chart, and the student's name is in one of the outer bubbles.

b) The assignment asks the student to put important people in a web chart with their name at the center. The chart should look like this:

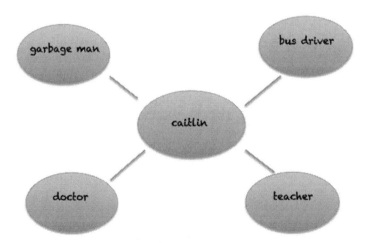

The importance of this web chart with the student's name at the center is to demonstrate that the student has the potential to become a beneficial community member like the ones they've listed. It also engages their knowledge of their own community and the people within it. In order to help the student understand this, I would draw another picture while explaining this concept, in case the student was more of an auditory learner or did better with a different picture. Then I would have the student draw a picture of themselves, indicating what community member they might want to be like one day and why. At the end, I would have them switch their name with the doctor, to show that a web chart demonstrates a central idea or character (the student) with ideas or characters branching off (what community member the student might want to be like one day).

Mathematics

Counting and Cardinality

Counting and cardinality are the foundation of mathematics. Understanding these two concepts allows students to comprehend why numbers are used, how they relate, and how they compare to one another. It is important for children that teachers focus early mathematical training on making sense of how numbers appear in everyday life. Basic ideas of counting, ordering, and comparing need to be understood before any work is done with operations and algebraic thinking. Knowing the correct vocabulary is crucial because that knowledge will help form the fundamentals necessary for learning more advanced concepts in the future. It will allow for future success in mathematics in grades 6-12, and proper exposure at this age lessens the chance for math anxiety.

Comparing, Ordering, and Connecting Numbers to Quantities

In the classroom, teachers can show that numbers represent how many of something exist, and that **natural numbers** and **whole numbers**—or **cardinal numbers**—represent items that can be counted.

Natural numbers are the set of numbers 1, 2, 3, ..., and the set of **whole numbers** are the set of natural numbers plus 0: 0, 1, 2, 3, ... Children learn that a numeral relates to a quantity of items they can see or touch, and this concept is known as **one-to-one correspondence**. Only one numeral can be matched to a given quantity of items.

For example, the number 4 relates to 4 fingers on one hand, and the number 10 relates to a box of 10 pens. Working with numbers up through 10 is taught first, and learning to count up to 10 items should be accomplished without any mistakes. Teaching children how to write the numbers simultaneously with what they are using in their vocabulary is important.

In counting, when a number appears *after* another number in order, that number will be 1 more. Conversely, when a number appears *before* another number in order, that number will be 1 less. This idea is useful when counting backward. Also, zero is a unique number that represents a situation in which there is none of something. This fundamental idea can be shown by taking away an entire quantity of something so that there are zero items left. Once counting up from 1 through 10 and backward from 10 to 1 are mastered, counting up to higher amounts can be practiced. Also, learning to count by tens starting at any number is a key concept. Once a new number is learned, learning how to read and write that number is also important.

Placing numbers in an order in which they are listed from smallest to largest is known as **ordering**. When items are listed by using numbers in order, the **ordinal numbers**, 1st, 2nd, 3rd, 4th, ..., can be used. Children initially learn to identify a first and last item in a list. That process allows for the ability to determine a lowest and highest ranking out of a set of numbers. Once that is accomplished, using the entire set of ordinal numbers for ranking purposes allows for the positioning of quantities in order, based on their numerical value.

Ordering numbers properly can help in the comparison of different quantities of items. Determining whether two amounts are equal or different is the basis for comparing numbers, and teachers can show two different quantities of items in the classroom and simultaneously discuss which amount is the lesser or greater amount. This exercise also can be used in order to classify quantities from the smallest amount to the largest amount.

Being able to compare any two whole numbers without a visual representation is also an important task. Each whole number relates to a specific quantity that can be ranked and compared. Knowing the proper vocabulary relating to ordering and comparing is imperative. The **equals sign** is =, and it shows that two quantities are the same on either side of the symbol. For example, 28 = 28. The symbols that are used for comparison are < to represent **less than,** > to represent **greater than,** ≤ to represent **less than or equal to,** ≥ to represent **greater than or equal to**, and ≠ to represent **not equal to**.

Comparing numbers with any number of digits can be accomplished using these symbols. For example, expressions such as 77 < 100, 44 > 23, and 22 ≠ 24 need to be introduced and understood as *77 is less than 100, 44 is greater than 23*, and *22 is not equal to 24*. Also, both $36 = 36$ and $36 \leq 36$ can be written because both "36 equals 36" and "36 is less than or equal to 36" are true.

Operations and Algebraic Thinking

The operations and algebraic thinking objective consists of building relationships between numbers, realizing patterns, learning different interactions between quantities, and understanding the component of change in application problems. The foundation of algebra consists of fully understanding relationships between different quantities and learning how to manipulate those relationships. Even though algebra is mainly taught in later years, elementary students can use algebraic reasoning as they work through their objectives. Learning how to evaluate numerical expressions, as well as how to read and write them, will assist students in problem solving.

Equations, Number Operations, and the Relationship Between the Operations and their Properties

Rearranging or reordering the items in a group does not change the quantity of items. This is the foundation of the idea of **equality**, which is the basis of an equation. This idea can be shown visually by using a group of items in the classroom. It can be shown that introducing more items or taking any items away will change the original quantity and result in a different number of objects given.

Being asked to quantify the new amount is the first type of addition or subtraction problem that children will face. The operation of acquiring more of something relates to addition, and the operation of losing something relates to subtraction. Vocabulary words such as *total, more, less, left*, and *remain* are common when working with these operations. The **+** sign means *plus,* and it displays that **addition** is happening, while the **−** sign means *minus,* and it displays that **subtraction** is happening. These and other symbols are important when writing equations.

A **number line** is a visual representation of all real numbers. It is a straight line on which any number can be plotted. The origin is 0, and the values to the right of the origin represent positive numbers. Values to the left of the origin represent negative numbers, but they are generally not introduced in this age group. Both sides extend indefinitely. Here is an example of a number line:

Number lines can be utilized for addition and subtraction, for example, using one to add 1 + 3. Starting at 1 on the line, adding 3 to 1 means to move three units to the right to end up at 4. Therefore, 3 + 1 is equal to 4. 5 − 2 can also be determined. Starting at 5 on the number line, subtracting 2 from 5 means moving to the left two units from 5 to end up at 3. Therefore, 5 − 2 is equal to 3.

The number line can also be used to show the identity property of addition and subtraction. What happens on the number line when one either adds or subtracts 0? In this case, there is no movement along the line. For example, 5 + 0 is equal to 5 and 4 − 0 is equal to 4. Zero (0) is known as both the **additive** and **subtractive identity** because it is the number that when added to or subtracted from any number does not change that original number.

Addition can also be defined in equation form. For example, 4 + 5 = 9 shows that 4 + 5 is the same as 9. Therefore, 9 = 9, and "four plus five equals nine." When two quantities are being added together, the result is called the **sum**. Therefore, the sum of 4 and 5 is 9. The numbers being added, such as 4 and 5, are known as the **addends**.

Addition adheres to the commutative property because the order of the quantities being added does not matter. For example, both 4 + 5 and 5 + 4 equal 9. The **commutative property of addition** states that for any whole numbers a and b, it is true that $a + b = b + a$. Also, addition follows the associative property because the sum of three or more quantities results in the same answer, no matter what order the addition is completed. Knowing that operations appearing within **grouping symbols**, such as parenthesis, are calculated first, it is true that 1 + (2 + 3) and (1 + 2) + 3 both equal 6. The **associative property of addition** states that for any whole numbers a, b, and c, $(a + b) + c = a + (b + c)$.

Subtraction also can be shown in equation form. For example, 9 − 5 = 4 shows that 9 - 5 is the same as 4 and that "9 minus 5 is 4." The result of a subtraction problem is known as a **difference**. The difference of 9 - 5 is 4, and 4 represents the quantity that is left once the subtraction is complete. Subtraction does not adhere to the commutative property because the order in which subtraction is completed does matter. For example, 9 − 5 and 5 − 9 do not have the same result. 5 − 9 results in a negative number. Also, subtraction does not adhere to the associative property. The order in which subtraction is completed is important if there are at least two quantities involved.

The relationship between addition and subtraction can be seen using fact families. **Fact families** are three numbers that are related. For example, 4 + 2 = 6 is the opposite of 6 − 2 = 4. A teacher can start with 4 apples and then add 2 more to visualize a total of 6. Then, 2 apples can be taken away to get back to a quantity of 4.

Here is an example of an addition and subtraction fact family worksheet:

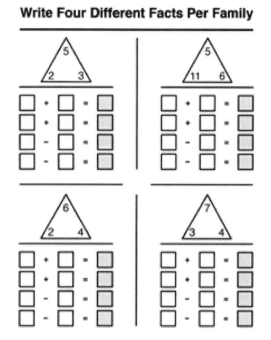

The foundation of multiplication is learned through adding equal quantities. The answer to a multiplication problem is called a **product** and represents the total quantity of items within different groups. The symbol for multiplication is $\times$ or $\cdot$, and we say 2×3 or $2 \cdot 3$ represents "2 times 3."

As an example, there are three sets of four apples, and the goal is to know how many apples there are in total. Three sets of four apples gives $4 + 4 + 4 = 12$. Also, three times four apples gives $3 \times 4 = 12$. Therefore, for any whole numbers a and b, where a is not equal to 0, $a \times b = b + b + \cdots b$, where b is added a times. Also, $a \times b$ can be thought of as the number of units in a rectangular block consisting of a rows and b columns. For example, 3×7 is equal to the number of squares in the following rectangle:

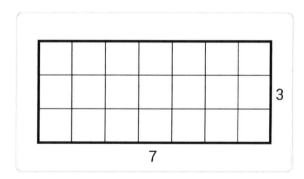

The answer is 21, and there are 21 squares in the rectangle.

In the consideration of anything times 1—for example, $8 \times 1 = 8$—the original amount does not change. Therefore, 1 is the **multiplicative identity**, and for any whole number a, $1 \times a = a$. Also, any number multiplied times 0 results in 0. Therefore, for any whole number a, $0 \times a = 0$.

Similar to addition, multiplication follows the commutative property. The order in which multiplication is calculated does not matter. For example, 3 x 4 and 4 x 3 both equal 12. Four sets of three apples and three sets of four apples both equal twelve apples. The **commutative property of multiplication** states that for any whole numbers a and b, $a \times b = b \times a$. Multiplication also follows the associative property because the product of three or more whole numbers is the same, no matter what order the multiplication is completed. The **associative property of multiplication** states that for any whole numbers a, b, and c, $(a \times b) \times c = a \times (b \times c)$. For example, $(2 \times 3) \times 4 = 2 \times (3 \times 4)$.

The **distributive property of multiplication over addition** is an extremely important concept that appears in algebra. It states that for any whole numbers a, b, and c, it is true that $a \times (b + c) = (a \times b) + (a \times c)$. Because multiplication is commutative, it is also true that $(b + c) \times a = (b \times a) + (c \times a)$. For example, $4 \times (3 + 2)$ is the same as $(4 \times 3) + (4 \times 2)$. Both result in 20.

The foundation of division is based on dividing a given quantity into parts. The simplest scenario involves dividing a quantity into equal parts. For example, if a pack of 20 pencils was to be divided among 10 children so that each child received the same number of pencils, one would have to divide 20 by 10. In this example, each child would receive 2 pencils.

The symbol for division is $\div$ or /, and the equation is written as $20 \div 10 = 2$ or 20 / 10 = 2 to say "20 divided by 10 is equal to 2." Division can be summarized as the following: for any whole numbers a and b, where b is not equal to 0, $a \div b = c$ if and only if $a = b \times c$. Therefore, division can be thought of as a multiplication problem with a missing part. For instance, calculating $20 \div 10$ is the same as asking the following: "If there are 20 items in total with 10 in each group, how many are in each group?" Therefore, 20 is equal to ten times what value? This question is the same as asking, "If there are 20 items in total with 2 in each group, how many groups are there?" The answer to each question is 2.

Within the division problem, a is known as the **dividend**, b is the **divisor**, and c is the **quotient.** 0 cannot be divided into parts, and therefore, for any nonzero whole number a, $0 \div a = 0$. Also, division by 0 is undefined. The scenario of dividing a quantity into 0 parts is impossible.

The more difficult division scenario involves dividing a quantity into equal parts, but having some left over. An example is dividing a pack of 20 pencils among 8 children so that each child received the same number of pencils. In this setting, each child would receive 2 pencils, and there would be 4 pencils leftover. 20 is the dividend, 8 is the divisor, 2 is the quotient, and 4 is known as the **remainder.** Within this type of division problem, for whole numbers a, b, c, and d, $a \div b = c$ with a remainder of d is true if and only if $a = (b \times c) + d$. When calculating $a \div b$, if there is no remainder, a is said to be **divisible** by b. **Even numbers** are all divisible by the number 2. **Odd numbers** are not divisible by 2, and an odd quantity of items cannot be paired up into groups of 2 without having 1 item leftover.

Mental math should always be considered as problems are worked through, and teachers should stress the importance of the ability for a child to perform operations in his or her head. If a problem is simple enough, such as 15 + 3 = 18, it should be completed mentally. The ability to do this will increase once addition and subtraction in higher place values are taught. Also, mental math is important in multiplication and division. The times tables multiplying all numbers from 1 to 12 should be memorized.

This will allow for division within those numbers to be memorized as well. For example, $121 \div 11 = 11$ because it should be memorized that $11 \times 11 = 121$. Here is the multiplication table to be memorized:

x	1	2	3	4	5	6	7	8	9	10	11	12	13	14	15
1	1	2	3	4	5	6	7	8	9	10	11	12	13	14	15
2	2	4	6	8	10	12	14	16	18	20	22	24	26	28	30
3	3	6	9	12	15	18	21	24	27	30	33	36	39	42	45
4	4	8	12	16	20	24	28	32	36	40	44	48	52	56	60
5	5	10	15	20	25	30	35	40	45	50	55	60	65	70	75
6	6	12	18	24	30	36	42	48	54	60	66	72	78	84	90
7	7	14	21	28	35	42	49	56	63	70	77	84	91	98	105
8	8	16	24	32	40	48	56	64	72	80	88	96	104	112	120
9	9	18	27	36	45	54	63	72	81	90	99	108	117	126	135
10	10	20	30	40	50	60	70	80	90	100	110	120	130	140	150
11	11	22	33	44	55	66	77	88	99	110	121	132	143	154	165
12	12	24	36	48	60	72	84	96	108	120	132	144	156	168	180
13	13	26	39	52	65	78	91	104	117	130	143	156	169	182	195
14	14	28	42	56	70	84	98	112	126	140	154	168	182	196	210
15	15	30	45	60	75	90	105	120	135	150	165	180	195	210	225

The values along the diagonal of the table consist of **perfect squares**. A perfect square is a number that represents a product of two equal integers.

Representing and Solving Problems Involving Addition and Subtraction to Help Students Gain Foundations for Multiplication and Division

Word and story problems should be presented in many different ways. Word problems present the opportunity to related mathematical concepts from the classroom into real-world situations. These types of problems are situations in which some parts of the problem are known and at least one part is unknown.

There are three types of instances in which something can be unknown: the starting point, the modification, or the final result can all be missing from the provided information.

- For an addition problem, the **modification** is the quantity of the new amount added to the starting point.
- For a subtraction problem, the **modification** is the quantity taken away from the starting point.

Keywords in the word problems can signal what type of operation needs to be used to solve the problem. Words such as *total, increased, combined*, and *more* indicate that addition is needed. Words such as *difference, decreased*, and *minus* indicate that subtraction is needed.

Regarding addition, the given equation is $3 + 7 = 10$.

The number 3 is the starting point. 7 is the modification, and 10 is the result from adding a new amount to the starting point. Different word problems can arise from this same equation, depending on which value is the unknown.

For example, here are three problems:

- If a student had three pencils and was given seven more, how many would he have in total?
- If a student had three pencils and a student gave him more so that he had ten in total, how many were given to him?
- A student was given seven pencils so that he had ten in total. How many did he start with?

All three problems involve the same equation, and determining which part of the equation is missing is the key to solving each word problem. The missing answers would be 10, 7, and 3, respectively.

In terms of subtraction, the same three scenarios can occur. The given equation is $6 - 4 = 2$.

The number 6 is the starting point. 4 is the modification, and 2 is the new amount that is the result from taking away an amount from the starting point. Again, different types of word problems can arise from this equation. For example, here are three possible problems:

- *If a student had six quarters and four were taken away, how many would be left over?*

- *If a student had six quarters, purchased a pencil, and had two quarters left over, how many quarters did she pay with?*

- *If a student paid for a pencil with four quarters and had two quarters left over, how many did she have to start with?*

The three question types follow the structure of the addition word problems, and determining whether the starting point, the modification, or the final result is missing is the goal in solving the problem. The missing answers would be 2, 4, and 6, respectively.

The three addition problems and the three subtraction word problems can be solved by using a picture, a number line, or an algebraic equation. If an equation is used, a question mark can be utilized to represent the unknown quantity. For example, $6 - 4 = ?$ can be written to show that the missing value is the result. Using equation form visually indicates what portion of the addition or subtraction problem is the missing value.

Similar instances can be seen in word problems involving multiplication and division. Key words within a multiplication problem involve *times, product, doubled,* and *tripled.* Key words within a division problem involve *split, quotient, divided, shared, groups,* and *half.* Like addition and subtraction, multiplication and division problems also have three different types of missing values.

Multiplication consists of a specific number of groups having the same size, the quantity of items within each group, and the total quantity within all groups. Therefore, each one of these amounts can be the missing value.

For example, the given equation is $5 \times 3 = 15$.

5 and 3 are interchangeable, so either amount can be the number of groups or the quantity of items within each group. 15 is the total number of items. Again, different types of word problems can arise from this equation.

For example, here are three problems:

- If a classroom is serving 5 different types of apples for lunch and has three apples of each type, how many total apples are there to give to the students?
- If a classroom has 15 apples of 5 different types, how many of each type are there?
- If a classroom has 15 apples with 3 of each type, how many types are there to choose from?

Each question involves using the same equation to solve, and it is imperative to decide which part of the equation is the missing value. The answers to the problems are 15, 3, and 5, respectively.

Similar to multiplication, division problems involve a total amount, a number of groups having the same size, and a number of items within each group. The difference between multiplication and division is that the starting point is the total amount, which then gets divided into equal quantities.

For example, the equation is $15 \div 5 = 3$.

15 is the total number of items, which is being divided into 5 different groups. In order to do so, 3 items go into each group. Also, 5 and 3 are interchangeable, so the 15 items could be divided into 3 groups of 5 items each. Therefore, different types of word problems can arise from this equation depending on which value is unknown. For example, here are three types of problems:

- *A student needs 48 pieces of chalk. If there are 8 pieces in each box, how many boxes should he buy?*

- *A student has 48 pieces of chalk. If each box has 6 pieces in it, how many boxes did he buy?*

- *A student has partitioned all of his chalk into 8 piles, with 6 pieces in each pile. How many pieces does he have in total?*

Each one of these questions involves the same equation, and the third question can easily utilize the multiplication equation $8 \times 6 = ?$ instead of division. The answers are 6, 8, and 48, respectively.

Writing, Interpreting, Analyzing, and Evaluating Numerical Expressions, Patterns, and Relationships

Learning proper vocabulary is necessary to be able to write, interpret, analyze, and evaluate numerical expressions. Being able to match a word phrase to an expression, or vice versa, is an integral part of mathematics. Being able to create a word phrase from an expression, or vice versa, is also important. Therefore, learning to read and write all numbers worked with in the classroom, as well as learning and understanding all terminology relating to mathematical operations, is key for success.

Determining whether an equation is true or false is an important concept within the concept of evaluating numerical expressions. For example, 4 + 2 = 2 + 4 is a **true statement** because the left-hand side of the equals sign equals the right-hand side. A **false statement** would be a situation in which the left-hand side of the equals sign does not equal the right-hand side. For example, 5 + 7 = 13 is a false statement. If the addition is completed on the left side, the equation shows that 12 = 13, which is false. This type of logic will be utilized mostly when checking answers after solving algebraic equations. If the correct answer has been found, it will result in a true statement once plugged into the original equation. Conversely, if an incorrect answer has been found, it will result in a false statement once plugged in.

Knowing the correct order of operations is essential in evaluating numerical expressions. As stated previously, when grouping symbols are present within a mathematical expression that needs to be evaluated, the expression existing within the symbols needs to be calculated first. Grouping symbols can also make an expression easier to read because they help clarify what operation needs to be performed first.

After the grouping symbols are taken care of, multiplication and division are performed working from left to right. Addition and subtraction are the last to be performed. Order of operations can be remembered easily using the abbreviation **PEMDAS**, which stands for Parenthesis, Exponents, Multiplication and Division, and Addition and Subtraction. It lists the exact order in which operations must be performed. *Please Excuse My Dear Aunt Sally* is a mnemonic that can help students memorize PEMDAS.

The order of operations must be used with the expression $2 \times 5 + 2 \div 2$. According to PEMDAS, multiplication is performed first. This gives $10 + 2 \div 2$. Next, division is performed, leaving $10 + 1$, which gives 11. Parentheses can be inserted in the original expression, which changes the order of operations: $2 \times (5 + 2) \div 2$. The parenthesis shows that the addition must be performed first. Therefore, the order is $2 \times 7 \div 2$. Next, multiplication and division are performed from left to right, resulting in $14 \div 2$, which equals 7. This example highlights the importance of following the correct order of operations.

Many relationships can exist between numbers. A number that can be divided into another number without a remainder is known as a **factor** of that number. For example, 2 is a factor of 20 because $20 \div 2 = 10$. The other factors of 20 are 1, 4, 5, 10, and 20. Due to the definition of multiplicative identity, 1 is a factor of any number. Any number is equal to 1 times itself. Also, 20 is known as a **multiple** of 2 because $2 \times 10 = 20$. A multiple of a number can be found by multiplying that number times any whole number. All multiples of 10 end in zero, and all multiples of 2 are even numbers. If two numbers have the same factor in common, it is known as a **common factor**. Similarly, if a number is a multiple of two numbers, it is known as a **common multiple.**

A number is either a **prime number** or comprised of a product of prime numbers. A prime number is a number greater than 0 where its only factors are itself and 1. A prime number can only be divided by itself and 1, having no remainder. For example, 3, 5, 7, 11, 13, 17, and 19 are prime numbers.

- Numbers greater than 2 and ending in 2 are never prime because they can always be divided by 2.

- Numbers greater than 5 and ending in 5 are never prime because they can always be divided by 5.

- A number that is not prime is known as a **composite number**. A composite number always has at least three factors. For example, 9 is a composite number because its factors are 9, 3, and 1.

Determining **patterns** is an important part of mathematics. When mathematical calculations are completed repeatedly, patterns can be recognized. Recognizing patterns is an integral part of mathematics because it helps one understand relationships between different concepts. For example, a sequence of numbers can be given, and recognizing the relationship between the given numbers can assist in extending the sequence.

For instance, given the sequence of numbers 7, 14, 21, 28, 35, ..., the next number in the sequence is 42 because the sequence lists all multiples of 7, starting at 7. Sequences can also be built from addition, subtraction, and division. Being able to recognize the relationship between the values that are given is the key to determining the next number in the sequence.

Numbers and Operations in Base 10

Children need to understand place value and the base ten system because these concepts are the foundation for operations among higher digit numbers. This framework will allow for further understanding of relationships between numbers containing multiple digits and decomposing those numbers. It also provides a basis for working with values less than 1 and allows students to be able to transition from additive thinking to multiplicative thinking. Knowing the **base 10** structure allows for thinking in scale, which is a big help in evaluating numerical expressions.

Place Value and the Properties of Operations

When numbers are counted, it is really counting groups of 10. That number is consistent throughout the set of natural numbers, whole numbers, etc., and is referred to as working within a base 10 numeration system. Only the numbers from 0 to 9 are utilized to represent any number, and the foundation for doing so involves **place value**. Numbers are written side by side, to show the amount is in each place value.

Teachers can first introduce the idea of place value by showing how the number 10 is different from 0 to 9. It has two digits instead of just one. The 1 in the first digit is in the tens' place, and the 0 in the second digit is in the ones place. Therefore, there is 1 group of tens and 0 ones. 11 is the next number that can be introduced because this number has 1 ten and 1 one. The introduction of numbers from 11 to 19 should be the next step. Anytime a new number is introduced, writing out the numbers as *eleven*, *twelve*, etc., should be done simultaneously. Each value within this range of numbers consists of one group of ten and a specific number of leftover ones. Counting by tens can be introduced once the tens column is understood. This process consists of increasing the number in the tens place by one. For example, counting by ten starting at 17 would result in the next four values being 27, 37, 47, and 57.

As children get older, higher place values are introduced. Base ten blocks can be utilized to help understand place value and assist with counting large numbers. They consist of cubes that help with the visualization of counting and operations. For example, here is a diagram of base ten blocks representing ones, tens, and a hundred:

Hundreds   Tens   Ones

Also, a place value chart should be utilized in the classroom for numbers containing higher digits.

In the number 1,234, there are 4 ones and 3 tens. The 2 is in the hundreds place, and the 1 is in the thousands place. Note that each group of three digits is separated by a comma. The 2 has a value that is 10 times greater than the 3. Every place to the left has a value 10 times greater than the place to its right. Also, each group of three digits is also known as a *period*. 234 is in the ones period.

The number 1,234 can be written out as *one-thousand, two hundred thirty-four*. The process of writing out numbers is known as the **decimal system** and is also based on groups of 10. The place value chart is a helpful tool in using this system. In order to write out or state a number, it always starts with the digit(s) in the highest period. For example, in the number 23,815,467, the 23 is in highest place and is in the millions' period. The number is read *twenty-three million, eight hundred fifteen thousand, four hundred sixty-seven*. Each period is written separately through the use of commas, and no "ands" are used within the number. Another way to think about the number 23,815,467 is through the use of an addition problem. For example, 23,815,467 = 20,000,000 + 3,000,000 + 800,000 + 10,000 + 5,000 + 400 + 60 + 7, and this expression is known as **expanded form**. The actual number 23,815,467 is known as being in **standard form**.

Once both the place value and decimal system are understood, positive numbers less than one can be introduced. Decimals and fractions are two ways that can be used to represent positive numbers less than one. Counting money—specifically, quantities less than one dollar—is a good method to introduce values less than one as problems involving change are important story problems that are applicable to real-world situations. For example, if a student had three quarters and a dime and wanted to purchase a cookie at lunch for 50 cents, how much change would she receive? The answer is found by first calculating the sum of the change as 85 cents and then subtracting 50 cents to get 35 cents. Money can also be utilized as a technique to learn the transition and relationship between decimals and fractions. For example, a dime represents $0.10 or $1/_{10}$ of a dollar. Problems involving both dollars and cents also can be introduced. For example, if someone has three dollar bills and two quarters, the amount can be represented as a decimal as $3.50.

Formally, a **decimal** is a number that has a dot within the number. For example, 3.45 is a decimal, and the dot is called a **decimal point**. The number to the left of the decimal point is in the ones place. The number to the right of the decimal point represents the portion of the number less than one. The first number to the right of the decimal point is the tenths place, and one tenth represents $1/_{10}$, just like a dime. The next place is the hundredths place, and it represents $1/_{100}$, just like a penny. This idea is continued to the right in the hundredths, thousandths, and ten thousandths places. Each place value to the right is ten times smaller than the one to its left. The place values to the right of the ones place can be added onto the chart above to get the following:

MILLIONS			THOUSANDS			ONES			.	DECIMALS		
billions	hundred millions	ten millions	millions	hundred thousands	ten thousands	thousands	hundreds	tens	ones	tenths	hundredths	thousandths

A number less than one contains only digits in some decimal places. For example, 0.53 is less than one. A **mixed number** is a number greater than one that also contains digits in some decimal places. For example, 3.43 is a mixed number. Adding a zero to the right of a decimal does not change the value of the number. For example, 2.75 is the same as 2.750. However, 2.75 is the more accepted representation of the number. Also, zeros are usually placed in the ones column in any value less than one. For example, 0.65 is the same as .65, but 0.65 is more widely used.

In order to read or write a decimal, the decimal point is ignored. The number is read as a whole number, and then the place value unit is stated in which the last digit falls. For example, 0.089 is read as *eighty-nine thousandths*, and 0.1345 is read as *one thousand, three hundred forty-five ten thousandths*. In mixed numbers, the word "and" is used to represent the decimal point. For example, 2.56 is read as *two and fifty-six hundredths*.

Rounding is an important concept dealing with place value. **Rounding** is the process of either bumping a number up or down, based on a specified place value. First, the place value is specified. Then, the digit to its right is looked at. For example, if rounding to the nearest hundreds place, the digit in the tens place is used. If it is a 0, 1, 2, 3, or 4, the digit being rounded to is left alone. If it is a 5, 6, 7, 8 or 9, the digit being rounded to is increased by one. All other digits before the decimal point are then changed to zeros, and the digits in decimal places are dropped. If a decimal place is being rounded to, all subsequent digits are just dropped. For example, if 845,231.45 was to be rounded to the nearest thousands place, the answer would be 845,000. The 5 would remain the same due to the 2 in the hundreds place. Also, if 4.567 was to be rounded to the nearest tenths place, the answer would be 4.6. The 5 increased to 6 due to the 6 in the hundredths place, and the rest of the decimal is dropped.

In order to compare whole numbers with many digits, place value can be used. In each number to be compared, it is necessary to find the highest place value in which the numbers differ and to compare the value within that place value. For example, $4,523,345 < 4,532,456$ because of the values in the ten thousands place. A similar process can be used for decimals; however, number lines can also be used. Tick marks can be placed within two whole numbers on the number line that represent tenths, hundredths, etc. Each number being compared can then be plotted, and The value farthest to the right on the number line is the largest.

Using Place-Value Understanding of Multi-Digit Numbers to Perform Multi-Digit Operations

Learning place value is important because it is utilized performing operations. Operations are completed within each place value. Adding and subtracting multiples of tens can be introduced first. When adding or subtracting 10 or a multiple of 10 to a number, the nonzero value in the ones place does not change. Only the digits in the tens place need to be added or subtracted. For example, $98 - 60 = 38$ is the result of keeping the 8 in the ones place and placing the solution of $9 - 6 = 3$ in the tens place.

Adding and subtracting other numbers with more than one digit involves place value and rewriting numbers in expanded form. In the addition problem $256 + 261$, 256 can be thought of as $200 + 50 + 6$ or 2 hundreds, 5 tens, and 6 ones. 261 can be thought of as $200 + 60 + 1$ or 2 hundreds, 6 tens, and 1 one. Adding the two numbers by place value results in 4 hundreds, 11 tens, and 7 ones. The 11 tens need to be regrouped as 1 hundred and 1 ten. This leaves 5 hundreds, 1 ten, and 7 ones, which is 517.

One method of subtraction involves a counting-up procedure. In the subtraction problem $476 - 241$, adding 9 to 241 gives 250, adding 50 to 250 gives 300, and adding 100 to 300 gives 400. Then we add the remaining 76 to 400 to reach 476. Therefore, the answer to the subtraction problem is $9 + 50 + 100 + 76 = 235$. The answer can be checked by adding $235 + 241$ to make sure it equals 476. Also, the place value technique used within addition can be used, by rewriting each number in expanded form and then subtracting within each place value. Therefore, $400 + 70 + 6 - (200 + 40 + 1) = 200 + 30 + 5 = 235$. If one of the subtraction problems is not possible within a place value, the next largest place value must be regrouped. For instance:

$$262 - 71 = 200 + 60 + 2 - (70 + 1) = 100 + 160 + 2 - (70 + 1) = 100 + 90 + 1 = 191$$

When adding and subtracting numbers with decimals, the decimals need to be lined up. Zeros need to be added onto the right of any number in the decimal places to ensure the same number of decimal places in both addends. Then, addition is performed in the same manner as with whole numbers, making sure to input the decimal point into the correct place in the answer. For example, $3.5 + 2.75 = 3.50 + 2.75 = 6.25$.

Multiplication and division are also completed using place value. When a number is multiplied times 10, the number shifts over one place value to the left, and a 0 is entered in the ones place. For example, $1,235 \times 10 = 12,350$. Similarly, when a number is multiplied times 100, the entire number is shifted over two place values to the left, and a 0 is entered in both the ones and tens places. For example, $15,634 \times 100 = 1,563,400$. This same technique can be used to multiply single digit numbers times factors of 10 and 100. For instance, 5×300 can be thought of as $5 \times 3 \times 100 = 15 \times 100 = 1,500$.

When a number is multiplied times any number with more than one digit, that number must be multiplied times each digit in the other number, and a zero placeholder must be used after the multiplication for each place value currently being multiplied. For example, when multiplying at the hundreds place value, one would use two zero placeholders. The results of all multiplication are then summed up to obtain the answer.

Another method of multiplication can be done with the use of an **area model**. An area model is a rectangle that is divided into rows and columns that match up to the number of place values within each number. Take the example 29×65. These two numbers can be split into simpler numbers: $29 = 25 + 4$ and $65 = 60 + 5$. The products of those 4 numbers are found within the rectangle and then summed up to get the answer. The entire process is: $(60 \times 25) + (5 \times 25) + (60 \times 4) + (5 \times 4) = 1,500 + 240 + 125 + 20 = 1,885$. Here is the actual area model:

	25	4
60	60x25 1,500	60x4 240
5	5x25 125	5x4 20

```
  1,500
    240
    125
+    20
  ─────
  1,885
```

Multiplying decimals involves the same procedure as multiplying whole numbers, but including the decimal places in the end result. The problem involves multiplying the two numbers together, ignoring the decimal places, and then inserting the total number of decimal places in the original numbers into the result. For example, given the problem 87.5×0.45, the answer is found by multiplying 875×45 to obtain 39,375 and then inputting a decimal point three places to the left because there are three total decimal places in the original problem. Therefore, the answer is 39.375.

Dividing a number by a single digit or two digits can be turned into repeated subtraction problems. An area model can be used throughout the problem that represents multiples of the divisor. For example, the answer to $8580 \div 55$ can be found by subtracting 55 from 8580 one at a time and counting the total number of subtractions necessary.

However, a simpler process involves using larger multiples of 55. First, $100 \times 55 = 5,500$ is subtracted from 8,580, and 3,080 is leftover. Next, $50 \times 55 = 2,750$ is subtracted from 3,080 to obtain 380. $5 \times 55 = 275$ is subtracted from 330 to obtain 55, and finally, $1 \times 55 = 55$ is subtracted from 55 to obtain zero. Therefore, there is no remainder, and the answer is $100 + 50 + 5 + 1 = 156$. Here is a picture of the area model and the repeated subtraction process:

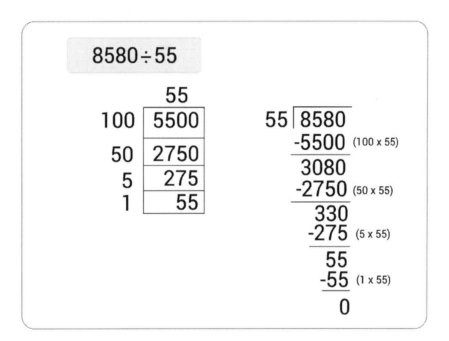

Checking the answer to a division problem involves multiplying the answer—the **quotient**—times the divisor to see if the dividend is obtained. If there is a remainder, the same process is computed, but the remainder is added on at the end to try to match the dividend. In the previous example, $156 \times 55 = 8580$ would be the checking procedure. Dividing decimals involves the same repeated subtraction process. The only difference would be that the subtractions would involve numbers that include values in the decimal places. Lining up decimal places is crucial in this type of problem.

Exponents with base 10 are also introduced in this age group. For example, 10×10 can be written as 10^2, and $10 \times 10 \times 10$ can be written as 10^3. The number of zeros in the product is equal to the **exponent**. For instance, $10^3 = 1,000$. Also, any number raised to a power of 0 results in a value of 1. For example, $10^0 = 1$.

Numbers and Fractions

Developing an Understanding of Fractions as Numbers

Fractions are a vital part of mathematics, and their understanding tends to be extremely challenging for students. Too often, steps are learned without understanding why they are being performed. It is important for teachers to make the concept of fractions less abstract and more tangible by providing concrete examples in the classroom. With this solid foundation and a lot of practice, learning will be easier, and success with fractions in later math classes will occur.

A **fraction** is a part of something that is whole. Items such as apples can be cut into parts to help visualize fractions. If an apple is cut into 2 equal parts, each part represents ½ of the apple. If each half is cut into two parts, the apple now is cut into quarters. Each piece now represents ¼ of the apple. In this example, each part is equal because they all have the same size. Geometric shapes, such as circles and squares, can also be utilized in the classroom to help visualize the idea of fractions.

For example, a circle can be drawn on the board and divided into 6 equal parts:

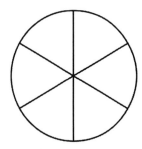

Shading can be used to represent parts of the circle that can be translated into fractions. The top of the fraction, the **numerator,** can represent how many segments are shaded. The bottom of the fraction, the **denominator,** can represent the number of segments that the circle is broken into. A pie is a good analogy to use in this example. If one piece of the circle is shaded, or one piece of pie is cut out, $1/_6$ of the object is being referred to. An apple, a pie, or a circle can be utilized in order to compare simple fractions. For example, showing that $1/_2$ is larger than $1/_4$ and that $1/_4$ is smaller than $1/_3$ can be accomplished through shading. A *unit fraction* is a fraction in which the numerator is 1, and the denominator is a positive whole number. It represents one part of a whole—one piece of pie.

A **proper fraction** is a fraction in which the numerator is less than the denominator. An **improper fraction** is a fraction in which the numerator is greater than the denominator. An example of a proper fraction is $5/_6$, and an improper fraction is $6/_5$. A proper fraction represents less than a whole pie or circle, and an improper fraction represents more than one whole pie or circle. Improper fractions can be written using whole numbers as *mixed numbers*. The bar in a fraction represents division. Therefore $6/_5$ is the same as $6 \div 5$. In order to rewrite it as a mixed number, division is performed to obtain $6 \div 5 = 1\ R1$. The remainder is then converted into fraction form. The actual remainder becomes the numerator of a fraction, and the divisor becomes the denominator. Therefore $1\ R1$ is written as $1\frac{1}{5}$, a mixed number. A mixed number can also decomposed into the addition of a whole number and a fraction.

For example:

$$1\frac{1}{5} = 1 + \frac{1}{5} \text{ and } 4\frac{5}{6} = 4 + \frac{1}{6} + \frac{1}{6} + \frac{1}{6} + \frac{1}{6} + \frac{1}{6}$$

Every fraction can be built from a combination of unit fractions.

Like fractions, or **equivalent fractions**, represent two fractions that are made up of different numbers, but represent the same quantity. For example, the given fractions are $^4/_8$ and $^3/_6$. If a pie was cut into 8 pieces and 4 pieces were removed, half of the pie would remain. Also, if a pie was split into 6 pieces and 3 pieces were eaten, half of the pie would also remain. Therefore, both of the fractions represent half of a pie. These two fractions are referred to as like fractions. **Unlike fractions** are fractions that are different and cannot be thought of as representing equal quantities. When working with fractions in mathematical expressions, like fractions should be simplified. Both $^4/_8$ and $^3/_6$ can be simplified into $^1/_2$.

Comparing fractions can be completed through the use of a number line. For example, if $^3/_5$ and $^6/_{10}$ need to be compared, each fraction should be plotted on a number line. To plot $^3/_5$, the area from 0 to 1 should be broken into 5 equal segments, and the fraction represents 3 of them. To plot $^6/_{10}$, the area from 0 to 1 should be broken into 10 equal segments and the fraction represents 6 of them.

It can be seen that $\frac{3}{5} = \frac{6}{10}$

Like fractions are plotted at the same point on a number line. Unit fractions can also be used to compare fractions. For example, if it is known that

$$\frac{4}{5} > \frac{1}{2}$$

and

$$\frac{1}{2} > \frac{4}{10}$$

then it is also known that

$$\frac{4}{5} > \frac{4}{10}$$

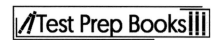

Also, converting improper fractions to mixed numbers can be helpful in comparing fractions because the whole number portion of the number is more visible.

Adding and subtracting mixed numbers and fractions can be completed by decomposing fractions into a sum of whole numbers and unit fractions. For example, the given problem is

$$5\frac{3}{7} + 2\frac{1}{7}$$

Decomposing into

$$5 + \frac{1}{7} + \frac{1}{7} + \frac{1}{7} + 2 + \frac{1}{7}$$

This shows that the whole numbers can be added separately from the unit fractions. The answer is

$$5 + 2 + \frac{1}{7} + \frac{1}{7} + \frac{1}{7} + \frac{1}{7} = 7 + \frac{4}{7} = 7\frac{4}{7}$$

Adding and subtracting fractions that have the same denominators involves adding or subtracting the numerators. The denominator will stay the same. Therefore, the decomposition process can be made simpler, and the fractions do not have to be broken into unit fractions.

For example, the given problem is:

$$4\frac{7}{8} - 2\frac{6}{8}$$

The answer is found by adding the answers to both

$$4 - 2 \text{ and } \frac{7}{8} - \frac{6}{8}$$

$$2 + \frac{1}{8} = 2\frac{1}{8}$$

A common mistake would be to add the denominators so that

$$\frac{1}{4} + \frac{1}{4} = \frac{1}{8} \text{ or } \frac{2}{8}$$

However, conceptually, it is known that two quarters make a half, so neither one of these are correct.

If two fractions have different denominators, equivalent fractions must be used to add or subtract them. The fractions must be converted into fractions that have common denominators. A **least common denominator** or the product of the two denominators can be used as the common denominator. For example, in the problem $\frac{5}{6} + \frac{2}{3}$, both 6, which is the least common denominator, and 18, which is the product of the denominators, can be used. In order to use 6, $\frac{2}{3}$ must be converted to sixths. A number line can be used to show the equivalent fraction is $\frac{4}{6}$. What happens is that $\frac{2}{3}$ is multiplied times a fractional form of 1 to obtain a denominator of 6. Hence, $\frac{2}{3} \times \frac{2}{2} = \frac{4}{6}$.

Therefore, the problem is now $\frac{5}{6} + \frac{4}{6} = \frac{9}{6}$, which can be simplified into $\frac{3}{2}$. In order to use 18, both fractions must be converted into having 18 as their denominator. $\frac{5}{6}$ would have to be multiplied times $\frac{3}{3}$, and $\frac{2}{3}$ would need to be multiplied times $\frac{6}{6}$. The addition problem would be $\frac{15}{18} + \frac{12}{18} = \frac{27}{18}$, which reduces into $\frac{3}{2}$.

When referring to coins, a dime is equal to $\frac{1}{10}$ of a dollar, and a penny is $\frac{1}{100}$ of a dollar. In decimal form, $\frac{1}{10} = 0.1$, *one-tenth*, and $\frac{1}{100} = 0.01$, *one-hundredth*. Other decimals can be expressed over a denominator of 10 and 100. For example, $\frac{3}{10} = 0.3$, *three-tenths*, and $\frac{56}{100} = 0.56$, *fifty-six hundredths*. Decimals can also be compared using a number line. The region from 0 to 1 can be broken up into either 10 or 100 segments, and the numbers can be plotted accordingly for comparison.

Multiplying and Dividing Fractions

Because multiplication is commutative, multiplying a fraction times a whole number is the same as multiplying a whole number times a fraction. The problem involves adding a fraction a specific number of times. The problem $3 \times \frac{1}{4}$ can be translated into adding the unit fraction 3 times: $\frac{1}{4} + \frac{1}{4} + \frac{1}{4} = \frac{3}{4}$. In the problem $4 \times \frac{2}{5}$, the fraction can be decomposed into $\frac{1}{5} + \frac{1}{5}$ and then added 4 times to obtain $\frac{8}{5}$. Also, both of these answers can be found by just multiplying the whole number times the numerator of the fraction being multiplied. The whole numbers can be written in fraction form as

$$\frac{3}{1} \times \frac{1}{4} = \frac{3}{4}$$

$$\frac{4}{1} \times \frac{2}{5} = \frac{8}{5}$$

Multiplying a fraction by a fraction involves multiplying the numerators together separately and the denominators together separately. For example,

$$\frac{3}{8} \times \frac{2}{3} = \frac{3 \times 2}{8 \times 3} = \frac{6}{24}$$

This can then be reduced to $^1/_4$. Dividing a fraction by a fraction is actually a multiplication problem. It involves flipping the divisor and then multiplying normally. For example,

$$\frac{22}{5} \div \frac{1}{2} = \frac{22}{5} \times \frac{2}{1} = \frac{44}{5}$$

The same procedure can be implemented for division problems involving fractions and whole numbers. The whole number can be rewritten as a fraction over a denominator of 1, and then division can be completed.

A common denominator approach can also be used in dividing fractions. Considering the same problem, $\frac{22}{5} \div \frac{1}{2}$, a common denominator between the two fractions is 10. $\frac{22}{5}$ would be rewritten as $\frac{22}{5} \times \frac{2}{2} = \frac{44}{10}$, and $\frac{1}{2}$ would be rewritten as $\frac{1}{2} \times \frac{5}{5} = \frac{5}{10}$. Dividing both numbers straight across results in $\frac{44}{10} \div \frac{5}{10} = \frac{44/5}{10/10} = \frac{44/5}{1} = \frac{44}{5}$.

Many real-world problems will involve the use of fractions. Key words include actual fraction values, such as half, quarter, third, fourth, etc. The best approach to solving word problems involving fractions is to draw a picture or diagram that represents the scenario being discussed, while deciding which type of operation is necessary in order to solve the problem. A phrase such as "one fourth of 60 pounds of coal" creates a scenario in which multiplication should be used, and the mathematical form of the phrase is $\frac{1}{4} \times 60$.

Measurement Concepts and Data

Measurement is the process by which an object's length, width, height, weight, and so on, are quantified. Measurement is related to counting, but it is a more refined and descriptive process. At this point, students are aware of length, weight, temperature, and time, and it is up to the teacher to develop these skills further. It is also up to the teacher to move the understanding of measurement from a physical sense to a more theoretical sense. This process will ensure success in the real-world application problems that appear so frequently in mathematics classes, and it will ensure success in real-world situations in which measurement is required.

Identifying, Classifying, Describing, and Comparing the Measurable Attributes of Objects

The United States units of measure are utilized within these age ranges. Standard units of length are *inches, feet,* and *yards*. Weight units can vary, based on whether the substance being measured is a liquid or a solid. Standard units of weight to measure liquids include *ounces, pints, quarts,* and *gallons*. Occasionally, solids can also be measured using pints and quarts. For example, both milk and berries can be measured in pints. Other units of weight for solids are *pounds* and *tons*.

An introduction to the **metric system** is also important in this age group. Units of mass within the metric system are *milligrams, grams,* and *kilograms*. Units of volume within the metric system are *milliliters* and *liters*. Finally, units of length within the metric system are *centimeters, meters,* and *kilometers*. Some other measures that are important in real-life settings are found in baking terminology, such as *teaspoons, tablespoons,* and *cups*, and temperature measures in *Celsius* and *Fahrenheit*. All of these units can be used to compare two objects within the classroom. Conclusions can be made that state an item is taller or heavier than another object, for example. Making sure students can utilize the proper units in order to talk about measurements is crucial.

Telling time is another important measurement and real-world application that needs to be introduced in this age group. Units of time such as *seconds, minutes, hours, days,* and *years*, etc., need to be familiarized. Clocks should be shown in the classroom, and the hour and minute hands should be used in order to tell the correct time. An analog clock can also help teach angle measurement.

Converting units within either the United States units of measure or the metric system is important in real-world application problems. It is important to make sure that all values are converted to the same units before any operations are performed. If two lengths are added that have different units, the answer would not make sense mathematically. Common length conversions within the U.S. system are that 1 foot is 12 inches, 1 yard is 3 feet, and 1 mile is 5,280 feet. Common length conversions within the metric system are that 1 centimeter is 10 millimeters, 1 meter is 100 centimeters, and 1 kilometer is 1,000 meters. In terms of volume, 1 liter is 1,000 milliliters. A meter stick is a good classroom tool to show students how to relate feet and meters.

Representing and Interpreting Data

Data can be represented in many ways including picture graphs, bar graphs, line plots, and tally charts. Students can be given the data, and the goal would be for them to be able to organize the data into categories that could be represented using one of these techniques. Also, students can record their own data, such as lengths of objects, to be plotted visually. Finally, being able to read these types of diagrams and interpret their meaning is also important in this age group.

A **picture graph** is a diagram that shows pictorial representation of data being discussed. The symbols utilized can represent the quantity of the objects being discussed. By using the key, it should be determined that each fruit symbol in the following graph represents a count of two fruits. One drawback of picture graphs is that they can be less accurate if each symbol represents a large number.

For example, if each banana symbol represented ten bananas, and students consumed 22 bananas, it may be challenging to draw and interpret two and one-fifth bananas as a frequency count of 22.

A **bar graph** is a diagram in which the quantity of items within a specific classification is represented by the height of a rectangle. Each type of classification is represented by a rectangle of equal width. Here is an example of a bar graph:

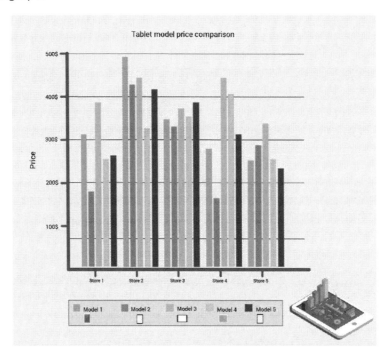

A **line plot** is a diagram that shows quantity of data along a number line. It is a quick way to record data in a structure similar to a bar graph without needing to do the required shading of a bar graph. Here is an example of a line plot:

A **tally chart** is a diagram in which tally marks are utilized to represent data. Tally marks are a means of showing a quantity of objects within a specific classification. Here is an example of a tally chart:

Number of days with rain	Number of weeks
0	II
1	HHT
2	HHT
3	HHT
4	HHT HHT HHT IIII
5	HHT I
6	HHT I
7	IIII

Data is often recorded using fractions, such as half a mile, and understanding fractions is critical because of their popular use in real-world applications. Also, it is extremely important to label values with their units when using data. For example, regarding length, the number 2 is meaningless unless it is attached to a unit. Writing 2 cm shows that the number refers to the length of an object.

Relating Addition and Subtraction to Length and Solving Problems Involving Measurements

Tools can be utilized in the classroom in order to measure the length of objects. Typical tools that can be utilized are rulers, yardsticks, and measuring tapes. They can be used to measure objects in the classroom, and comparisons can be made to show how something is longer or shorter than another item, based on either estimated or exact measurements. Such tools are based on an iterative concept that a length measurement is based on the repetition of the same unit.

For example, in order to determine the length of an object in centimeters, the answer equals the total number of centimeters from end to end of the object – basically an addition of a finite number of centimeters. Distance measurement consists of the same idea. Distance equals a measurement from the beginning to the end, with no gaps in between. Subtraction needs to be used to determine how much shorter an object is when comparing it to another object.

When students are given a problem involving measurements, it is important for them to pay attention to what units the final answer needs to be written in. All measurements should be converted to the same units initially before any calculations are completed. For example, if measurements are provided in both inches and feet, and the end result must be in inches, the measurements in feet must be converted to inches before manipulating it in calculations.

Perimeter and Area

Area is a concept relating to two-dimensional geometric shapes. It is first introduced as the total number of equally-sized squares within an object. Basically, a given figure is partitioned into two-dimensional units, and the number of units needed to cover the figure is counted. Area is measured using square units, such as square inches, feet, centimeters, or kilometers. Initially in the classroom, in order to calculate area of squares and rectangles, square units can be placed on top of a shape, and the total can be calculated to define its area. Other strategies will be necessary in order to calculate less straightforward shapes, such as triangles and parallelograms.

The **perimeter** of a two-dimensional shape is the sum of the length of the sides. It is a length measurement and is measured in inches, feet, centimeters, or kilometers. In the classroom, the perimeter of a given closed side would be found by first measuring the length of each side and then calculating the sum of all sides.

Once the concepts are understood, formulas can be used to calculate area and perimeter. Recall that multiplication can be taught by adding up squares of a rectangle. In a similar manner, the area of a rectangle is found by multiplying its length, l, times its width w. Therefore, the formula for area is $A = l \times w$. An equivalent expression is found by using the term *base*, b, instead of length, to represent the horizontal side of the shape. In this case the formula is $A = b \times h$. This same formula can be used for all parallelograms. Here is a visualization of a rectangle with its labeled sides:

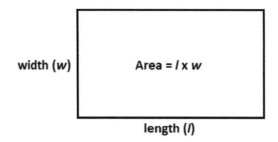

Because a square has four equal sides with the length s, its length is equal to its width, and the formula for the area of a square is $A = s \times s$. Finally, the area of a triangle is calculated by dividing the area of the rectangle that would be formed by the base, the altitude, and height of the triangle. Therefore, the area of a triangle is $A = \frac{1}{2} \times b \times h$. Formulas for perimeter are derived by adding length measurements of the sides of a figure. The perimeter of a rectangle is the result of adding the lengths of the four sides. Therefore, the formula for perimeter of a rectangle is $P = 2 \times l + 2 \times w$, and the formula for perimeter of a square is $P = 4 \times s$. The perimeter of a triangle is the sum of the lengths of the three sides.

Angles and Volume

Initially, an **angle** is defined as a corner and later is defined as the formation of two rays connecting at a vertex that extend indefinitely. Angles are measured in **degrees**, and their measurement is a measure of rotation. A **full rotation** equals 360 degrees and represents a circle. Half of a rotation equals 180 degrees and represents a half-circle. Subsequently, 90 degrees represents a quarter-circle. Similar to the hands on a clock, an angle begins at the center point, and two lines extend indefinitely from that point in two different directions.

A clock can help teach how to measure angles. At 3:00, the big hand is on the 12 and the small hand is on the 3. The angle formed is 90 degrees and is known as a **right angle**. Any angle less than 90 degrees, such as the one formed at 2:00, is known as an **acute angle**. Any angle greater than 90 degrees is known as an **obtuse angle**. The entire clock represents 360 degrees, and each clockwise increment on the clock represents an addition of 30 degrees, since there are twelve numbers and 360 degrees divided equally over the twelve segments is 30 degrees. Therefore, 6:00 represents 180 degrees, 7:00 represents 210 degrees, etc. Angle measurement is additive. When an angle is broken into two non-overlapping angles, the total measure of the larger angle is equal to the sum of the measurements of the two smaller angles.

Volume is a measurement of capacity. Whereas area is calculated by counting squares within a two-dimensional object, volume is calculated by counting cubes within a three-dimensional object. It is a measure of the space a figure occupies. Volume is measured using cubic units, such as cubic inches, feet, centimeters, or kilometers. Centimeter cubes can be utilized in the classrooms in order to promote understanding of volume.

For instance, if 10 cubes were placed along the length of a rectangle, with 8 cubes placed along its width, and the remaining area was filled in with cubes, there would 80 cubes in total, which would equal a volume of 80 cubic centimeters. Its area would equal 80 square centimeters. If that shape was doubled so that its height consists of two cube lengths, there would be 160 cubes, and its volume would be 160 cubic centimeters. Adding another level of cubes would mean that there would be $3 \times 80 = 240$ cubes. This idea shows that volume is calculated by multiplying area times height. The actual formula for volume of a three-dimensional rectangular solid is $V = l \times w \times h$, where l represents length, w represents width, and h represents height. Volume can also be thought of as area of the base times the height. The base in this case would be the entire rectangle formed by l and w. Here is an example of a rectangular solid with labeled sides:

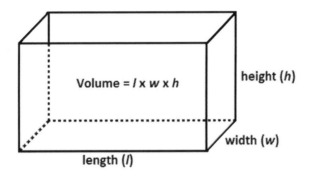

A **cube** is a special type of rectangular solid in which its length, width, and height are the same. If this length is s, then the formula for the volume of a cube is $V = s \times s \times s$.

Geometry

The portion of mathematics that deals with shapes and their properties is referred to as **geometry**. Geometry involves knowing the names and properties of shapes, but it is also closely linked to measurement and number operations. The foundations of geometry involve being able to classify and describe shapes and their properties, and that knowledge will eventually lead to working with formulas such as area, perimeter, and volume, which will help students to solve word problems involving shapes.

Shapes and their Attributes

Flat or two-dimensional shapes, such as circles, triangles, and rectangles need to be shown first. Then, three-dimensional solid shapes, such as spheres and cubes, can be introduced. A shape can be classified based on whether it is open like the letter U or closed like the letter O. Further classifications involve counting the number of sides and **vertices**—the corners—on the shapes. These categorizations will allow for methods to help students verbally distinguish between different types of shapes.

In geometry, a **line** connects two points, has no thickness, and extends indefinitely in both directions beyond the points. If it does end at two points, it is known as a **line segment** and is said to have two **endpoints**. It is important to distinguish between a line and a line segment. Students can be taught to draw **polygons** by sketching a finite number of line segments that eventually meet to create a closed shape. In addition, they can be taught to draw **triangles** by sketching a closed region using only three line segments. **Quadrilaterals** are closed shapes with four line segments. Note that a triangle has three vertices, and a quadrilateral has four vertices.

In order to teach students how to draw **circles**, one curved line segment must be created that has only one endpoint, creating a closed shape. Given such direction, every point on the line would be the same distance away from its center. The line segment created from placing an endpoint at the center of the circle and the other endpoint on the circle is known as the **radius.** The plural form of radius is **radii**. The line segment created by placing an endpoint on the circle, drawing straight through the radius, and placing the other endpoint on the circle is known as the **diameter**. A **compass** can be used in the classroom to further teach students how to draw circles, especially those with specific measurements.

Graphing Points on the Coordinate Plane

The **coordinate plane** consists of the intersection of two number lines. As discussed previously, a number line is a straight line in which numbers are marked at evenly spaced intervals with tick marks. The horizontal number line in the coordinate plane represents the **x-axis**, and the vertical number line represents the **y-axis**. The coordinate plane represents a representation of real-world space, and any point within the plane can be defined by a set of **coordinates** (x, y). The coordinates consist of two numbers, x and y, which represent a position on each number line. The coordinates can also be referred to as an **ordered pair**, and (0, 0) is the ordered pair known as the **vertex**, or the **origin,** the point in which the axes intersect. Positive x-coordinates go to the right of the vertex, and positive y-coordinates go up. Negative x-coordinates go left, and negative y-coordinates go down.

Here is an example of the coordinate plane with a point plotted:

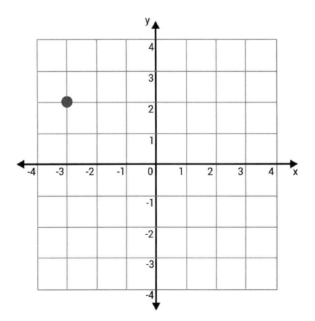

In order to plot a point on the coordinate plane, each coordinate must be considered individually. The value of x represents how many units away from the vertex the point lies on the x-axis. The value of y represents the number of units away from the vertex that the point lies on the y-axis.

For example, given the ordered pair (5, 4), the x-coordinate, 5, is the distance from the origin along the x-axis, and the y-coordinate, 4, is the distance from the origin along the y-axis. This is determined by counting 5 units to the right from (0, 0) along the x-axis and then counting 4 units up from that point, to reach the point where $x = 5$ and $y = 4$. In order to graph the single point, the point should be marked there with a dot and labeled as (5, 4). Every point on the plane has its own ordered pair.

Data can be recorded using a coordinate plane. Graphs are utilized frequently in real-world applications and can be seen in many facets of everyday life. A relationship can exist between the x- and y-coordinates that are plotted on a graph, and those values can represent a set of data that can be listed in a table. Going back and forth between the table and the graph is an important concept, and defining the relationship between the variables is the key that links the data to a real-life application.

For example, temperature increases during a summer day. The *x*-coordinate can be used to represent hours in the day, and the *y*-coordinate can be used to represent the temperature in degrees. The graph would show the temperature at each hour of the day. Time is almost always plotted on the *x*-axis and utilizing different units on each axis, if necessary, is important. Labeling the axes with units is also important.

Drawing and Identifying Lines and Angles and Classifying Shapes by Properties of Their Lines and Angles

A **ray** is a straight path that has one endpoint on one side and extends indefinitely in the other direction. Lines are known as being **coplanar** if they are located in the same plane. Similar to the coordinate plane, coplanar lines exist within the same two-dimensional surface. Two lines are **parallel** if they are coplanar, extend in the same direction, and never cross. They are known as being **equidistant** because they are always the same distance from each other. If lines do cross, they are known as **intersecting lines** because they intersect at one point. As discussed previously, angles are utilized throughout geometry, and their measurement can be seen by using an analog clock. An angle is formed when two rays begin at the same endpoint. **Adjacent angles** can be formed by creating two angles out of one shared ray. They are two side-by-side angles that also share an endpoint.

Perpendicular lines are coplanar lines that form a right angle at their point of intersection. A triangle that contains a right angle is known as a **right triangle**. The sum of the angles within any triangle is always 180 degrees. Therefore, in a right triangle, the sum of the two angles that are not right angles is 90 degrees. Any two angles that sum up to 90 degrees are known as **complementary angles**. A triangle that contains an obtuse angle is known as an **obtuse triangle,** and a triangle that contains three acute angles is known as an **acute triangle**. Here is an example of a 180-degree angle, split up into an acute and obtuse angle:

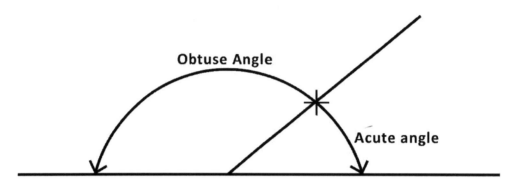

The vocabulary regarding many two-dimensional shapes is an important part of this age range. Many four-sided figures can be identified using properties of angles and lines. A **quadrilateral** is a closed shape with four sides. A **parallelogram** is a specific type of quadrilateral that has two sets of parallel lines that have the same length. A **trapezoid** is a quadrilateral having only one set of parallel sides. A **rectangle** is a parallelogram that has four right angles. A **rhombus** is a parallelogram with two acute angles, two obtuse angles, and four equal sides. The acute angles are of equal measure, and the obtuse angles are of equal measure. Finally, a **square** is a rhombus consisting of four right angles. It is important to note that some of these shapes share common attributes. For instance, all four-sided shapes are quadrilaterals. All squares are rectangles, but not all rectangles are squares.

Symmetry is another concept in geometry. If a two-dimensional shape can be folded along a straight line and the halves line up exactly, the figure is **symmetric**. The line is known as a **line of symmetry**. Circles, squares, and rectangles are examples of symmetric shapes.

Practice Questions

1. How will the number 847.89632 be written if rounded to the nearest hundredth?
    a. 847.90
    b. 900
    c. 847.89
    d. 847.896

2. What are all the factors of 12?
    a. 12, 24, 36
    b. 1, 2, 4, 6, 12
    c. 12, 24, 36, 48
    d. 1, 2, 3, 4, 6, 12

3. A construction company is building a new housing development with the property of each house measuring 30 feet wide. If the length of the street is zoned off at 345 feet, how many houses can be built on the street?
    a. 11
    b. 115
    c. 11.5
    d. 12

4. Given the value of a given stock at monthly intervals, which graph should be used to best represent the trend of the stock?
    a. Box plot
    b. Line plot
    c. Line graph
    d. Circle graph

5. The area of a given rectangle is 24 square centimeters. If the measure of each side is multiplied by 3, what is the area of the new figure?
    a. 48 cm^2
    b. 72 cm^2
    c. 216 cm^2
    d. 13,824 cm^2

Answer Explanations

1. A: 847.90. The hundredths place value is located two digits to the right of the decimal point (the digit 9 in the original number). The digit to the right of the place value is examined to decide whether to round up or keep the digit. In this case, the digit 6 is 5 or greater so the hundredth place is rounded up. When rounding up, if the digit to be increased is a 9, the digit to its left is increased by one and the digit in the desired place value is made a zero. Therefore, the number is rounded to 847.90.

2. D: 1, 2, 3, 4, 6, 12. A given number divides evenly by each of its factors to produce an integer (no decimals). The number 5, 7, 8, 9, 10, 11 (and their opposites) do not divide evenly into 12. Therefore, these numbers are not factors.

3. A: 11. To determine the number of houses that can fit on the street, the length of the street is divided by the width of each house: $345 \div 30 = 11.5$. Although the mathematical calculation of 11.5 is correct, this answer is not reasonable. Half of a house cannot be built, so the company will need to either build 11 or 12 houses. Since the width of 12 houses (360 feet) will extend past the length of the street, only 11 houses can be built.

4. C: The scenario involves data consisting of two variables: month and stock value. Box plots display data consisting of values for one variable. Therefore, a box plot is not an appropriate choice. Both line plots and circle graphs are used to display frequencies within categorical data. Neither can be used for the given scenario. Line graphs display two numerical variables on a coordinate grid and show trends among the variables, so this is the correct choice.

5. C: 216cm. Because area is a two-dimensional measurement, the dimensions are multiplied by a scale that is squared to determine the scale of the corresponding areas. The dimensions of the rectangle are multiplied by a scale of 3. Therefore, the area is multiplied by a scale of 3^2 (which is equal to 9):

$$24cm \times 9 = 216cm$$

Science

Characteristics of Science

Scientific Investigation Skills and Communication

Designing a Science Investigation

Human beings are, by nature, very curious. Long before the scientific method was established, people have been making observations and predicting outcomes, manipulating the physical world to create extraordinary things—from the first man-made fire in 6000 B.C.E. to the satellite that orbited Pluto in 2016. Although the history of the scientific method is sporadic and attributed to many different people, it remains the most reliable way to obtain and utilize knowledge about the observable universe. Designing a science investigation is based on the scientific method, which consists of the following steps:

- Make an observation
- Create a question
- Form a hypothesis
- Conduct an experiment
- Collect and analyze data
- Form a conclusion

The first step is to identify a problem based on an observation—the who, what, when, where, why, and how. An **observation** is the analysis of information using basic human senses: sight, sound, touch, taste, and smell. Observations can be two different types—qualitative or quantitative. A **qualitative observation** describes what is being observed, such as the color of a house or the smell of a flower. **Quantitative observations** measure what is being observed, such as the number of windows on a house or the intensity of a flower's smell on a scale of 1-5.

Observations lead to the identification of a problem, also called an **inference**. For example, if a fire truck is barreling down a busy street, the inferences could be:

- There's a fire.
- Someone is hurt.
- Some kid pulled the fire alarm at a local school.

Inferences are logical predictions based on experience or education that lead to the formation of a hypothesis.

Hypothesis

Valid experiments must start with a valid hypothesis. There must be one independent variable for any scientific question and a measurable dependent variable that is used to investigate the question. The **hypothesis** is a statement that explains how changing the **independent variable** would affect the dependent variable, and is often stated as an *if (*independent variable plus verb*), then (*dependent variable plus verb*)* sentence. At the early childhood level, before developing a hypothesis, it's important to emphasize valid dependent variables.

Dependent variables must be measurable. Common dependent variables include mass (measured with a balance or scale), length (measured with a ruler), and volume (measured with a graduated cylinder or the more familiar tablespoons, cups, and pints for young students).

It is also important to develop an independent variable with at least two known conditions. The normal condition is called the **control group**, and other conditions different from the control group are called **experimental groups**.

For example, a simple experiment could entail investigating how fertilizer affects plant growth.

Here are examples of valid hypotheses that collect quantitative data:

- If fertilizer is added to the soil, then plant height will increase.
- If fertilizer is added to the soil, then the number of leaves on the plant will increase.

Here are examples of invalid hypotheses:

- If fertilizer is added to the soil, then the plant will grow better.
- If the plant soil changes, then the plant will grow better.

Notice in the valid hypothesis that there's a clear independent variable: the addition of fertilizer to soil. Also, both dependent variable options are quantitative and can be measured. Height can be measured with a ruler, and the number of leaves can be measured by counting.

The invalid hypotheses contain immeasurable changes. "Growing better" isn't specific enough and can't be measured. "Soil changes" isn't specific enough and could involve many different changes, including amount of soil, type of fertilizer, or amount of fertilizer.

Variable Development

After developing a valid hypothesis with specific changes and measurements, the details of the experiment must be confirmed before developing a procedure. That means defining constants, a control group, experimental groups, and measurement methods/devices.

With the proposed hypothesis in mind (*If fertilizer is added to the soil, then plant height will increase*), several constants should be defined. The type of plant is important. Some plants grow faster than others, so all the plants included in the experiment should be of the same type (Wisconsin fast plants are an excellent choice). The brand and amount of soil should be the same; the shape and type of pot should be the same; and the amount of watering and light exposure should be consistent between all test groups. If any one of these factors is different, it will be impossible to tell which factor caused an observable change as opposed to the independent variable. The independent variable (the addition of fertilizer) should be the only changed factor.

A control group is also important to include in all experiments. In this case, the control group would be soil with no added fertilizer. There would be no way to know if the fertilizer was actually helpful unless the experiment included the unaffected condition. Including at least two experimental conditions of the manipulated variable is important if it is desirable to see varying amounts of change. Good options in this case would be to include soil with 5% fertilizer and 10% fertilizer.

The dependent variable should be something easy for young students to measure. In this experiment, a good dependent variable is length. It's important for children to know that the measurement should consist of stretching out the plant and measuring its length with a string, then using the ruler to measure the length of the straightened string. This method of measurement will account for possible drooping and will be more accurate. Discussing with students why such a procedure is important offers an opportunity for students to analyze and come up with the reason for this measuring procedure on their own, enhancing their high-level analysis skills.

Finally, it's important to include multiple trials of each test group—in this case, multiple seeds in each fertilizer condition. Students must be able to have confidence in their results; some experiments inevitably go wrong through forces of nature (such as a dud seed), so this is a critical part of any experiment.

Procedure

Developing a procedure could be a class process. For this particular experiment, several parameters should be kept in mind:

- The experiment should last for at least a week so the plants have a chance to grow.
- Water and light should be a critical part of plant care and should be uniform in all conditions.
- The string/ruler measurement system is important.

Example procedure:

Day 1
1. Place 2 cups of soil without fertilizer (0% fertilizer)* into the pot.
2. Add five seeds in the pattern exemplified below.

3. Pour ½ cup of tap water over seeds.
4. Sprinkle ¼ cup of soil over watered seeds.
5. Place the group name on the pot (label the pot appropriately).
6. Repeat steps #1-5 with:
    a. Low fertilizer mix (5% fertilizer)*
    b. High fertilizer mix (10% fertilizer)*
7. Lastly, put the pots in the light box.

*For young students, percentages are a concept that can be omitted, depending on their level. The purpose of this experiment is teaching the scientific process (not math), so "no fertilizer," "low fertilizer," and "high fertilizer" are sufficient experimental group descriptions.

Days 2-14
1. Water the plants with 1/3 cup of water every school day.
2. Day 14: Carefully pull each plant out of the soil. Carefully stretch it out and measure its length with a piece of string. Then measure the piece of string against a ruler and record the value.

At the early elementary level, it's important to know that qualitative data based on the senses (sight, taste, touch, smell, hearing) should be used in investigation as well as quantitative data (numerical data). As a class, discussing data about plants such as color, number and size of leaves, and root structure adds to the learning experience.

Developing the procedure as a class has many benefits. There is opportunity for students to make choices and further discussion. For example, if they want to use only one seed, it's a good opportunity to talk about the importance of multiple trials.

Data Collection and Results
At a young age, students will need guidance with data collection as well as communicating results. A great way to model data collection is having a data table on the blackboard and asking each group to walk up and fill in their data. Teachers should be sure to guide them so they know where to put their numbers. For example:

Amount of Fertilizer	Plant height (cm)					
	Group 1	Group 2	Group 3	Group 4	Group 5	Average
None						
Low						
High						

If students aren't familiar with the concept of averaging, it might be more appropriate to do that for them and instead to place on the board a simplified table like the one below (with mock data):

	Plant Height (cm)*
No fertilizer	5
Medium Fertilizer	12
High Fertilizer	19

*Note that figures are rounded to the nearest integer. Rounding is fine for early childhood experiments and a good point of discussion. More advanced students can write numbers to the tenths place in their data collection.

A concept that students should eventually develop on their own is how to make and present a graph; however, this should be modeled by the teacher for younger students by giving them the actual graph on paper for them to color. For older or more advanced students, an empty graph without the data bars would be sufficient, so students can draw and color the bars themselves. Teachers should emphasize to students that the independent variable should be the x-axis and the dependent variable should be the y-axis so the results are easy to interpret.

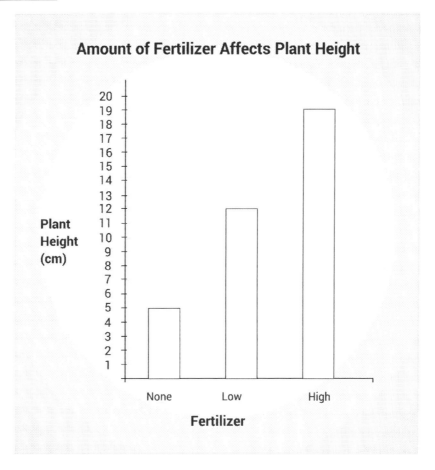

Communicating the results with a graph is simple because either the fertilizer affected the plants or it didn't, and the trend in the graph will illustrate the answer. A simple conclusion sentence can be written to wrap up the investigation. Students should decide whether the hypothesis was proven true or false, such as, "*When fertilizer was added to the soil, plant growth increased.*"

Systems, Models, Changes, and Scale's Role in Science and Technology

Visual representation and hands on-learning through the development of models is critical for students' conceptual understanding at a young age. A **system** is a set of smaller things that work together to form a larger whole. A Styrofoam ball model can demonstrate the role of planets in the larger solar system. Verbal discussion of ecosystems and food chains isn't as effective as drawing pictures of food chains and watching and discussing video clips of feeding relationships. Illustrating how plants need nutrients in their soil could be emphasized by an experiment such as the one described above.

The *scale* of science simply means its breadth, and for students to gain perspective of scale, they need models. For example, a class project involving constructing a globe would be a meaningful activity to show the land to water ratio of the Earth. Discussing destruction of rainforests and how this changes the Earth's environment by using magic markers to color affected areas on the globe is another way to show the scope of science.

A project at the University of North Texas investigated conservation habits and their effect on water bills. Children wore a bracelet to remind themselves of a promise they made to turn off the water when they brushed their teeth. Their conservation habit involved using a toothbrush that gave a signal after two minutes from starting to brush. Then, after a significant portion of time (a month or more), students had their parents bring in their water bills, and they measured and graphed the consumption decrease from month to month. The project extended further in that it actually obtained the entire city's water consumption levels, and the data indeed showed that the small changes made at home resulted in a significant conservation of water. Including technological resources into science lessons provides the opportunity for deeper understanding.

Scientific Process

Science is a process that always begins with a question or a problem. For early childhood, students must be able to perform experiments, collect quantitative and qualitative data, and communicate results visually and verbally.

The classic scientific process can be demonstrated by the development of modern genetics. Why offspring resemble parents is the question that led Gregor Mendel to experiment with pea plants and ultimately elucidate the mechanism behind heredity. Mendel proposed that there were two alleles per trait, and that an organism receives one allele from each parent. He proposed that there was a **dominant allele** and a **recessive allele**, and an organism's appearance is determined by the presence of the overpowering dominant allele. After many experiments with pea plants, Mendel found that round seeds were dominant over wrinkled seeds because if the round allele was present (even if the wrinkled allele was present), the organism appeared round.

He replicated his data not only with seed shape, but also with leaf color and plant height, among other traits, and consistently noticed that dominant alleles were overpowering.

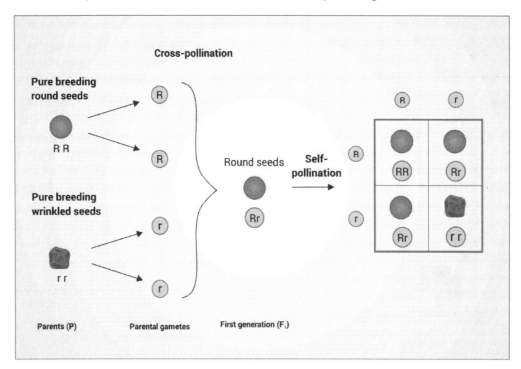

Phenotype: 3:1 round:wrinkled

Genotype: 1 RR : 2 Rr : 1 rr

Like any scientist, Mendel analyzed the question via valid experimentation and multiple trials. He performed thousands of crosses of pea plants and observed data that supported the dominant/recessive/two genes per trait idea. After the results confirming the predicted ratio, he confidently concluded that traits are determined by dominant and recessive alleles, and that every individual has two genes per trait.

In the late 1800s and early 1900s, Mendel's ideas were rejected because the prevailing idea was that an individual's traits were simply a blend of his or her parents' traits.

Modern genetics confirms that humans are **diploid**, meaning that they have two chromosomes and therefore two genes for every trait, which affirms Mendel's notion of **heredity**. A **karyotype**—a picture of all of an organism's chromosomes—is visual proof that has become possible with modern tools.

Mendel's journey exemplifies the scientific process and experimental development: problem/question, hypothesis, valid experimentation, data collection, multiple trials, and conclusions. Scientific conclusions are continually tested as technology advances. For example, Mendel's pea plant conclusions were retested and validated by visualization of chromosomes with modern microscopes.

Earth Science

Day/Night and Climate Patterns

Day, night, and climate are easy concepts to demonstrate with a globe and a light source. The notion that the Earth spins on a vertical axis is a critical piece, and a model showing the Sun and Earth's location will explain why the areas that are "day" are light because they face the Sun. The part of the globe that is "night" is simply the part facing away from the Sun.

The climate portion of an early education curriculum can be demonstrated with string and a large ball. If the wall is the Sun, three strings that start from the same point on the wall can be used to demonstrate distances of locations on Earth. One string can be stretched from the wall to the **equator** (the belt dividing the Earth in half), one from the wall to the North Pole, and one from the wall to the area halfway between. Measuring the string afterwards shows that areas closer to the equator are closer to the Sun, and that fact can easily explain why those areas have hotter climates. It makes sense that beaches like Cancun and Hawaii are hotter because they are close to the equator. Areas farthest away from the Sun (the ones that have the longest string), get less sunlight, so they're really cold (like the North Pole).

Weather Patterns

Weather is different from climate because it varies from day to day and is the result of wind and heat changes. Weather can be mild rain and snow, but it can also be dangerous thunderstorms, hurricanes, tornadoes, and blizzards. Students should be able to recognize simplified concepts of different forms of weather including:

- **Rain:** water falling from clouds
- **Snow:** snowflakes falling from clouds
- **Thunderstorms:** rainstorms with lightning
- **Tornadoes:** fast-spinning wind that looks like water going down a drain
- **Hurricanes:** huge storms that start in the ocean with massive winds that can be very destructive
- **Blizzards:** ferocious snowstorms with very high winds

Another important aspect of weather is that so much of it has to do with precipitation and the water cycle. Most of the phenomena listed above involve rain and snow.

These severe weather conditions can easily be investigated and modeled. There are 2-liter bottle experiments designed to exhibit rain and tornadoes. Hurricanes can also be researched. Hurricanes Alicia in 1983, Katrina and Rita in 2005, and Ike in 2008 are all devastating storms that can not only be used to illustrate the weather phenomenon, but can also be tied to cities and their economies.

Changes in Environment

The primary relevant changes in the environment involve destruction of forests, pollution, and global warming. The following are examples of these changes:

- **Forest destruction:** Plants provide most of the oxygen that people breathe, and destroying them changes the Earth's atmosphere. Destroying a forest also destroys an entire ecosystem (all of the plants and animals in it). It could eventually result in endangered and even extinct species.

- **Pollution:** Introducing contaminants into the air creates adverse change to the environment. Burning fossil fuels (oil and natural gas) releases fumes into the environment that cause health issues for many people and contributes to global warming.

- **Global warming:** The changing gases in the atmosphere from human activity are causing the Earth to slowly warm, which is altering ecosystems and can result in species extinction and extreme weather.

Reduce, reuse, recycle is an excellent campaign for young students that makes the concept of conservation more tangible.

Rocks, Soil, and Fossils

Rocks are solid blocks composed of a combination of minerals. There are three different types of rocks: igneous, sedimentary, and metamorphic.

Igneous rocks are formed from magma in the Earth's mantle or lava that has cooled after volcanic eruptions. **Sedimentary rocks** are little pieces of igneous rocks that break off and then they combine in layers many times at the bottom of oceans. **Metamorphic rocks** are the rocks underneath layers and layers of either sedimentary or igneous rocks that meld together and transform due to the pressure of the layers and the heat radiating upward from the Earth's core.

The differences in the appearances of rocks are called their **physical properties**. Some are shiny and some are dull. Others are hard and don't scratch easily, while still others are soft and can be scratched. They come in a range of colors, and some are even metallic. Many rocks can be found every day in houses. Igneous rocks, like granite, are found on many kitchen countertops, and pumice stones are used in foot care. Metamorphic rock, such as marble, is often found in bathroom countertops. Limestone, a sedimentary rock, is commonly found in cement. See the example below:

Types of Rocks

Igneous		Metamorphic		Sedimentary	
Granite	Gabbro	Marble	Chlorite Schist	Conglomerate	Shale
Pumice	Basalt	Phyllite	Mica Schist	Limestone	Sandstone
Obsidian		Slate	Quartzite		

To demonstrate the differences between rocks, activities in the classroom could involve taking qualitative data on the rocks while having a theme of the day. For example, igneous rock formation can be demonstrated by making erupting papier-mâché volcanoes. On that day, the class could be full of igneous rocks. Students can use their senses to record properties of the rocks and the proximity and connection to the volcano will help them remember that igneous rocks come from lava.

In order to connect metamorphic rocks to the concept that they are changed due to heat and pressure, metamorphic rocks can be scattered around the room with a stack of books over each one. Students can temporarily remove the "pressure" and examine the look and feel of the rock, recording qualitative data.

Students can investigate sedimentary rocks by digging for buried sedimentary rocks in a sandbox. The physical properties of the rocks can be recorded, and the proximity to the sand communicates that sedimentary rocks are formed by the erosion of subsequent compression of layers of sediment from other rocks. Precipitation and the water cycle results in the weathering and breakdown of rocks. **Erosion** involves runoff that carries them away to where they pile up into the layers of sediments that form sedimentary rock.

Fossils show Earth's changing history and are trapped in sedimentary rocks. The lower the fossil, the older the organism because it has been buried deeper and deeper over time.

There is an entire field of science called **paleontology** that specifically studies fossils. Fossils can be completely intact organisms, like the mosquito preserved in the sap in the movie *Jurassic Park*. Fossils can also include remnants of an organism left behind, such as bones and teeth. Structures like these have remained intact due to minerals seeping inside and preserving them like the process that occurs in petrified wood. **Trace fossils** like a footprint are also considered fossils even though they aren't actual remains—they are simply evidence that the organism was there.

Trace fossils   Remain   Layer Analysis

Using the sandbox to hunt for fossils will enhance the learning experience. If students also get their hands dirty with soil, the next day, they can compare and contrast soil with sand. While sedimentary rock is the result of erosion and compaction of sediments, soil is the result of weathered rock mixing with decomposing dead organisms to form a loose mix conducive to plant growth. Liquid flows in soil, and air seeps through it as well. Sedimentary rock does not have the same amount of vulnerability to liquids and gases.

Earth's Surface Features

Ultimately, the **topography** of the Earth changes for two reasons: plate movement and the water cycle.

The Earth is divided into **plates**, which are kind of like puzzle pieces in that they are huge chunks of the Earth's surface (both water and land) that piece together to cover the surface of the planet.

These boundaries are cracks in the globe that cause many different physical changes. If the plates separate or **diverge**, a trench can form and magma can erupt from sites of volcanic activity. If two plates in the water **converge,** there will be a subduction zone where one buckles under the other. If two plates on land converge, they will buckle together and form mountains. There is also sideways movement between **transform boundaries**, which can cause cracks in the Earth's surface.

The **water cycle** also accounts for the Earth's changing features. Rivers, glaciers, and run-off cause ravines, and the sediment deposited by rivers as they converge with larger bodies of water cause large, spread-out deltas. Erosion also alters the landscape by chipping off bits of rocks and soil.

All surface changes can be labeled as either **constructive** (building) or **destructive** (destroying).

Constructive	Destructive
Mountains Volcanoes Sediment deposits result in deltas and sand dunes	Ravines Trenches Weathering followed by erosion

Demonstrating these concepts to students can be used with puzzle pieces to represent tectonic plates as well as using clay to make various landforms.

Physical Science

Properties of Objects

Properties can be broken down into two types, physical and chemical. **Chemical properties** are important in knowing how to handle a substance because they describe its behavior (radioactive, corrosive, flammable, reactive). **Physical properties** are important in identifying and describing the substance.

Examples of physical properties include:

- Color
- Luster (shine)
- Magnetism
- Density
- Boiling point
- Melting point
- Hardness (Can it be scratched?)
- Conductivity of heat
- Conductivity of electricity
- Brittleness (Does it shatter or break in chunks?)
- Malleability (pliability)

Young students should be able to identify simple physical properties such as color, magnetism, hardness, and malleability, which can easily be tied to the rock activity above. These properties will be meaningful to include in discussing differences and similarities of elements like copper, iron, sulfur, and carbon (coal).

It's also important that students identify extensive physical properties and rank substances based on weight, size, and dimensions. Which is larger? Which is heaviest? Which takes up the most space? These questions seem easy, but for early childhood students, such comparisons can require high-level thinking. Extending the rock activity above by having students weigh the rocks and rank them in order by mass can be a meaningful exercise. Measuring the rocks with a ruler, and even measuring their volume by **displacement** (putting them in a container of water and measuring how much the water moves), are other ways of communicating the concept of physical properties.

Importance of Physical Science Concepts

Awareness of the physical environment is important in understanding the world. Important concepts for early elementary students include:

- Location: Classifying objects in terms of nearness or where they are found
- Heat energy: Measuring temperature
- Light energy: Absorbed by plants to make food and illuminates the environment
- Magnetic forces: Important to describe push and pull forces
- Object movement: Observing and recording movements and relative movement speed

Activities to develop concepts above can include:

- Location and object movement: Students can move toy cars at different speeds to identify which move faster and, as a result, which stop farther away. This could be developed with an experiment investigating the hypothesis *If cars are pushed harder, then they will travel farther.* (Although force isn't the most specific independent variable, it can still be used at this level.) The dependent variable of length would be easy to measure with the string/ruler procedure. If resources are available, generating loop tracks and emphasizing above and below would also be a way to emphasize object relationships to each other.

- Heat energy: This can be demonstrated with boiling water. As water is heated up, its temperature increases and it boils because its particles are moving faster.

- Light energy: Coloring pictures of rainbows is a way to emphasize the visible light spectrum. Using prisms and flashlights illustrates that adding light makes more color visible. Also, plant experiments with varying amounts of light as the independent variable can emphasize how plants are dependent on light energy.

- Magnetic forces: Using magnets and comparing magnetic objects with non-magnetic objects is a way to emphasize that magnetism is a physical property. Magnets can even be applied to the same object at different sizes to compare heavier and lighter objects.

Students should be familiar with the tenet "**matter** is anything that has mass and takes up space." Understanding matter means knowing that all matter is made of atoms. Teachers can introduce a basic understanding of **atoms** by discussing their structure (a nucleus with protons and neutrons in its center, and tiny electrons that orbit around the nucleus, like how planets orbit around the sun). This concept – that small parts join to make larger structures – can easily be demonstrated with Lego blocks. An

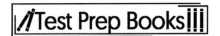

extension of this discussion is explaining that **electrons** are negatively charged and **protons** are positively charged, and demonstrating the idea with magnets.

Life Science

Characteristics of Living and Non-Living Things

There are several common traits among all living organisms, including:

- They are comprised of cells
- The contain DNA, the genetic code of life
- They grow and develop
- They reproduce
- They need food for energy
- They maintain homeostasis
- They react to their surroundings
- They evolve as a population

There are two types of cells that make up living things: simple bacterial cells (**prokaryotes**) and the complicated cells of protists, fungi, plants, and animals (**eukaryotes**). All of these have a set of instructions, DNA, which codes for the proteins that allow organisms to grow. In the case of bacteria and single-celled eukaryotes, there is simple development, such as creating structures like DNA, **ribosomes** (protein factories), and a cell membrane. Bacteria do not have complex development because they simply divide once and make a new organism; however, multicellular organisms develop more complex structures—for examples, humans have hearts, stomachs, brains, etc. A human starts as one fused cell called a **zygote**. In nine months, that zygote has developed so much that it has all the internal organs needed to support life.

Organisms cannot live without energy to fuel the necessary reactions to grow and develop. They get the energy they need either by making it themselves (if they are **producers/autotrophs** like plants) or consuming it (like animals and fungi) from an outside source. Not only do organisms use that food to grow and develop, but they also use it to stay healthy and maintain homeostasis. For example, the human body has a constant temperature of 98.6 degrees. If the temperature goes above that, the body starts to sweat to cool off. Much below that temperature, the body will shiver in order to generate energy to heat up. For survival, all organisms must be highly regulated to function, kind of like a car. Every single part has to work together in harmony in order to function properly.

Living things, such as humans, respond to their surroundings. If someone hears a loud noise, his or her head turns toward it. If something gets thrown at one's face, the person will blink. Even plants grow towards sunlight. Living things also evolve as a population. Humans today are nothing like our ancestors of long ago because as a species, humans had to continually adapt to the Earth's changing environment.

An extensive explanation of these characteristics of life is beyond an early childhood curriculum, but it's helpful for the teacher to know them because delineating living and nonliving objects can be tricky. A teacher needs to know why fire, a dead grasshopper, and a robot are not alive, because these are common student misconceptions. Although a fire can grow, it does not have DNA. Although a dead grasshopper is made of cells and has DNA, it can't grow or reproduce. A robot doesn't have DNA and isn't made of cells, although it can react to its environment. Conversely, some students don't believe that plants are alive because they don't walk around. To illustrate that they are alive, simple experiments can be used to show that they can reproduce, develop, and grow, such as planting seeds and using light-boxes to show that plants grow toward light.

Teachers must be able to explain that not all organisms move. Plants are alive because they are made of cells, have DNA, grow independently, and meet all of the other characteristics of life. Tiny germs are alive for the same reasons.

These nuances are complicated, but young students should be able to explain that living things grow and nonliving things don't. They should be able to identify mushrooms, plants, and animals as living, and fire, desks, and robots as nonliving.

Life Cycle and Organism Interaction with Habitats

Human **development** starts when sperm fertilizes an egg to create a zygote, which will develop into an embryo. Pregnant women carry an **embryo** inside their bodies for nine months before giving birth to a live baby. Human reproduction is a concept best left for an older age, but mentioning that babies come from eggs that grow inside a mom is a concept that can be briefly discussed because all the organisms below develop from external eggs. It will provide a good contrast to emphasize the following life cycles:

Chicken	Hens are female chickens, and they lay about one egg per day. If there is no rooster (male chicken) around to fertilize the egg, the egg never turns into a chick and instead becomes an egg that we can eat. If a rooster is around, he mates with the female chicken and fertilizes the egg. Once the egg is fertilized, the tiny little embryo (future chicken) will start as a white dot adjacent to the yolk and **albumen** (egg white) and will develop for 21 days. The mother hen sits on her clutch of eggs (several fertilized eggs) to incubate them and keep them warm. She will turn the eggs to make sure the embryo doesn't stick to one side of the shell. The embryo continues to develop, using the egg white and yolk nutrients, and eventually develops an "egg tooth" on its beak that it uses to crack open the egg and hatch. Before it hatches, it even chirps to let the mom know of its imminent arrival!
Frog	Frogs mate similar to the way chickens do, and then lay eggs in a very wet area. Sometimes, the parents abandon the eggs and let them develop on their own. The eggs, like chickens', will hatch around 21 days later. Just like chickens, a frog develops from a yolk, but when it hatches, it continues to use the yolk for nutrients. A chicken hatches and looks like a cute little chick, but a baby frog is actually a **tadpole** that is barely developed. It can't even swim around right away, although eventually it will develop gills, a mouth, and a tail. After more time, it will develop teeth and tiny legs and continue to change into a fully grown frog! This type of development is called **metamorphosis.**
Fish	Most fish also lay eggs in the water, but unlike frogs, their swimming sperm externally fertilize the eggs. Like frogs, when fish hatch, they feed on a yolk sac and are called *larvae*. Once the larvae no longer feed on their yolk and can find their own nutrients, they are called **fry,** which are basically baby fish that grow into adulthood.
Butterfly	Like frogs, butterflies go through a process called **metamorphosis**, where they completely change into a different looking organism. After the process of mating and internal fertilization, the female finds the perfect spot to lay her eggs, usually a spot with lots of leaves. When the babies hatch from the eggs, they are in the larva form, which for butterflies is called a **caterpillar**. The larvae eat and eat and then go through a process like hibernation and form into a **pupa**, or a **cocoon**. When they hatch from the cocoon, the butterflies are in their adult form.
Bugs	After fertilization, other bugs go through **incomplete metamorphosis**, which involves three states: eggs that hatch, nymphs that look like little adults without wings and molt their exoskeleton over time, and adults.

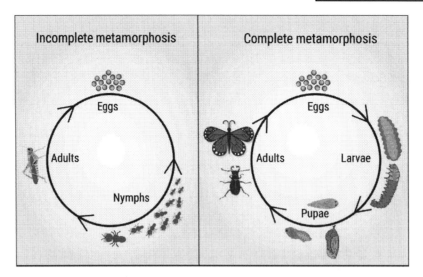

All of these organisms depend on a proper environment for development, and that environment depends on their form. Frogs need water, caterpillars need leaves, and baby chicks need warmth in order to be born.

Engaging ways to introduce the life cycle are books like *Rainbow Fish* by Marcus Pfister and *The Very Hungry Caterpillar* by Eric Carle.

Interactions of Organisms and Their Environments

An **ecosystem** consists of all living (**community**) and nonliving components (abiotic factors) in an area. **Abiotic factors** include the atmosphere, soil, rocks, and water, which all have a role in sustaining life. The atmosphere provides the necessary gasses, soil contains nutrients for plants, rocks erode and affect topography, and water has many different roles.

An ecosystem not only involves living things interacting with nonliving things, but also involves the community interacting with each other. **Food chains** depict one type of community interaction, like the one shown here:

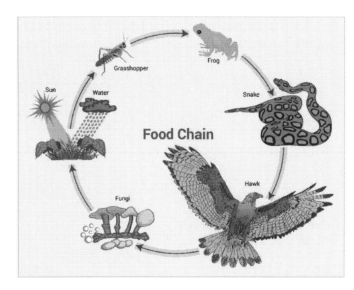

Food chains show the transfer of energy as one organism eats another. They also show an organism's eating habits. **Herbivores** eat plants and **carnivores** eat meat. A lion in grassland with no available animal prey will starve to death even though there is lots of grass because lions don't eat grass; that isn't their role in their habitat.

Food webs not only show predator-prey relationships, but they also show another relationship called **competition**.

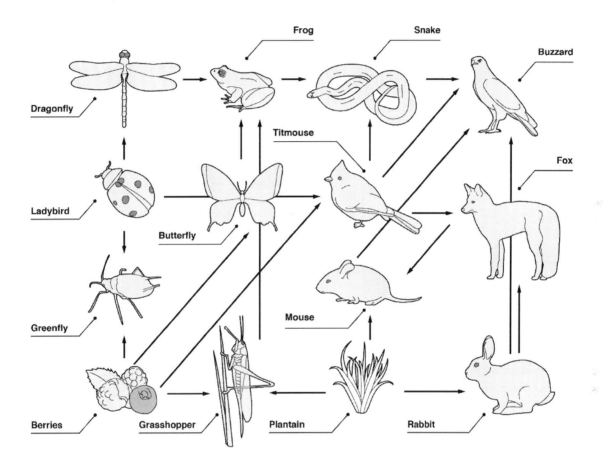

This food web shows that mice and frogs are competing for grasshoppers. If there is a scarcity of grasshoppers, the mouse and frog populations will decrease.

The final three types of community relationships all fall under the blanket term **symbiosis** and are described in the table below.

	Mutualism	**Commensalism**	**Parasitism**
Definition	Both organisms benefit from the relationship	One organism benefits from the relationship	One organism benefits from the relationship, and the other is harmed
Example	Birds and flowers	Whale and barnacle	Dog and flea
Explanation	Birds get nectar. Plants get pollinated.	Barnacle gets a free ride and access to food. Whale doesn't care because the barnacle is just latched on and isn't hurting anything.	Flea sucks dog's blood and gets nutrients. Dog is itchy and gets its blood drained.

The important knowledge for students to retain is:

- Plants need soil and sunlight to survive. This can be demonstrated by growing plants in the classroom.

- Animals in an area can have relationships other than predator-prey.

- Animals have niches in their environment. Some are herbivores (eat plants only), some are carnivores (eat meat only), and some are **omnivores** like humans (eat both plants and animals).

Inherited Traits, Learned Behaviors, and Organism Survival

Many characteristics are inherited from the DNA obtained from an individual's parents, including skin color, eye shape, hair color, and color-blindness, among others. Learned behavior isn't related to genetics and is a result of training. For example, a dog catching a stick is learned. The overall intelligence of the dog, however, has to do with its genes.

An organism's survival depends on its **fitness** relative to the environment, and any trait that helps it survive is called an **adaptation**. Whale blubber and shark teeth are examples of adaptations. Blubber keeps whales warm, and a shark's many teeth ensures it's better able to capture prey. Whales don't decide to grow blubber, and sharks don't decide to grow teeth. These characteristics have been inherited from their parents.

Discussion of adaptations can involve showing pictures of various organisms and identifying which of their characteristics would be helpful and why. See below for some ideas for discussion.

Organism	Adaptation to identify	Why it's helpful
Cactus	Spikes	Help protect from water thieves
Peacock	Feathers	Help scare off predators (look like eyes); also help attract mates
Elephant	Trunk	Helps suck up water
Skunk	Smelly secretions	Help protect from predators

Practice Questions

1. How many daughter cells are formed from one parent cell during meiosis?
    a. One
    b. Two
    c. Three
    d. Four

2. What is the total mechanical energy of a system?
    a. The total potential energy
    b. The total kinetic energy
    c. Kinetic energy plus potential energy
    d. Kinetic energy minus potential energy

3. What does the Lewis Dot structure of an element represent?
    a. The outer electron valence shell population
    b. The inner electron valence shell population
    c. The positioning of the element's protons
    d. The positioning of the element's neutrons

4. Which rock is formed from cooling magma underneath the Earth's surface?
    a. Extrusive sedimentary rocks
    b. Sedimentary rocks
    c. Igneous rocks
    d. Metamorphic rocks

5. Which of the following is most abundant in the Earth's atmosphere?
    a. Carbon dioxide
    b. Oxygen
    c. Nitrogen
    d. Water

Answer Explanations

1. D: Meiosis has the same phases as mitosis, except that they occur twice—once in meiosis I and once in meiosis II. During meiosis I, the cell splits into two. Each cell contains two sets of chromosomes. Next, during meiosis II, the two intermediate daughter cells divide again, producing four total haploid cells that each contain one set of chromosomes.

2. C: In any system, the total mechanical energy is the sum of the potential energy and the kinetic energy. Either value could be zero but it still must be included in the total. Choices *A* and *B* only give the total potential or kinetic energy, respectively. Choice *D* gives the difference in the kinetic and potential energy.

3. A: A Lewis Dot diagram shows the alignment of the valence (outer) shell electrons and how readily they can pair or bond with the valence shell electrons of other atoms to form a compound. Choice *B* is incorrect because the Lewis Dot structure aids in understanding how likely an atom is to bond or not bond with another atom, so the inner shell would add no relevance to understanding this likelihood. The positioning of protons and neutrons concerns the nucleus of the atom, which again would not lend information to the likelihood of bonding.

4. C: Igneous rocks are formed from the cooling of magma, both on and below the Earth's surface, which are classified as extrusive and intrusive, respectively. Sedimentary rocks are formed from deposition and cementation on the surface, and metamorphic rocks are formed from the transformation of sedimentary or igneous rocks through heat and pressure.

5. C: Nitrogen is the most abundant element in the atmosphere at 78%. Carbon dioxide and water don't make up a large percentage. Oxygen makes up only 21% of the atmosphere.

Health Education, Physical Education, and the Arts

Health and Physical Education Concepts and Influences

Health Promotion and Disease Prevention

Early childhood educators should be able to incorporate health and physical education concepts into the classroom for the overall health, wellness, and growth of their students. Physical activity is especially important at young ages, and children need at least sixty minutes of moderate to vigorous physical activity daily according to the U.S. Surgeon General's Recommendations. There are five components of health-related **physical fitness**: cardiovascular fitness, muscular strength, muscular endurance, flexibility, and body composition. All five areas should be addressed in physical education classes. With cardiovascular training, as the heart enlarges, the volume of the chambers increase, allowing for a greater **stroke volume** (the volume of blood ejected in each heart beat) and cardiac output. This also enables the heart to be more efficient, with a resultant lowering of the resting and submaximal exercise heart rate and blood pressure, which increases the body's exercise duration and intensity tolerance. Blood volume—both in terms of plasma and hemoglobin—increases oxygen-carrying capacity and lactic acid metabolism improves, which allows the aerobic system to more effectively metabolize substrates for usable energy. Muscle glycogen storage, another important form of energy storage in the body, also increases. Vasculature increases as well, improving the blood perfusion of muscles.

Other positive results of physical fitness include increased bone mineral density, improvements in body composition, and neural adaptations. Resistance training, even with body weight alone (such as squats and push-ups), affords strength, power, and coordination improvements and leads to greater efficiency of the anaerobic metabolic systems. Nervous system adaptations occur quickly with training as **motor units** (connections between the spine and other muscles throughout the body) become conditioned to activate more quickly and more often. As a greater number of motor units activate together and coordinate with each other, a higher percentage of fibers in a muscle contract simultaneously, increasing strength. Over time, muscle fibers increase in size and bone mineral density increases in load-bearing bones. Flexibility training increases elasticity and resting length of muscle and connective tissues and joint range of motion (ROM) before the stretch reflex is initiated (muscle spindle adaptation), reducing injury risk.

Health education – even beginning at preschool ages – has been shown to have a significant positive impact on an individual for maintaining healthy behaviors as an adolescent and adult. Preschool children who receive high-quality physical and health education may have improved nutrition and exercise habits and are more likely to receive routine medical and dental care as adults. Early childhood educators can start laying the groundwork for a lifetime of healthier behaviors and attitudes by fostering an environment of enjoyment of physical activity, an understanding of nutrition and hydration, and methods of disease and injury prevention.

Educators can talk with older children about the types, causes, and characteristics of chronic, degenerative, communicable, and non-communicable diseases, as well as ways to detect and prevent them. Students can learn about modifiable risk factors for various diseases and conditions such as diabetes, coronary artery disease, cardiovascular disease, and obesity.

The Relation Between Healthy Behaviors and a Healthy Person

Early childhood educators can introduce young children to a wide variety of healthy behaviors that will help improve overall health. An important concept to begin teaching students is that optimal health is brought about through routine practice of daily healthy behaviors and an overall commitment to a healthy lifestyle. For example, educators can discuss the importance of establishing regular physical activity and daily healthy eating habits and that, through these habits, students can control their body weight and help avoid obesity. Obesity is a modifiable risk factor for many diseases including insulin-resistant Type 2 diabetes mellitus and cardiovascular disease. It is important and empowering for children to start to understand their roles and responsibilities in healthy habits and disease prevention. By giving them the necessary knowledge and tools to put the information into practice in their lives, educators can increase the self-efficacy and behaviors of even young children. In this way, early childhood educators can be instrumental in bringing about a healthier generation of young children who have an awareness of their health and an understanding of their own influence on risk factors for certain diseases. The following are healthy behaviors that can lead to a healthy body and mind:

Nutrition

Children should be taught how to identify foods and the importance of consuming a daily variety of food within each healthy food group. The benefits of trying new foods, especially those from other cultures, can help students understand diversity and challenge their preconceived notions about different cultures and flavors. Older children can learn how to prepare simple foods, recognize the USDA recommended daily allowances of each food group in order to keep the body healthy, and classify foods based on their group and health benefits. Older students can also learn about the role of various nutrients in the body such as fat, fiber, and protein, and how to select nutrient-dense foods from a given list. Children benefit from understanding what makes a food healthy and knowing options for healthy meals and snacks. By the third grade, students can start learning how to read nutrition labels, how to compare foods based on nutrition labels, and how to modify food choices to improve healthfulness, such as replacing low-fiber foods with higher fiber choices, like opting for apples instead of applesauce. When students are in the fourth grade, educators can start talking about portion sizes and the relationship between food consumption and physical activity on energy balance and weight control. In the context of introducing the basics about calories, prevention of obesity and the ramifications of an unhealthy diet can also be discussed. Children in the fifth and sixth grades can learn about the differences in types of fats, examples of common vitamins and minerals and food sources of these nutrients, the disadvantages of "empty-calories," and how to recognize misleading nutrition information.

Physical Activity

In childhood, regular physical activity improves strength and endurance, helps build healthy bones and muscles, controls weight, reduces anxiety and stress, increases self-esteem, and may improve blood pressure and cholesterol. Children should get at least sixty minutes of physical activity daily. Typically, young children are less concerned about their physical fitness and more concerned about having fun; therefore, physical education should center on fun and play as a means to engage the body in activity. Play-centered physical education programs are an effective means to promote children's movement development and meet their requisite activity needs for health. Early childhood educators should develop physical education programs that focus on the enjoyment of movement rather than sport-specific skill mastery for two reasons. Firstly, play-centered activity will help the child be more engaged and likely to adopt a positive attitude towards exercise; and secondly, in early childhood, basic general fitness and movement skills are more important than mastery of highly specialized skills unique to certain sports. Young children also tend to lack the gross and fine motor skills and perceptual abilities needed for such highly specialized skills, which can lead to frustration or simply an inability to perform the activity.

For optimal results, it is best for early childhood educators to establish an environment of student-centered learning in regards to physical education. Because young children at any given age can have vastly different motor and physical abilities from each other, it is imperative that the educator simply set standards of enjoyment, movement, and physical discovery rather than specific mastery of skills. This prevents boredom in more physically advanced children and bewilderment and demotivation in less skilled children. It is prudent for educators to provide a variety of options within every activity and game so that children can figure out what appeals and works for them at their own developmental level. This also starts children on the path to understanding themselves and evaluating choices at a young age within a fun, playful environment and begins to get their minds processing not just what to do but how to do it as well.

Educators should use simple instructions that are age-appropriate in terms of the steps and level of complexity, visual demonstrations of movements, and drills that help reinforce the skill. During practice and exploration of the new skill, educators should focus on positive feedback and evaluation to guide the children in learning. When teaching new skills, especially to toddlers and young children, instructions lasting longer than twenty seconds or that contain more than just a couple of steps will cause students to lose interest or get overwhelmed. It is typically advantageous to have very short instructional periods interspersed between longer breaks to play and try out the skills. To help manage a large group of small, active children, simple rules and expectations should be laid out with consequences for improper behavior.

Children should learn about the methods and benefits of a proper warm-up and cool-down, how to set goals to make exercise part of their daily routine, and the benefits of physical activity. Older children can learn about the effects of exercise on the heart and how to locate their pulse during and after exercise, how to stay physically active through more than just sports, and how to create a personal fitness plan.

Sleep

Early childhood educators should talk about the importance of sleep and why parents set a "bedtime," as well as healthy sleep hygiene and establishing a sleep schedule. Children can learn about how much sleep they need and ways to improve the quality of sleep, such as physical activity and avoiding screen time before bed. Young children who may experience nightmares can benefit from learning relaxation techniques as well as talking about their fears and feelings to trusted adults.

Stress Management

Students should be educated about stress management and exposed to techniques such as mental imagery, relaxation, deep breathing, aerobic exercise, and meditation. Children can be guided through progressive muscle relaxation and should be taught signs of excessive nervousness and stress, how to manage test and performance anxiety, and when and how to get help with excessive stress.

Healthy Relationships

Healthy family and social relationships are important to overall health and happiness. Studies have pointed to a negative impact of parental fighting on a child's wellbeing, including sleep and exercise habits, nutrition choices, stress, and social adjustment. Early childhood educators should talk about aspects of healthy relationships such as communication, emotional support, sharing, and respect. Younger children should learn skills that are helpful in making friends, cultivating relationships, and resolving conflict, especially as they relate to peers and siblings. Cooperation, taking turns, using words rather than physical means to communicate feelings, and exploring feelings are helpful concepts to instill. Older children should begin to be exposed to dating etiquette and forming healthy romantic relationships. Educators should work to create a classroom environment of inclusion where students have an awareness of peers who may feel left out and work to include everyone. Within discussions of healthy relationships, educators should talk about accepting and appreciating diversity, including differences in cultures, religions, families, physical appearance and abilities, interests, intellect, emotions, lifestyle, and, in older children, sexual orientations. Life skills – such as having self-esteem, making decisions, calming oneself when angry or upset, and using listening skills – should be addressed.

Hydration

Early childhood educators should teach students about the importance of hydration and signs of dehydration as well as healthy choices for fluids, with a special emphasis on water. Children and their parents should be encouraged to send kids to school with a water bottle, and classrooms or hallways should be equipped with water fountains that children can access and use with limited supervision or assistance.

Safety Behaviors

Children should learn basic safety behaviors and the importance of following rules to prevent common injuries. Basic safety behaviors include wearing sunscreen and sunglasses when going outdoors; wearing protective gear in sports such as bicycle helmets, reflective vests, appropriate pads and cups, etc.; and using a car seat and/or always wearing a seat belt. Young children should learn about household safety such as not touching burners and not putting their fingers in electrical sockets nor opening the door to strangers. Educators should have children practice the "no, go, and tell" procedure for unsafe situations. For example, if a stranger offers the child an unknown substance, the child should know how to firmly refuse, carefully leave the situation, and tell a trusted adult. In this lesson, educators should also help children to identify trusted adults in their families and communities.

Educators can also discuss community safety measures such as using sidewalks, contacting city services (police, fire, and ambulance) in emergencies, and crossing the street safely by using crosswalks, holding hands, and looking both ways before crossing. Children should also learn about the health consequences of smoking, how to avoid secondhand smoke, and how to identify and avoid poisonous household substances. Fire safety such as "stop, drop, and roll" and emergency evacuation procedures should be rehearsed. Older children can learn about safety rules for various types of weather and how weather affects their personal safety, what different traffic signs mean, water/swim safety rules, and the importance of weighing consequences before taking risks.

Hygiene

Young children should learn about germs and the spread of infections. Older children can learn about bacteria and viruses. The importance of washing hands (including appropriate demonstration) cannot be overstated in elementary and preschool classrooms.

Other aspects of hygiene such as covering the mouth while coughing and covering the nose while sneezing, not sharing cups, practicing clean bathroom habits, showering and bathing, and, in older children, using deodorants, antiperspirants, and facial cleansers should be included in the curriculum.

Learning to Seek Health Care

Early childhood educators can play an instrumental role in the lifelong practice of seeking routine medical and dental care as well as medical support during illness and injury by setting positive attitudes towards such care and explaining the benefits to young children. Not all children will necessarily have health insurance, so information regarding local free and affordable options should be made available to parents. It is important that children learn to identify signs of illness and injury such as sore throats, headaches, stomachaches that do not go away, swelling, etc.

Consistent Feelings of Sadness, Anxiety, Loneliness, and Stress

Just as it is important to get professional help for medical issues, it equally important to seek help with mental and emotional issues. Educators should talk about feelings and emotions and how it is normal to feel sad or anxious at various times, but that if such feelings persist, help may be necessary. Teachers can lead the class through stress management techniques to combat anxiety and talk about the role of physical activity, sound nutrition, and good sleep for mood stabilization. Young children should learn about identifying and communicating their emotions.

Lingering Pains or Aches
Children should be instructed to tell a trusted adult when they have pains, aches, or symptoms that persist for several days so that the adult can help determine if medical attention is needed. Children can also learn basic first-aid such as how to wash a cut and put on a Band-Aid or when and how to use **RICES** (Rest, Ice, Compression, Elevation, and Stabilization) after an injury.

Prevention of Common Injuries and Health Problems
One critically important component of health and safety education is the prevention of common injuries and illnesses. By practicing safety and exercising caution, many common injuries and illnesses can be avoided. For example, wearing helmets and seat belts can reduce the risk of injury during automobile or bicycle accidents. Washing hands thoroughly and frequently with antibacterial soap can help prevent the spread of germs, and thus safeguard against viral and bacterial infections. Even very young children should be encouraged to wash hands thoroughly before and after eating, after using the bathroom, after coming in from outdoor play, and when transitioning to a new activity. It is sometimes helpful to demonstrate how to wash in between each finger, under the fingernails, and up to the wrists, modeling not only how to wash hands but for how long. The common song "Row, Row, Row Your Boat" repeated three times is sometimes used to measure the appropriate length of time for hand washing.

By instilling an attitude of mindfulness and awareness, educators can help children to develop practices of safety, which will ultimately keep them healthy. Other longer-term behavioral and lifestyle principles – such as keeping a healthy weight through caloric balance and a healthy diet – will help prevent disease risk factors such as obesity, high triglycerides, hypercholesterolemia, and high blood sugar. Children should be informed about the dangers of smoking and the detrimental health consequences of tobacco products, including ingestion of secondhand smoke. Other simple safety practices include wearing proper footwear, practicing good hygiene, remaining alert when out in traffic, using sidewalks and pedestrian walkways, and wearing sunscreen.

Wearing Seat Belts and Helmets
Children should be informed that they should always wear a seat belt in the car. Children under eighty pounds should be in an appropriate car seat as well to maximize safety in moving vehicles. Many unfortunate traffic injuries and fatalities could have been prevented had the victim appropriately worn a seat belt. Riding bicycles, skateboarding, using scooters, and rollerblading are examples of excellent exercise and recreational pursuits; however, helmets and appropriate padding and protection on elbows and knees should always be worn. Children or their supervisors often neglect to fasten on a helmet when the child is simply trying out a skateboard or scooter around the driveway or park. This is quite dangerous because falls are inevitable in the learning process and even minor head bumps can be damaging. Helmets should fit snugly with the band clipped securely under the chin and the dome of the helmet should cover the entire forehead. Helmets should not move freely on the head and should be snug enough to stay in place. They should be sized appropriately to the child's head with use of additional padding if necessary. Kneepads and shoulder pads are great adjuncts to safety gear for rollerblading, skateboarding, and scooters. Children riding in bicycle trailers should also wear helmets, and children should never ride on the handlebars of a bicycle. Although more stable, tricycles and bicycles with training wheels still require helmets with their use.

Drugs, Alcohol, and Tobacco

Drugs, alcohol, and tobacco are unhealthy substances that early childhood educators should begin informing young children about. Exposure to drugs, cigarettes, and alcohol happens at increasingly younger ages, particularly when children have older siblings. By educating children about the risks and consequences of such substances at young ages, teachers can begin to thwart the risks of unhealthy behaviors. The Drug Abuse Resistance Education (D.A.R.E.) program is often helpful at introducing such substances, their health consequences, and how to navigate social situations involving peer pressure. The difference between alcohol abuse and alcohol in moderation should also be discussed.

Routine Preventative Medical and Dental Care

By practicing routine medical and dental care and adhering to recommended guidelines regarding the frequency of preventative healthcare, certain risks for various diseases and dental issues (such as cavities and gingivitis) can be reduced. It is typically recommended the children see their pediatrician and get dental cleanings at least once every six months. In between these appointments, healthy habits continue to safeguard against health issues. Examples include thoroughly brushing teeth at least twice a day and flossing daily, getting at least sixty minutes of moderate to vigorous exercise a day, meeting healthy sleep requirements (the National Sleep Foundation recommends ten to thirteen hours for preschoolers and nine to eleven hours for elementary school children), consuming an adequate amount of water, and following nutritional guidelines. By keeping children on a routine schedule of preventive care with consistency in providers of that care, the health and wellbeing of each child can be tracked during their growth to ensure health issues do not slip through the cracks.

Food Preparation Choices

Early childhood educators should devote instructional attention to the methods of food preparation and how various choices in preparation affect the nutritive value of the food. For example, baking and steaming are healthier than pan frying, deep frying, and sautéing. Eating whole foods is healthier than eating their processed counterparts because the whole foods retain a greater percentage of the inherent nutrients. For example, apples are healthier than applesauce because applesauce strips away much of the fiber and the vitamins in the apple skin. Similarly, whole grain bread is healthier than refined white breads, which remove the bran from the grain, thereby reducing the fiber, protein, and B vitamin content. Foods that are organic do not have the pesticides and chemicals used with certain **conventional** (non-organic) foods. This is an important consideration for thin-skinned fruits and vegetables such as spinach, tomatoes, and berries, which can absorb harmful chemicals.

Influence of Family, Peers, Culture, and Media on Health Behaviors

Health behaviors are heavily influenced by a child's environment, including family, friends, peers, media, and technology. These factors can shape the child's ideas of health, nutrition, and fitness, as well as influence subsequent health behaviors. It is important for educators to help children identify and cultivate positive influences while avoiding or modifying negative ones.

Educators should work with students to develop self-efficacy for healthy behaviors to help safeguard against any negative environmental influences. Children should learn about peer pressure, substance use, wearing seat belts, and how to make independent decisions and stick to them despite peer pressure or group dynamics. Discussed below are a few examples of potential environmental and situational influences.

Family

Family factors include health insurance status, safety and injury prevention education and care, nutritional meal planning and diet composition, family dynamics and stress, family culture during leisure time such as activity vs. inactivity, child care situation, and parental and sibling modeled behavior.

Peers

The peer group that surrounds a child can affect his or her health behaviors depending on those of the group. Example behaviors and influences include the use of helmets and seat belts, interests and activities, inclusion on sports teams or during recess and physical education, aggression and bullying or teasing.

School and Community

Factors in this domain include things such as the availability and choices of food in vending machines, school breakfast and lunch programs, health education and screenings, first aid and AED (automated external defibrillator) access, bike paths and walking trails, parks and community fitness and sports programs, crosswalks, and non-smoking zones.

Public Policy and Government

Tobacco and alcohol sales and policies, seat belt and helmet enforcement, child care laws, and other such regulations fall under the domain of public policy and governmental influences.

Media

Media use and exposure can have a significant impact on young minds. Children have not necessarily developed the critical thinking skills needed to evaluate the truthfulness of media claims. Television programming and commercials, PSAs, advertising, exposure to celebrities, knowledge of current events, and consumer skills all fall under this domain.

Technology

Technological factors including Internet access, handicap accessibility such as audio signals at crosswalks and wheelchair ramps and lifts, health technology apps, and pedometer availability can affect health behaviors.

Advocating for Personal, Family, and Community Health

Students have a lot to gain by cultivating advocacy skills, especially as they relate to promoting healthy behaviors. Students can learn how to advocate for personal, family, and community health resources and opportunities and establish health-enhancing messages that encourage others to also adopt and maintain a healthy lifestyle. Young children can work on how to advocate for healthy policies in their own schools and communities, such as ensuring easy access to drinking water and banning smoking on school grounds. They can also work on ways to encourage peers to make positive health choices, focusing on supporting one another and getting everyone to join the "team" of good health advocates. Older students can research and learn about various health issues and then make presentations to other students and family members to share accurate health information. The following are a few specific advocacy skills that educators should work to enhance in their students:

Locate Valid Health Resources in the Home, School, Community, and Media

One of the greatest challenges for children and adults alike is vetting various health resources in the home, school, community, and especially media for their validity and accuracy. Unfortunately, fad diets are popularized in the media daily. The weight loss industry is a multi-billion-dollar industry for a reason: people are desperate to lose weight and are often looking for the "quick fix" that many of these diets and exercise gadgets promise. However, many of these fad diets are dangerous, have not been developed by health professionals, or do not have sufficient scientific research to validate their safety or efficacy. For instance, fad diets often eliminate entire food groups or claim that the diet is some sort of health panacea. Other unhealthy methods promising rapid weight loss in popular culture include exercise in saunas or steam rooms to "sweat off pounds," starvation or liquid diets, cleanses, and mega doses of dietary supplements. These can cause dangerous dehydration, overdoses on certain micronutrients, and electrolyte imbalances leading to arrhythmias, and a reduced resting metabolic rate as the body senses starvation, which makes subsequent weight loss harder.

Educators should teach students how to critically evaluate information, particularly from the media, and judge its accuracy. School resources may include things such as the physical education department and health education resources, the Great Body Shop health curriculum, the infirmary or nurse's office, the D.A.R.E. program, and other health-informing programs. In the community, additional resources include S.A.D.D. (Students Against Destructive Decisions), the Red Cross, local medical and health offices, and WIC (Women, Infants, and Children) offices.

In the media, students should look for reliable sources of information such as myplate.gov and other government-sponsored health resources, peer-reviewed research journals, PBS or NOVA documentaries, TED Talks, course content from colleges and universities, etc. Students should not only be informed about correct and accurate information, but should also develop the skills to independently determine the validity of resources when they are faced with new information.

Develop Sound Opinions about Health Issues

A critical skill for children to develop is the ability to form informed opinions and back up their opinions with sound evidence. This need extends beyond the realms of health and fitness and can apply to all facets of life, but health information and behaviors are some of the more approachable and applicable topics for young children. Behaviors such as the choice not to smoke or consume drugs and alcohol, the practice of engaging in an active lifestyle over a sedentary one, the consumption of home-cooked or lower fat food choices over fried or fast foods, the intake of water over sodas and juices, and even safety behaviors such as wearing a helmet are all choices and issues that children can begin to consider and establish their own personal standards for.

Early childhood educators can help guide children to the healthful choices by presenting the information and facts about each choice and its consequences as well as engage children in brainstorming sessions to come up with ideas and tactics to support their choices for healthy behaviors. For example, if a family typically stops at the local fast food drive-through after soccer practice, children can talk to their parents about packing healthy snacks for the car ride home instead and even work with parents in the kitchen to make snacks such as vegetable sticks and hummus and cheese and apple slices. Children can even make posters or perform skits to defend their healthy opinions and share such information with younger grades.

The ability to not only form an opinion but also explain and support the reasoning behind it will serve students well throughout their education and lives in general. At the same time, educators should encourage students to keep an open mind and practice critical listening and analytical skills so that they remain open to other people's opinions and can modify their own with changes in research or situations. Particularly in the fields of health and nutrition, where research and science are constantly evolving, the "healthy option" does tend to change. Considering dietary recommendations alone, macronutrient (nutrients required in large amounts, like protein and carbohydrates) intake is constantly changing and the thinking about the healthfulness of saturated fats and carbohydrates shifts. The educated consumer is one who stays abreast of the research and also has the ability to alter his or her own opinions based on changes in the information.

Help Assist Others in Making Healthy Choices

One component of advocacy is supporting and assisting others in making healthy choices. Once students have formulated educated opinions about health-related topics like diet, exercise, safety habits, and substance use, they can become educators and advocates themselves. Students can then share their knowledge and reasoning with peers, family, friends, neighbors, and the community. For example, students can create posters with health information they have learned and hang them in their schools, homes, or other community areas. Students with younger siblings can help them develop good hygiene and safety habits.

Use Effective Communication Skills

Early childhood educators are instrumental in developing effective communication skills in their students. Verbal and nonverbal communication skills are important in setting a positive, educational, supportive environment to optimize learning. They are equally important for students to master for use in their own daily lives. When communicating with others, students should be mindful to be fully attentive, make eye contact, and use encouraging facial expressions and body language to augment positive verbal feedback. Postures including hands on hips or crossed over the chest may appear standoffish, while smiling and nodding enhance the comfort and satisfaction of the other party. **Active listening** is the process of trying to understand the underlying meaning in someone else's words, which builds empathy and trust. Asking open-ended questions and repeating or rephrasing in a reflective or clarifying manner is a form of active listening that builds a positive, trusting relationship.

In tandem with different communication styles, educators and students alike should be aware of different learning styles. **Auditory learners** learn through hearing, so the educator can use verbal descriptions and instructions. **Visual learners** learn through observation, so the educator can use demonstrations, provide written and pictorial instructional content, and show videos. **Kinesthetic learners** learn through movement, involvement, and experience, so the educator can prepare lessons with hands-on learning, labs, or games with a physical component.

An important skill for children is the ability to communicate effectively with adults, and developing this comfort from a young age will be helpful throughout life. Educators can facilitate this through providing experiences where children need to talk to adults in the community. For example, educators may take the class on a field trip to the local community library, where students must ask the librarian for help locating certain health resources. Students might also prepare a health fair and invite parents, community members, and those from senior centers to come learn from posters, demonstrations, and presentations. Children can also work on developing communication skills using an array of technologies such as telephone, written word, email, and face-to-face communication.

Motor Skills and Movement Patterns in Children

Educators should be familiar with physical and neurological development, especially in terms of motor skills and development, to provide developmentally appropriate motor movement tasks. As young children grow and mature, they develop the ability to handle increasingly complex motor skills. Children learn to move and move to learn and, for this reason, physical activity is especially important in the classroom for young children. As children grow, their physical abilities gradually increase, and educators can begin to modify lessons and activities to continue to challenge and improve new movement patterns and abilities. What looks like "play" actually consists of meaningful movement patterns that help the child move his or her body and use large muscle groups to develop physical competency. This is known as movement education. Children should learn basic movement patterns and skills for daily life so that they can maneuver safely and appropriately in their environment in relation to other people and objects. After basic skills are mastered, more specific sport-related skills can be achieved. Movement competency is the successful ability of the child to manage his or her body in both basic and specialized physical tasks despite obstacles in the environment, while perceptual motor competency includes capabilities involving balance, coordination, lateral and backward movements, kinesthetic sense, and knowledge of one's own body and strength.

Educators should be able to assess the level at which students can control specific movements and identify patterns of physical activity that have been mastered. This information can be used to plan developmentally-appropriate movement tasks and activities. In addition, early childhood educators can be helpful in identifying students who seem to be lagging behind in age-appropriate motor abilities. In such cases, early intervention programming and resources may be beneficial.

There are three general categories of basic skills: locomotor, non-locomotor, and manipulative skills; more complex movement patterns combine skills from multiple categories. **Locomotor skills** – such as walking, running, jumping, and skipping – are the movement skills that children need to travel within a given space or get from one space to another. **Non-locomotor skills** are typically completed in a stationary position – such as kneeling, pushing, twisting, bouncing, or standing – and help control the body in relation to gravity. **Manipulative skills** usually involve using the hands and feet, although other body parts may be used. These skills help the child handle, move, or play with an object. Manipulating objects helps advance hand-eye and foot-eye coordination so that the child can more successfully participate in sports activities like throwing, batting, catching, and kicking.

Young children can begin to learn these skills with balls and beanbags at a less challenging level and progress to more difficult levels and activities with practice and development. Early stages usually involve individual practice first and then progress to involve partners and groups. Throwing and catching are actually quite complex skills that can be as challenging to teach as they are to learn. Early childhood educators should emphasize skill performance and principles such as opposition, following objects with the eyes, weight transfer, follow through, and, eventually, striking targets. **Motor planning** is the ability of the child to figure out how to complete a new motor task or action and depends on both the sensory motor development of the child as well as his or her thinking and reasoning skills.

Motor Development
Typical motor development milestones for various age groups are as follows:

Ages three to four: have mastered walking and standing and are now developing gross motor skills such as single foot hopping and balancing, unsupported ascent and descent of stairs, kicking a ball, overhand throwing, catching a ball off of a bounce, moving forward and backward with coordination, and riding a tricycle. Fine motor skills begin to progress including using scissors with one hand, copying capital letters and more complex shapes, and drawing basic shapes from memory.

Ages four to five: tackling increasingly complex gross motor skills that require some coordination and multiple movement patterns combined together such as doing somersaults, swinging, climbing, and skipping. They also can use utensils to eat independently, dress themselves with clothing containing zippers and buttons, and begin to tie shoelaces. Mastery of fine motor skills begins to progress more rapidly, including cutting and pasting, and drawing shapes, letters, and people with heads, bodies, and arms. They tend to engage in long periods of physical activity followed by a need for a significant amount of rest. Physically, bones are still developing. Girls tend to be more coordinated while boys are stronger, but both sexes lack precise fine motor skills and the ability to focus on small objects for a long time.

Children Enjoy Exercise with Games Like Tag

Age six to eight: skating, biking, skipping with both feet, dribbling a ball. By the end of grade two, children should be able to make smoother transitions between different locomotor skills sequenced together. They can also accomplish more complicated manipulative skills such as dribbling a soccer ball with their feet and can better control their bodies during locomotion, weight-bearing, and balance. Students can begin to use feedback to hone motor skills from a cognitive perspective.

Ages nine to eleven: Children begin to get stronger, leaner, and taller as they enter the pre-adolescent stage and growth accelerates with the beginnings of secondary sex characteristics. Attention span and gross and fine motor skills improve. By the end of grade five, most children can achieve more performance-based outcomes such as hitting targets and can complete specialized sports skills such as fielding baseballs and serving tennis balls. They are also able to combine movements in a more dynamic environment such as moving rhythmically to music. From a cognitive perspective, they can begin to take concepts and feedback learned in other skills or sports and apply them to a new game. An example of this is increasing body stability by bending the knees to lower the center of gravity in basketball during a pick drill; this skill can also be reapplied on the ski slope. Additionally, children begin to observe peers more and can provide feedback to others.

Promoting Physical Fitness, Responsible Behavior, and Respect in Physical Activity Settings

The youngest students enjoy being physically active for the fun of movement itself, and they particularly enjoy non-structured activities in moderate and high intensities followed by sufficient rest. By the end of second grade, students will likely voluntarily incorporate activities from physical education class to leisure time activity and, although they are not typically concerned with structured exercise or activity recommendations for health, they do recognize the physical and mental benefits of activity and they self-select game-like play they enjoy. They are able to recognize the physiologic indicators of exercise such as elevated heart rate, sweating, and heavy breathing; they have a general understanding that physical fitness improves health; and they know that there are five components of health-related fitness: cardiovascular endurance, muscular strength, muscular endurance, flexibility, and body composition.

By the end of fifth grade, students should be aware that participation in regular physical activity is a conscious decision, and they should choose activities based on both enjoyment and health benefits. At this age, they begin to develop an awareness of resources and opportunities in the school and community to support activity and may become more interested in healthy food choices, realizing that personal responsibility and their own choices can affect their health. They also become more aware of their body and voice in a complex dynamic environment with others, and have greater focus towards controlling parts of their body and their movements within an environment with others. Students should also begin to take an interest in improving aspects of fitness for better sports' performance or health indicators, and should apply the results of fitness assessments to gain a deeper understanding of their own personal fitness and health compared with peers and standards. Older students also understand that success comes with practice and effort, and they also enjoy broadening their skills and activities by learning new sports and skills based on prior mastery. They can engage in mutual physical activity with students of differing ability levels.

It is important that educators continually address the issues of personal and social behavior, especially as it relates to accepting and respecting differences in abilities, ideas, lifestyles, cultures, and choices. By the end of second grade, students should know how to follow the rules and safety procedures in physical education classes and during activities with little to no need for reinforcement. They also understand the social benefits of playing with others and how activities are more fun while interacting with other people. They should be able to effectively communicate during group activities in a respectful way, and enjoy working collaboratively with others to complete motor tasks or goals by combining movements and skills from many people together. By the end of fifth grade, students should be able to work independently or in small or large groups during physical activities in a cohesive and agreeable manner, understanding that the group can often achieve more than the individual alone. However, individually, the student should understand that he or she is also responsible for personal health behaviors and movements.

The Arts

Foundations of Art Education

The four general categories of **arts** are visual arts, dance, music, and theater arts. As children progress through elementary school, they should be exposed to the basic foundations, creative expression and production of each type of art, and the ability to critically analyze a work of art and make connections within a cultural and historical context. Art education should build progressively during childhood so that older children are able to eventually take on these more sophisticated and advanced applications.

There are a wide variety of visual and performing arts that can enhance a child's creativity and learning experience. It is optimal to expose young children to many different types of art – both as a creator and observer – for well-rounded cultural, creative, and comprehensive learning. Depending on the child's age, early childhood educators can tailor art assignments and activities to meet the child's interests, motor skills, attention, and needs.

Visual Arts

Visual arts include things like drawing, painting, sketching, collage, sculpture, etc. Before the age of three, most artwork is produced less in an artistic way and more in a scientific and sensory way. Children at these youngest ages are more interested in the textures, colors, and shapes of what they create rather than expressing any sort of emotion or symbol. There are a variety of crafting activities that young children enjoy and can benefit from including finger painting, pasting, modeling with Play-Doh and clay, folding paper for origami, tracing and making models, and using a variety of craft supplies in creative ways including pom-poms, googly eyes, glitter, pipe cleaners, felt, and yarn. Craft activities help small children develop fine motor skills as they use instruments such as scissors and try to make precise movements like stringing beads and coloring within boundaries. As children develop, they can focus for longer periods of time and can handle more precise movements with smaller materials and areas. For example, a three- to four-year-old child may make simple Play-Doh snakes or snowmen, while a six- to eight-year-old child can add spots, a tongue, and facial features to the snowman with smaller bits of material laid in more exact locations. Through arts and crafts, young children can learn about colors and observe colors in the world around them, recognizing things such as green grass and blue sky. Working on arts and crafts projects helps children develop skills in planning, attention and focusing, problem-solving, and originality. It also helps them learn how to observe the world around them, be appreciative of other people's interpretations and ideas, deal with frustrations when things do not go as planned, and develop hand-eye coordination.

Early childhood educators should strive to expose children to a vast array of arts and craft materials and different types of arts. Activities should be age-appropriate. For example, four- to five-year-old children are likely unable to use small beads and fine pencils and markers, and do better with wider drawing utensils and larger beads that are easier to grasp and manipulate. Children who are ten to twelve are able to work with more intricate objects and may be bored with crayons and coloring books. There are a variety of other art forms that students may view or try to create such as jewelry, pottery, stained glass, wire art, sewing, quilting, knitting, and decoupage.

Music

Studies show that learning an instrument, especially at a young age, improves thinking, mathematical skills, attention, and brain activity. Children benefit from being exposed to a variety of instruments and musical genres including woodwinds, strings, brass, piano, vocals, jazz, blues, classical, folk, etc. Older children can learn basic music theory and how to read music, and may be able to take on more advanced instrument lessons and play or sing collaboratively in groups. As children mature, their attention spans, fine motor skills, ability to understand and maintain rhythm and pitch, and musical fluency improve. Activities and expectations should be age-appropriate. Smaller versions of some instruments are also manufactured and available to very young children to fit their small bodies and fingers.

For young children, learning to identify and maintain rhythm and beat is an important early skill and can be practiced by listening to music accompanied by physical movements such as clapping, stomping, dancing, or following the beat with percussive instruments like tambourines or small drums. They can learn to recognize **musical notes** and the position of the notes on a staff as well as the various characteristics of basic note types such as eighth notes, quarter notes, half notes, and whole notes. Singing and learning basic traditional and folk songs are simple ways to expose children to music as an easy, low-cost group activity. As children get older and more experienced, the group can be divided into sections to create harmonies and maintain separate singing roles within a varied group, which is a more advanced skill requiring concentration, attention, and group coordination.

Dance

Dance incorporates not only music, creativity, and arts, but also physical activity, which is very important to young children. Dance can help improve **kinesthetic sense** or awareness of one's body in space, rhythm and mathematical thinking, fluidity of motion, and coordination and balance. There are many varieties of dance, and educators should pick age-appropriate music and dances. The youngest children tend to do best with free movement to music or simple choreographed dances such as the hokey pokey, which are accompanied by easy sing-along songs.

Theater

Educators can expose young children to theater, both as participants and audience members. Young children may enjoy puppets, and older children can begin to take on roles and learn and memorize short lines. Memorization and recitation skills are transferable to educational activities in other subjects such as spelling words, learning history dates, and memorizing state capitals. Theater activities provide opportunities for imaginative play for children who enjoy dressing up, pretending to be various characters, imagining and acting out scenes, improvising lines, and mimicking jobs, characters, and roles in society. This is healthy and developmentally-appropriate.

Fundamental Concepts Related to the Arts

Artists, regardless of medium, typically rely on the following six main principles in art: emphasis, rhythm, balance, contrast, harmony, and movement.

Emphasis

Artists often want to make one part of their work stand out from the rest and guide viewers to pay attention to specific components of their piece. For example, lines and textures in paintings and sculptures may direct viewers to specific details or target features, and altering the texture of one area may make it stand out in contrast to the rest of the work.

Rhythm

Rhythm involves repeating elements within a work such as colors, shapes, lines, notes, or steps to create a pattern of visual or auditory motion.

Balance

Balance is positioning objects or using size, color, shape and lighting in the artwork so that all of the elements are equally present with no particular component overpowering the rest. Symmetrical balance is when two halves of an image create a mirror image, so that if the work is folded in half, each half is the same. Balance can also be **asymmetrical,** wherein the composition is balanced but the two halves are not the same. For example, a large central object is balanced by a smaller figure on one edge.

Contrast

Contrast exemplifies differences between two unlike things such as loud and soft music, major and minor tones, fast and slow dancing movements, and light and dark colors.

Harmony

Somewhat opposite of contrast, **harmony** highlights the similarities in separate but related parts of a composition. Rather than emphasizing their dissimilarities, harmony shows that different things can actually be related to each other and blend together.

Movement

Artwork that contains a sense of motion or action has **movement**. Even stationary art, like painting and sculpture, can imply movement based on the positioning of objects or the artist's use of lines, which draw the viewer's eye to different areas of the artwork.

Art Terminology

Each of the four forms of art have a vast list of terminology unique to that art form. Educators should be familiar with such terms to help effectively communicate with and educate students and, more importantly, to empower students to have intelligent and meaningful conversations about artwork with peers, artists, and community members. Listed below are some examples of common terms to introduce at age-appropriate levels with each of the various forms of art:

Visual Arts

Early learners can focus on the basic vocabulary of visual art like identifying colors and shapes. Older students can be exposed to more nuanced terms in the world of visual art. Some visual art is **representational** and depicts objects as they appear in the real world. One visual tool that heightens the realistic accuracy of visual art is **perspective**, an artistic technique that creates the illusion of depth through the use of line (for example, lines in the foreground converge in the background), size and placement of objects (objects that are supposed to be closer to the viewer appear larger than objects that are further away), or color (for example, a hill that is close to the viewer is depicted in a vibrant green, while a distant mountain appears with a more muted, hazy color).

In contrast to representational art, other visual art is **abstract**. When artists use abstraction, they use line, color, and other elements to communicate the presence of objects and emotions rather than realistically portraying the objects. For example, a swirl of **warm colors** like red and orange might represent anger or anxiety; **cool colors** like blue and gray could communicate sadness or passivity. In this way, the artist's **palette**, or range of colors used in their work, can communicate a mood or emotion to the viewer. Some works are **monochromatic,** meaning that they only use one color (although the artist might use different shades of the same color—for example, dark blue and light blue). Different shades of color can also create the illusion of shape or represent different lighting.

Other tools of both abstract and representational visual art include **contrast** (the pairing of dissimilar elements to make each other stand out), **positive** and **negative space** (positive space refers to the areas of the artwork occupied by its subject, whereas negative space includes all the areas that do not contain any subject), **balance**, and **symmetry**. Some artistic techniques to introduce to students might include caricature, collage, painting, sculpture, portraiture, landscape, and still life. If educators are able to take students on museum field trips, students should know museum-related vocabulary terms like *gallery, exhibit,* and *curator.*

Music

Students should be familiar with terms related to **meter,** which is the repeating pattern of stressed and unstressed sounds in a piece of music. While meter is a somewhat complex concept, students can easily understand the idea of a musical beat, which is the audible result of meter. In written music, meter is noted by a **time signature**, which looks like a fraction with one number on the top and one number on the bottom, like ¾. The bottom number expresses the **beat** as a division of a whole note (for example, the number four means that it is a quarter note), while the top number shows how many beats make up a **bar** (so ¾ means that three quarter note beats make up one bar).

In addition to patterns of stress, music also contains an arrangement of sounds, known as its melody. **Melody** refers to the development of a single tone; when many tones are combined simultaneously in a way that sounds pleasing to the listener, it is referred to as **harmony**. Other sound elements related to tone include **chords** (the combination of musical tones), **keys** (the principal tone in a piece of music), and **scales** (a series of tones at fixed intervals, either ascending or descending, usually beginning at a certain note). These elements can be described as either major or minor.

Words to describe the **tempo**, or the speed of a piece of music, include, from slowest to fastest: *largo, adagio, andante, allegro, vivace,* and *presto.* In terms of the intensity of the sound, **piano** refers to music that is played softly whereas **forte** means played with force. Students should also be familiar with vocabulary terms that describe different instruments, different genres of music, and different musical periods.

Dance

In dance, a **step** is one isolated movement, and **choreography** refers to the arrangement of a series of steps. Even young students can learn simple choreography that they rehearse with an instructor and perform with classmates as a group. Older students can learn about different styles of dance such as the waltz, tap, jazz, and ballet, as well as more contemporary styles like **lyrical dance** (combining ballet and jazz) or **fusion dance** (a highly rhythmical dance form). Students of ballet should be familiar with terms like **pirouette** (spinning on one foot or on the points of the toes), **arabesque** (standing on one leg while extending one arm in front and the other arm and leg behind), **plié** (bending at the knees while holding the back straight), **elevé** (rising up from flat foot to pointed feet), and **pivot** (turning the body without traveling to a new location; a pirouette is a type of pivot). Students can also learn about folk dances, partner dances, and line dances.

Theater Arts

Students can become familiar with a host of terms related to theater productions. In terms of people working in theater, there is the **director** leading the production and **actors** performing it. The **cast** is comprised of a group of actors, and an organization of actors and other theater workers is known as a

company. During the casting process, actors usually need to **audition** for parts in a play, and they may get a **callback** if their audition goes well! In addition to a main performer, leading roles in a production might also have an **understudy,** an actor who can step into the role when the main performer is unable to appear in the show.

On the technical side, students can learn about props, sets, costumes and wardrobe, effects, and staging. Theater arts education also presents an opportunity to teach students about the literary aspects of a play, such as the narrator, act and scene divisions, and stage directions contained in the script. Students can also become familiar with different dramatic modes like comedy and tragedy. They can learn about the structure of classic drama as well as more open ended structures like ad lib and improvisation.

Basic Techniques, Tools, and Materials for Producing Art

Art has **personal** (self-expression, gratification, narrative functions), **social** (collective meaning for a group of people, such as symbolic art honoring a god or political art), and **physical** (such as a pottery mug for tea) functions that often overlap within a single piece of work. As children go through elementary school, they become familiar with an increasing variety and complexity of visual art forms beginning with things like drawing, painting, and sculpting, then adding printmaking, sponge painting, film animation, and graphics in third and fourth grades, and dabbling in environmental design and art based on personal experience and observation by the fifth grade. They may also try computer-generated art, photography, metalworking, textile arts, and ceramics. Materials include scissors, brushes, papers, glue, beads, clay, film, and computers.

Instruments used in the early education classroom typically fall into one of the following categories: **melodic instruments** (melody bells, xylophones, flutes, and recorders), **rhythmic instruments** (drums, triangles, tambourines, and blocks), or **harmonic instruments** (chording instruments such as the autoharp). The key elements of music include rhythm, melody, harmony, **form** (the structure or design of the music, usually referring to the music's different sections and their repetition, such as **binary** (AB), **ternary** (ABA), theme and variation and **rondo** (ABACA), and the musical phrases), and expression [**dynamics** (volumes) and timbre].

The main skills of the theatrical arts are literary, technical, and performance elements. For theater, teachers can use a variety of techniques to incorporate dramatic arts into the classroom, including the following:

Theater-in-Education (TIE)
This is performed by teachers and students using curriculum material or social issues. Participants take on roles that enable them to explore and problem-solve in a flexible structure that is also educational. TIE productions are conducted with clear educational objectives, such as teaching facts or communicating a lesson to the audience.

Puppetry
Puppetry can be used for creative drama with either simple puppets and stages made of bags, cardboard, socks, or more elaborate, artistic materials. Using puppets in theater allows students to tell stories about a wide variety of characters and settings without requiring large and complex costumes, props, or sets. Telling stories with puppets also allows children to develop their motor skills.

More formal theater works for children are typically product-oriented and audience-centered, and children can be either participants or audience members. Such forms may include the following:

Traditional Theater

Actors use characters and storylines to communicate and the audience laughs, applauds, or provides other feedback. The performers and audience are separate entities and the acting takes place on a stage, supported by technical workers.

Participation Theater

Students can engage their voices or bodies in the work by contributing ideas, joining the actors, or contributing in other ways. This is more interactive than traditional theater.

Story Theater

Often told with simple sets, story theater can take place easily in the classroom with minimal scenery and costumes. Due to the sparse use of sets, props, and costumes, story theater often incorporates improvisational strategies to communicate character and setting to the audience. The actors function as characters and narrators and play multiple parts, often commenting on their own actions in their roles.

Readers' Theater

Readers perform a dramatic presentation while reading lines (typically from children's literature), enabling performance opportunities in the absence of elaborate staging or script memorization. This allows students to focus on emotional expression and speaking skills while reading their lines. The students can sit or stand but no movement is needed.

Readers' Theater

Dance simultaneously incorporates a variety of elements, including the following:

Body: refers to *who* – the dancer – and may describe the whole body or its parts, the shape of the body (such as angular, twisted, symmetrical), the systems of the body and its anatomy, or inner aspects of the body such as emotions, intention, and identity.

Action: refers to *what* – the movement created in the dance such as the steps, facial changes, or actions with the body – and can occur in short bouts or long, continuous actions.

Time: refers to *when*, and may be metered or free. Time may also refer to clock time or relationships of time such as before, after, in unison with, or faster than something else.

Space: refers to *where* through space, and how the dancer fills the space and interacts with it. For example, it can refer to whether the dancer's body is low to the ground or up high; moving or in place; going forward, backwards, or sideways; in a curved or random pattern; in front or behind others; or in a group or alone.

Energy: refers to *how*. It is with energy that a force or action causes movement. Dancers may play with flow, tension, and weight. Their energy may be powerful or it may be gentle and light.

Self-Expression and Communication through Art

One of the fundamental benefits of the arts is their ability to be used as forms of self-expression, creativity, and self-identity, and a means to communicate emotions, culture, and personal and societal narratives. While the youngest students may not fully grasp the ability to express themselves through art, even fairly young children can use art to communicate ideas, stories, and feelings. Early childhood educators can encourage students to use all forms of art for self-expression and should engage children in active critical thinking and analysis to uncover the meanings and emotions behind artwork generated by others. For example, educators can play a variety of music clips with different tempos, moods, tones, and keys and ask students to explain how the music makes them feel and what they think the composer was trying to express. Compositions in minor keys, at slower largo and adagio tempos, and music with harmonic dissonance may evoke feelings of sadness, trepidation, anxiety, or fear, whereas lively, spirited songs in major keys at faster allegro tempos are likely expressing happier feelings. Students can begin to contrast different moods and types of music and talk about how the moods are conveyed by differences in the music.

Similarly, the students can look at visual artwork and analyze the artist's use of different colors, textures, brushstrokes, etc. to express the feelings behind the artwork. Students can also try to discern the narrative within art, particularly in theater, music, and dance. They can try to understand how stories can be told abstractly and recognize that not every story is told through concrete narrative writing. For example, operatic works and ballets often tell elaborate stories with few or no words. Yet, even when they are presented in foreign languages, operas and ballets can be universally understood by varying audiences due to the emotions and movements present on stage. While these abstract concepts are likely too complex for young children, as students mature and develop, they will gradually become more aware of the nuances and arts' function as a vehicle of expression. Young children are able to understand how their pictorial drawings or paintings convey a narrative in their mind; from there, they can begin to understand how artwork generated by another person conveys his or her storyline. Educators can also encourage students to use art as a cathartic release when they are feeling sad, angry, frustrated, or nervous. Dance, visual arts, and music are constructive, safe, and appropriate ways to temper difficult emotions. Children can use dance choreography and improvisation to express feelings and ideas as well.

Strategies to Promote Critical Analysis and Understanding of the Arts

Early childhood educators should use techniques that foster their students' ability to critically analyze a variety of art forms. Students should develop a toolbox with the appropriate language and terminology to be able to intelligently discuss artwork from a critical standpoint with others. Each form of art has its own unique terms that are important for students to understand, both for their own appreciation and fluency in the arts and for their ability to communicate with others about arts. As students mature and develop their own interests, they will become increasingly able to effectively talk about why they may or may not enjoy a piece of artwork and how it makes them feel. Educators should emphasize that the artistic process is creative and subjective and that each person will have his or her own opinions about various art forms, but that in every case, the universal principles of respect, diversity, and acceptance apply.

Although generally there is no "right or wrong" in art, the ability to critique creative works is a skill that takes time, maturity, exposure, and intellectual understanding and appreciation of art. Early childhood educators can best help students improve these skills through a broad exposure to many arts, detailed explanations about the intricacies of various types of artwork, and discussions about self-expression through art. For example, a young student may inherently not enjoy a classical piece of music arranged in a quartet, but he or she can learn to critique it from an unbiased position based on that type of music. By understanding the details taking place in the piece (such as how the composer changes the key from major to minor halfway through to invoke sadness or mystery, or how the cello and violin feed off each other as if conversing), students can become more impartial and able to understand art for art's sake.

Educators should instruct students to evaluate questions such as: what was the artist's purpose in creating the work, and is the purpose achieved? Is the style the artist chose appropriate for the expressed purpose of the work? Does the artist have a unique idea in their work? The dialogue underlying these lessons should always focus on showing respect for artwork and creative ideas that are different from the student's own and celebrating diversity of preferences and art forms.

Arts in Various Cultures and Throughout History

It is imperative that early childhood educators focus on the fact that artwork has been used throughout history and in every culture as a means of expression and storytelling. Even seemingly new forms of art were not created out of nowhere, but rather, they have evolved from other previously existing forms of art. One of the best ways to discuss art is actually through embedding it in discussions of history and culture. The evolution of music can easily be discussed through various time periods. For example, the assassination of President John F. Kennedy, the Hippie movement, the Vietnam War, and the Beatles coexisted in the same time period, so students can find similarities and differences among these social and artistic ideals within their historical context.

Students can also study different time periods of art and architecture. In the **Classical period**, Greek artists focused on physical beauty and the human form, paying particular attention to Olympian gods and their idealized proportions in their works. The **Medieval period** that occurred in Europe from 500-1400 CE saw a flourish of Romanesque style art that shifted the emphasis from portraying realism to conveying a message, particularly symbolic Christian ideals. Students should also learn about the history of art in other countries such as China, with its jade, pottery, bronze, porcelain, and calligraphy. Educators should focus on how various influences over time affected the predominant artwork each period. For example, Buddhism in the early first century BCE increased calligraphy on silks, the Song dynasty created landscape paintings that were popular, and the Ming and Qing dynasties developed color painting and printing with an evolution towards individualism. As China became increasingly influenced by Western society in the nineteenth and early twentieth centuries, social realism predominated. In addition to covering other Asian nations, educators should expose students to traditional African art, which generally demonstrates moral values, focuses on human subjects, and seeks to please the viewer. Educators can also introduce art from the American Indians such as woodcarving, weaving, stitchery, and beading. Art in American Indian populations varies widely from tribe to tribe but tends to beautify everyday objects and create items of spiritual significance. Students should be exposed to music and theater from other cultures and observe the costumes, movements, instruments, and themes in performing arts from places like the Caribbean islands, Japan, Mexico, Australia, Africa, Italy, and Russia.

Practice Questions

1. Which of the following is NOT considered one of the five main components of health-related physical fitness?
     a. Muscular power
     b. Flexibility
     c. Muscular endurance
     d. Body composition

2. Balance is facilitated by _____ the base of support and _____ the center of mass.
     a. widening, lowering
     b. widening, raising
     c. lowering, widening
     d. raising, raising

3. Where did the waltz originate?
     a. Paris
     b. Copenhagen
     c. Venice
     d. Vienna

4. Which of the following is true regarding the origin of the tango?
     a. It has its roots in 19th century Buenos Aires
     b. It began in Cuba in the 19th century
     c. It is a recently developed dance from Argentina
     d. It is a modern popular ballroom dance from Cuba

5. Engaging in physical movements such as clapping, stomping, or dancing while listening to music is one way that educators can help students do which of the following?
     a. Learn about melody and harmony
     b. Figure out the key in which the song is played
     c. Learn about rhythm and tempo
     d. Learn about instruments and chords

Answer Explanations

1. A: The five main components of health-related physical fitness are cardiovascular fitness, muscular strength/endurance, flexibility, body composition, and flexibility. Muscular power is related to exercise performance and is a measure of strength to speed. It isn't one of the five components of fitness that directly relates to health.

2. A: Balance is the ability to control the center of mass within the base of support without falling. The wider the base of support and the lower the center of gravity, the easier it is to maintain balance. Center of gravity is the location of a theoretical point that represents the total weight of an object. Base of support is the part of an object that serves as the supporting surface, often thought of as feet in contact with the ground. The base of support also refers to the area between the feet as well, not just the physical structures of the body in contact with the supporting surface. Choice C is incorrect because a person cannot easily widen the center of gravity of the body. The center is a fixed point, so it can be moved, but not expanded. Choices B and D would make it harder to balance if the center of mass is raised.

3. C: Waltzes first appeared in Venetian ballrooms in the 13th century.

4. A: The tango is an energetic ballroom dance originating in the suburbs of Buenos Aires in the late ninetieth century. It quickly gained popularity in other cultures.

5. C: Teachers can help students learn about the rhythm or tempo of a piece of music by accompanying the listening experience with physical movements such as clapping, stomping, dancing, or following the beat with percussive instruments like tambourines or small drums. The other answer choices pertain to the melodic arrangement of the particular pitches or sounds so stomping or clapping (a rhythmic activity) would not facilitate learning these concepts.

Practice Test

Reading and Language Arts

1. What is the method called that teachers use before and after reading to improve critical thinking and comprehension?
   - a. Self-monitoring comprehension
   - b. KWL charts
   - c. Metacognitive skills
   - d. Directed reading-thinking activities

2. When a student looks back at a previous reading section for information, he or she is using which of the following?
   - a. Self-monitoring comprehension
   - b. KWL charts
   - c. Metacognitive skills
   - d. Directed reading-thinking activities

3. Reading fluency involves what key areas?
   - a. Accuracy, rate, and prosody
   - b. Accuracy, rate, and consistency
   - c. Prosody, accuracy, and clarity
   - d. Rate, prosody, and comprehension

4. When a student looks at a word and is able to tell the teacher that the letters spell C-A-T, but the student cannot actually say the word, what is the spelling stage of the student?
   - a. Alphabetic Spelling
   - b. Within Word Pattern Spelling
   - c. Derivational Relations Spelling
   - d. Emergent Spelling

5. Predicting, Summarizing, Questioning, and Clarifying are steps of what?
   - a. Reciprocal teaching
   - b. Comprehensive teaching
   - c. Activation teaching
   - d. Summative teaching

6. When a student asks, "What do I know?" "What do I want to know?" and "What have I learned?" and records the answers in a table, he or she is using which of the following?
   - a. Self-monitoring comprehension
   - b. KWL charts
   - c. Metacognitive skills
   - d. Directed reading-thinking activities

7. What technique might an author use to let the reader know that the main character was in a car crash as a child?
   a. Point of view
   b. Characterization
   c. Figurative language
   d. Flashback

8. A graphic organizer is a method of achieving what?
   a. Integrating knowledge and ideas
   b. Generating questions
   c. Determining point of view
   d. Determining the author's purpose

9. A student is trying to decide if a character is telling the truth about having stolen candy. After the student reads that the character is playing with an empty candy wrapper in her pocket, the student decides the character is guilty. This is an example of what?
   a. Flashback
   b. Making inferences
   c. Style
   d. Figurative language

10. What is the method of categorizing text by its structure and literary elements called?
   a. Fiction
   b. Non-Fiction
   c. Genre
   d. Plot

11. A reader is distracted from following a story because he's having trouble understanding why a character has decided to cut school, so the reader jumps to the next page to find out where the character is headed. This is an example of what?
   a. Self-monitoring comprehension
   b. KWL charts
   c. Metacognitive skills
   d. Directed reading-thinking activities

12. Phonemic Awareness, Phonics, Fluency, Vocabulary, and Comprehension are the five basic elements of what?
   a. Bloom's Taxonomy
   b. Spelling instruction
   c. Reading education
   d. Genre

13. A child reads the story Little Red Riding Hood aloud. He easily pronounces the words, uses an apprehensive tone to show that the main character should not be leaving the path, adds a scary voice for the Big Bad Wolf, and reads the story at a pace that engages the class. What are these promising signs of?
    a. Reading fluency
    b. Phonemic awareness
    c. Reading comprehension
    d. Working memory

14. A student is trying to read the word "preferred." She first recognizes the word "red" at the end, then sounds out the rest of the word by breaking it down into "pre," then "fer," then "red." Finally she puts it together and says "preferred." This student is displaying what attribute?
    a. Phonemic awareness
    b. Phonics
    c. Fluency
    d. Vocabulary

15. A class silently reads a passage on the American Revolution. Once they are done, the teacher asks who were the two sides fighting, why were they fighting, and who won. What skill is the teacher gauging?
    a. Orthographic development
    b. Fluency
    c. Comprehension
    d. Phonics

16. Poems are often an effective device when teaching what skill?
    a. Fluency
    b. Spelling
    c. Writing
    d. Word decoding

17. What allows readers to effectively translate print into recognizable speech?
    a. Fluency
    b. Spelling
    c. Phonics
    d. Word decoding

18. A teacher wants to help her students write a nonfiction essay on how the Pueblos built their homes. Before they write, she helps the students make clay from corn starch and water, draw a plan for the house with a ruler, and build it using the clay and leaves from the schoolyard. These exercises are examples of what?
    a. Proficiency
    b. Collaboration
    c. Constructive writing
    d. Cross-curricular integration

19. A student has quickly written a story and turned it in without reading it. To help reinforce the POWER strategy, the teacher tells the student go back and read his story. This POWER stage is called what?
    a. Prewriting
    b. Evaluating
    c. Organizing
    d. Revising

20. During which stage of the POWER strategy are graphic organizers used?
    a. Pre-writing
    b. Organizing
    c. Writing
    d. Evaluating

21. A teacher wants his students to write a story over two weeks. They are instructed to write a draft the first day. On each of the following days, he asks the students to develop and edit the story for one of the following: ideas, organization, voice, word choice, sentence fluency, conventions, and presentation. What does this teaching technique incorporate?
    a. Ideas
    b. POWER strategy
    c. Cross-curricular integration
    d. 6+1 Traits

22. Which trait teaches students to build the framework of their writing?
    a. Conventions
    b. Word choice
    c. Ideas
    d. Organization

23. Which trait ultimately forms the content of the writing?
    a. Conventions
    b. Word choice
    c. Ideas
    d. Voice

24. Which trait is most commonly associated with giving individuality and style to writing?
    a. Voice
    b. Word choice
    c. Presentation
    d. Ideas

25. A teacher asks a student to describe a beautiful day. The student says the flowers were pretty, the air was warm, and animals were running. The teacher asks the student to specify how many flowers there were—just a few hopeful buds or an abundance of blossoms? Was the air still or breezy? How did it feel? The teacher is developing which trait in the student?
    a. Voice
    b. Word choice
    c. Organization
    d. Presentation

26. Writing practice for the sole purpose of communicating refers to what kind of writing?
    a. Persuasive
    b. Informational
    c. Narrative
    d. Purposeful

27. A second-grade student brings a book to read to a group. It is about a caterpillar counting its food each day of the week before becoming a butterfly. Realizing the group is very familiar with their days and numbers, the teacher uses the story to explore the "moral" of the story and proper nutrition. This is an example of what?
    a. Modeling
    b. Encouragement
    c. Acknowledgement
    d. Challenging

28. A student is struggling with reading, especially aloud. When it is his turn to read to the class, the teacher offers an easier book she knows the student likes and is very familiar with. When the student reads aloud well and with enthusiasm, the teacher praises him to the class, then gives a more challenging book the next time. What is this called?
    a. Acknowledgement
    b. Providing feedback
    c. Encouragement
    d. Effective assistance

29. Preparation, Presentation, Application, and Evaluation are the four steps of what?
    a. Demonstration
    b. Modeling
    c. Explanation
    d. Challenging

30. Students are asked to pretend to prepare a meal. At various classroom stations, they must draw a picture, engage in pretend play, or write a list of instructions: one for grocery shopping, cooking, and cleanup. The teacher helps each student choose which task to pair with which station, encouraging autonomy and self-motivation. This is an example of what instruction technique?
    a. Challenging
    b. Modeling
    c. Giving feedback
    d. Giving assistance

31. Throughout the day, a teacher used language priority, beginning each subject by asking students to volunteer five related words that start with the letter "P." Then, during a reading exercise, the teacher partnered with a small group to turn their words from the day into a cover illustration for a story. This is an example of what?
    a. Giving directions
    b. The Abecedarian Approach
    c. Developmentally appropriate practice
    d. Autonomy

32. Speaking, listening, reading, and writing are four essential elements of what?
    a. Developmentally appropriate practice
    b. The Abecedarian Approach
    c. Literacy development
    d. Task, purpose, and audience

33. A teacher is about to read a story. He tells the class they will be quizzed and need to pay attention. He instructs them to focus by clearing everything else from their desks, to look at his face for clues about the story's tone, and to think about the adjectives used to describe the characters to learn more about them. What skill is he teaching?
    a. Writing
    b. Reading
    c. Speaking
    d. Listening

34. Since teachers must be communicators, educators, evaluators, models, and agents of socialization, this is considered to be mastery of what?
    a. Conventions
    b. Spelling
    c. Speaking
    d. Listening

35. Synonyms, Antonyms, and Homonyms are examples of what?
    a. Syntax relationships
    b. Pragmatic relationships
    c. Semantic relationships
    d. Morphology relationships

36. What is the most valuable strategy for helping children understand new words?
    a. Phonics instruction
    b. Pre-teaching
    c. Self-monitoring
    d. Context clues

Social Studies

1. An elementary teacher is planning a social studies lesson on individuals who have had an important historical influence to the state of Georgia. All EXCEPT which of the following individuals should be discussed in this lesson?
    a. Andrew Jackson
    b. John White
    c. William T. Sherman
    d. Booker T. Washington

2. Which member of British parliament convinced King George II in 1732 to colonize the area that is now Georgia with individuals from Britain's overflowing debtor prisons?
    a. James Oglethorpe
    b. Button Gwinnett
    c. George Walton
    d. Lyman Hall

3. A fourth-grade teacher is having students work in small groups to research and present about historical figures instrumental in leading the charge for discussion at the Constitutional Convention held in Philadelphia in 1787. Which of the following gentlemen would NOT be assigned to a group for this project?
    a. George Washington
    b. Alexander Hamilton
    c. Thomas Jefferson
    d. James Madison

4. A text read in a third-grade classroom is introducing readers to an American Indian tribe that led a nomadic lifestyle and lived in teepees that were easily moved from place to place. In which region did this tribe likely live?
    a. Plains
    b. Southwest
    c. Eastern
    d. Northwest

5. What was Britain's first permanent settlement in North America?
    a. Plymouth, Massachusetts
    b. Roanoke, Virginia
    c. Jamestown, Virginia
    d. L'Anse Meadows, Newfoundland

6. What was the controlling act imposed by the British on American colonists that taxed imported lead, glass, paints, paper, and tea, and prompted the colonies to unite against British rule?
    a. The Stamp Act
    b. The Sugar Act
    c. The Currency Act
    d. The Townsend Act

7. Fourth-grade students are creating timelines with landmark events of the American Revolution. Under which of the following events should they notate as where the first shot took place?
    a. At the Boston Massacre
    b. During the Boston Tea Party
    c. On Lexington Green
    d. At the Battle of Trenton

8. The Revolutionary War's final battle took place on October 19, 1781, when British General Lord Cornwallis surrendered to Washington's troops at what location?
    a. Yorktown, Virginia
    b. Valley Forge, Pennsylvania
    c. Trenton, New Jersey
    d. Saratoga, New York

9. What important U.S. structure was burned during the War of 1812?
    a. The Washington Monument
    b. Independence Hall
    c. The White House
    d. The Statue of Liberty

10. Who was elected President of the Confederate States of America during the Civil War?
    a. Robert E. Lee
    b. Jefferson Davis
    c. William T. Sherman
    d. Abraham Lincoln

11. The period of business and industrial growth from 1876 through the turn of the twentieth century was deemed by author Mark Twain as what?
    a. Manifest Destiny
    b. The Columbian Exchange
    c. The New Deal
    d. The Gilded Age

12. A fifth-grade teacher is leading a discussion with his class about cause and effect. He is drawing upon historical examples. Which of the following sets comprises a primary cause and effect of the American Revolution that he could introduce to his students?
    a. A cause was the taxation of the colonies, and an effect was the civil rights movement.
    b. A cause was the Declaration of Independence, and an effect was the Constitution.
    c. A cause was the French and Indian War, and an effect was the Bill of Rights.
    d. A cause was the debate over slavery, and an effect was the Seven Years' War.

13. Which of the following countries was a U.S. ally during World War II?
    a. The Soviet Union
    b. Italy
    c. Germany
    d. Japan

14. The North Atlantic Treaty Organization (NATO) was formed between which countries or regions?
    a. Canada, the U.S., and South America
    b. Western Europe, the U.S., and Canada
    c. The U.S., Western Europe, Canada, and the Soviet Union
    d. Asia, the U.S., and Western Europe

15. All EXCEPT which of the following would have a place in a social studies discussion in a fifth-grade classroom about the driving forces for the passage of the Civil Rights Act in 1964?

    a. *Brown vs. the Board of Education*
    b. Freedom rides
    c. The G.I. Bill
    d. The Montgomery bus boycott

16. What program launched by the U.S. government under President Ronald Reagan was designed to shield the U.S. from nuclear attack by the Soviet Union?

    a. The Strategic Arms Limitation Talks (SALT I and II)
    b. The Strategic Defense Initiative (SDI)
    c. The Iran-Contra Affair
    d. *Glasnost*

17. After the terrorist attacks initiated by Islamic fundamentalist Osama bin Laden on September 11, 2001, President George W. Bush ordered bombing raids on various locations in what country in an attempt to bring down bin Laden and his al-Qaeda network?

    a. Afghanistan
    b. Iraq
    c. Kuwait
    d. Pakistan

18. What are the two largest rivers in the U.S. called?

    a. The Mississippi and the Colorado
    b. The Mississippi and the Missouri
    c. The Missouri and the Ohio
    d. The Mississippi and the Ohio

19. What is used to pinpoint location on a map?

    a. Scale and longitude
    b. Contour lines and scale
    c. Latitude and longitude
    d. Latitude and contour lines

20. Under America's democratic form of government, which of the following are citizens NOT obligated to do?

    a. Obey the law
    b. Pay taxes
    c. Serve on a jury if asked to do so
    d. Vote in elections

21. How many times has the U.S. Constitution been amended in order to accommodate changes and updates?

    a. Fourteen
    b. Eighteen
    c. Twenty-one
    d. Twenty-seven

22. What is interaction of consumers, households, and companies within individual markets and the relationships between them called?
   a. Macroeconomics
   b. Microeconomics
   c. Boom and bust
   d. Economic output

23. A third-grade teacher is planning a lesson on life in the United States during WWII. Which of the following would be an applicable primary source to include in the lesson?
   a. A recording of one of FDR's Fireside chats
   b. A picture book about the Treaty of Versailles
   c. A movie about life in Germany under the Nazi regime
   d. A documentary of Eisenhower's Inaugural Address

24. What is the business sector of the economy that provides consumer or business services, including industries such as entertainment, travel and tourism, and banking called?
   a. Primary
   b. Secondary
   c. Tertiary
   d. Quaternary

25. Consumers must make choices regarding the goods and services to buy with their limited income. By purchasing one good or service, they are giving up the chance to purchase another. This is referred to as which of the following?
   a. The circular flow model
   b. Opportunity cost
   c. Savings account
   d. Assets

Mathematics

1. Which of the following could be used in the classroom to show $\frac{3}{7} < \frac{5}{6}$ is a true statement?
   a. A bar graph
   b. A number line
   c. An area model
   d. Base 10 blocks

2. A teacher is showing students how to evaluate $5 \times 6 + 4 \div 2 - 1$. Which operation should be completed first?
   a. Multiplication
   b. Addition
   c. Division
   d. Subtraction

3. What is the definition of a factor of the number 36?
   a. A number that can be divided by 36 and have no remainder
   b. A number that 36 can be divided by and have no remainder
   c. A prime number that is multiplied times 36
   d. An even number that is multiplied times 36

4. Third graders are calculating how many 1 cm³ sugar cubes fit inside boxes of various sizes during a math activity. What topic are they most likely learning about?
    a. Volume
    b. Area
    c. Perimeter
    d. Measuring length

5. What is the next number in the following series: 1, 3, 6, 10, 15, 21, ... ?
    a. 26
    b. 27
    c. 28
    d. 29

6. A student is asked to give the coordinates of the point plotted on the grid. Which of the following responses would provide evidence that she is understanding how to interpret the coordinate plane?

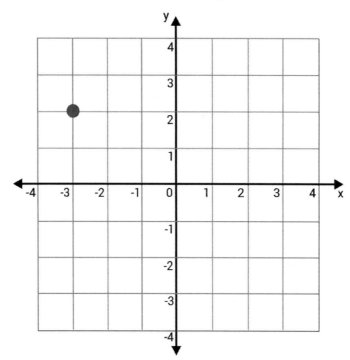

    a. (-3, 2)
    b. (2, -3)
    c. (-3, -2)
    d. (2, 3)

7. The perimeter of a 6-sided polygon is 56 cm. The length of three sides are 9 cm each. The length of two other sides are 8 cm each. What is the length of the missing side?
    a. 11 cm
    b. 12 cm
    c. 13 cm
    d. 10 cm

8. Rewriting mixed numbers as improper fractions can help students perform operations on mixed numbers. Which of the following is a mixed number?

    a. $16\frac{1}{2}$

    b. 16

    c. $\frac{16}{3}$

    d. $\frac{1}{4}$

9. If a teacher was showing a class how to round 245.2678 to the nearest thousandth, which place value would be used to decide whether to round up or round down?

    a. Ten-thousandth

    b. Thousandth

    c. Hundredth

    d. Thousand

10. Carey bought 184 pounds of fertilizer to use on her lawn. Each segment of her lawn required $12\frac{1}{2}$ pounds of fertilizer to do a sufficient job. If a student were asked to determine how many segments could be fertilized with the amount purchased, what operation would be necessary to solve this problem?

    a. Multiplication

    b. Division

    c. Addition

    d. Subtraction

11. Students should line up decimal places within the given numbers before performing which of the following?

    a. Multiplication

    b. Division

    c. Subtraction

    d. Exponents

12. Which of the following expressions best exemplifies the additive and subtractive identity?

    a. $5 + 2 - 0 = 5 + 2 + 0$

    b. $6 + x = 6 - 6$

    c. $9 - 9 = 0$

    d. $8 + 2 = 10$

13. Which of the following is an equivalent measurement for 1.3 cm?

    a. 0.13 m

    b. 0.013 m

    c. 0.13 mm

    d. 0.013 mm

14. Katie works at a clothing company and sold 192 shirts over the weekend. One third of the shirts that were sold were patterned, and the rest were solid. Which mathematical expression would help a student calculate the number of solid shirts Katie sold over the weekend?

a. $192 \times \frac{1}{3}$

b. $192 \div \frac{1}{3}$

c. $192 \times (1 - \frac{1}{3})$

d. $192 \div 3$

15. Third graders are classifying shapes. Which four-sided shape is always a rectangle?

a. Rhombus
b. Square
c. Parallelogram
d. Quadrilateral

16. A rectangle was formed out of pipe cleaner. Its length was $\frac{1}{2}$ feet and its width was $\frac{11}{2}$ inches. What is its area in square inches?

a. $\frac{11}{4}$ inch^2

b. $\frac{11}{2}$ inch^2

c. 22 inch^2

d. 33 inch^2

17. A teacher cuts a pie into 6 equal pieces and takes one away. What topic would she be introducing to the class by using such a visual?

a. Decimals
b. Addition
c. Fractions
d. Measurement

18. Which item taught in the classroom would allow students to correctly find the solution to the following problem: A clock reads 5:00 am. What is the measure of the angle formed by the two hands of that clock?

a. Each time increment on an analog clock measures 90 degrees.
b. Each time increment on an analog clock measures 30 degrees.
c. Two adjacent angles sum up to 180 degrees.
d. Two complementary angles sum up to 180 degrees.

19. Which of the following represent one hundred eighty-two billion, thirty-six thousand, four hundred twenty-one and three hundred fifty-six thousandths?

a. 182,036,421.356
b. 182,036,421.0356
c. 182,000,036,421.0356
d. 182,000,036,421.356

20. A solution needs 5 mL of saline for every 8 mL of medicine given. How much saline is needed for 45 mL of medicine?

    a. $\frac{225}{8}$ mL

    b. 72 mL

    c. 28 mL

    d. $\frac{45}{8}$ mL

21. What other operation could be utilized to teach the process of dividing 9453 by 24 besides division?

    a. Multiplication

    b. Addition

    c. Exponents

    d. Subtraction

22. What unit of volume is used to describe the following 3-dimensional shape?

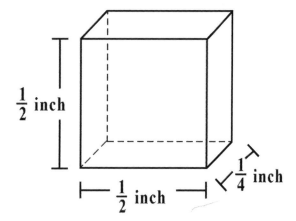

    a. Square inches

    b. Inches

    c. Cubic inches

    d. Squares

23. A fourth-grade student was asked to add $\frac{2}{3} + \frac{3}{5}$. He determined the solution to be $\frac{5}{8}$. If the student was then asked to add $\frac{1}{4} + \frac{1}{3}$, which of the following would likely be his solution?

    a. $\frac{2}{7}$, which is correct.

    b. $\frac{2}{7}$, which is incorrect.

    c. $\frac{7}{12}$, which is correct.

    d. $\frac{7}{12}$, which is incorrect.

24. What operation are students taught to repeat to evaluate an expression involving an exponent?

    a. Addition

    b. Multiplication

    c. Division

    d. Subtraction

25. Which of the following formulas would correctly calculate the perimeter of a legal-sized piece of paper that is 14 inches long and $8\frac{1}{2}$ inches wide?

    a. $P = 14 + 8\frac{1}{2}$

    b. $P = 14 + 8\frac{1}{2} + 14 + 8\frac{1}{2}$

    c. $P = 14 \times 8\frac{1}{2}$

    d. $P = 14 \times \frac{17}{2}$

26. Which of the following are units that would be taught in a lecture covering the metric system?
    a. Inches, feet, miles, pounds
    b. Millimeters, centimeters, meters, pounds
    c. Kilograms, grams, kilometers, meters
    d. Teaspoons, tablespoons, ounces

27. Which important mathematical property is shown in the expression: $(7 \times 3) \times 2 = 7 \times (3 \times 2)$?
    a. Distributive property
    b. Commutative property
    c. Associative property
    d. Multiplicative inverse

28. A grocery store is selling individual bottles of water, and each bottle contains 750 milliliters of water. If 12 bottles are purchased, what conversion will correctly determine how many liters that customer will take home?
    a. 100 milliliters equals 1 liter
    b. 1,000 milliliters equals 1 liter
    c. 1,000 liters equals 1 milliliter
    d. 10 liters equals 1 milliliter

29. If a student evaluated the expression $(3 + 7) - 6 \div 2$ to equal 2 on an exam, what error did she most likely make?
    a. She performed the operations from left to right instead of following order of operations.
    b. There was no error. 2 is the correct answer.
    c. She did not perform the operation within the grouping symbol first.
    d. She divided first instead of the addition within the grouping symbol.

30. What is the solution to $(2 \times 20) \div (7 + 1) + (6 \times 0.01) + (4 \times 0.001)$?
    a. 5.064
    b. 5.64
    c. 5.0064
    d. 48.064

31. A cereal box has a base 3 inches by 5 inches and is 10 inches tall. Another box has a base 5 inches by 6 inches. What formula is necessary for students to use to find out how tall the second box would need to be in order to hold the same amount of cereal?
    a. Area of a rectangle
    b. Volume of a rectangular solid
    c. Volume of a cube
    d. Perimeter of a square

32. An angle measures 54 degrees. In order to correctly determine the measure of its complementary angle, what concept is necessary?
    a. Two complementary angles sum up to 180 degrees.
    b. Complementary angles are always acute.
    c. Two complementary angles sum up to 90 degrees.
    d. Complementary angles sum up to 360 degrees.

33. The diameter of a circle measures 5.75 centimeters. What tool could be used in the classroom to draw such a circle?
    a. Ruler
    b. Meter stick
    c. Compass
    d. Yard stick

34. A piggy bank contains 12 dollars' worth of nickels. A nickel weighs 5 grams, and the empty piggy bank weighs 1050 grams. What is the total weight of the full piggy bank?
    a. 1,110 grams
    b. 1,200 grams
    c. 2,250 grams
    d. 2,200 grams

35. $\frac{3}{4}$ of a pizza remains on the stove. Katie eats $\frac{1}{3}$ of the remaining pizza. In order to determine how much of the pizza is left, what topic must be introduced to the students?
    a. Converting fractions to decimals
    b. Subtraction of fractions with like denominators
    c. Addition of fractions with unlike denominators
    d. Division of fractions

36. Last year, the New York City area received approximately $27\frac{3}{4}$ inches of snow. The Denver area received approximately 3 times as much snow as New York City. How much snow fell in Denver?
    a. 60 inches
    b. $27\frac{1}{4}$ inches
    c. $9\frac{1}{4}$ inches
    d. $83\frac{1}{4}$ inches

37. Joshua has collected 12,345 nickels over a span of 8 years. He took them to bank to deposit into his bank account. If the students were asked to determine how much money he deposited, for what mathematical topic would this problem be a good introduction?
    a. Adding decimals
    b. Multiplying decimals
    c. Geometry
    d. The metric system

38. Which of the following would be an instance in which ordinal numbers are used in the classroom?
    a. Katie scored a 9 out of 10 on her quiz.
    b. Matthew finished second in the spelling bee.
    c. Jacob missed 1 day of school last month.
    d. Kim was 5 minutes late to school this morning.

39. If students are given the problem $9 \times 9 \div 9 + 9 - 9 \div 9$, which of the following is likely the focus of the lesson?
    a. Identity property of 1
    b. Associative property
    c. Commutative property
    d. Order of operations

40. A student answers a problem with the following fraction: $\frac{3}{15}$. Why would this be considered incorrect?
    a. It is not expressed in decimal form.
    b. It is not simplified. The correct answer would be $\frac{1}{5}$.
    c. It needs to be converted to a mixed number.
    d. It is in the correct form, and there is no problem with it.

Science

1. A teacher presents a science lesson to her class of second graders about physical and chemical properties. After the lesson, students create posters that highlight examples of each. Which of the following would fall off the list of examples of chemical properties?
    a. Color
    b. Malleability
    c. Reactivity
    d. Luster

2. A second-grade science activity is developed to differentiate qualitative and quantitative measurements. Which of the following TWO choices are qualitative measurements in an experiment?
    a. Length
    b. Mass
    c. Width
    d. Smell
    e. Texture

3. Which of the following happens first in the scientific method?
   a. Procedure
   b. Hypothesis
   c. Observation
   d. Data collection

4. Students in a fourth-grade class are brainstorming testable hypotheses. Which of the following suggestions offered by a student is a valid hypothesis?
   a. If a cat is happy, then it purrs.
   b. If pants are softer, then they feel more comfortable.
   c. If light exposure increases, then plant height will increase.
   d. If calories are added to a dog's diet, then it will grow.

5. An elementary teacher is about to begin a new science unit of seasons and weather. As part of various a activities to gauge students' background knowledge, he asks. Each student to share what they believe to be the difference between seasons and weather. The responses of four students are presented below. Which of these students is most accurate?
   a. Carter: Seasons depend on wind and heat patterns.
   b. Darrel: Weather depends on proximity to the sun.
   c. Gloria: Seasons are day-to-day weather.
   d. Dimitri: Weather involves the water cycle.

6. Which is the best way to teach the concept of day and night to early childhood students?
   a. Showing an animated PowerPoint
   b. Going outside and talking about the Sun's location
   c. Modeling with flashlights and tennis balls
   d. Reading a book where the Sun and moon are friends

7. Why is Florida hotter than Alaska?
   a. Florida is next to the ocean.
   b. Florida is a peninsula.
   c. Alaska is farther from the equator.
   d. Alaska is larger than Florida.

8. Which of the following is an example of a constructive landform?
   a. Weathered rocks
   b. Mountains
   c. Ravines
   d. Trenches

9. Which of the following weather phenomena do NOT directly involve the water cycle?
   a. Hurricanes
   b. Tornados
   c. Snow
   d. Rain

10. Plate tectonic movement contributes to the Earth's topography by doing which of the following?
    a. Causing volcanoes
    b. Stimulating evaporation
    c. Forming deltas
    d. Stopping tornadoes

11. Which type of rock is formed by the pressure of many rock layers above and heat from below the Earth's surface?
    a. Sedimentary
    b. Metamorphic
    c. Igneous
    d. Hardened magma

12. Which type of rocks contain fossils?
    a. Sedimentary
    b. Metamorphic
    c. Igneous
    d. Hardened magma

13. Which type of fossil is considered a "trace fossil"?
    a. Bone
    b. Footprint
    c. Shell
    d. Tooth

14. Which characteristic isn't required for an organism to be considered alive?
    a. Contains DNA
    b. Moves
    c. Grows
    d. Reproduces

15. Which organism is a producer?
    a. Mushroom
    b. Human
    c. Plant
    d. Insect

16. Which of the following organism goes through a life cycle that contains a pupa stage?
    a. Chicken
    b. Frog
    c. Human
    d. Butterfly

17. An assessment question asks: *Tadpoles are part of which organism's life cycle*? Students are given the choices of chickens, frogs, humans, or butterflies. A first-grade student responds "chicken." Of the provided choices, for which type of assessment would this response be least concerning to the teacher?
    a. Standardized test
    b. Formative assessment
    c. Diagnostic assessment
    d. Summative assessment

18. Which statement is true regarding atomic structure?
   a. Protons orbit around a nucleus.
   b. Neutrons have a positive charge.
   c. Electrons are in the nucleus.
   d. Protons have a positive charge.

19. Why is camouflage considered an adaptation for lizards?
   a. It helps them absorb heat.
   b. It makes them less visible to predators.
   c. It's part of the molting process.
   d. It only occurs in the winter.

Questions 20 & 21 are based on the food web below:

20. How many omnivores are shown in this food web?
   a. 0
   b. 3
   c. 4
   d. 8

21. The food web shows that the warthog and the gazelle have which type of relationship?
   a. Predator-prey
   b. Competitive
   c. Symbiotic
   d. Mutualistic

22. Which of the following is a characteristic that is NOT inherited by an organism's parents?
    a. Eye color
    b. Blood type
    c. Musical achievements
    d. Susceptibility to heart disease

23. Which of the following are changing the environment and contributing to endangered species?
    a. Global warming
    b. Forest destruction
    c. Combustion
    d. All of the above

Health Education, Physical Education, and the Arts

1. Which of the following would NOT be included on a list of nutrition recommendations for children?
    a. Replace higher fat foods with lower-fat alternatives
    b. Replace higher fiber foods with lower-fiber options
    c. Reduce intake of sugary beverages
    d. Replace refined foods with foods in their more natural form

2. Mr. Lopez is working on planning the physical education curriculum for his five- to six-year-old students. He know that it should optimally focus on which of the following?
    a. Movement for enjoyment
    b. Sport-specific skills
    c. Hand-eye coordination
    d. Low intensity, endurance activities

3. Which of the following is true regarding classroom instruction of new movement skills for young children?
    a. It should occur in one long session at the beginning of the class, followed by time for children to play and attempt the skill.
    b. It should contain many small steps for the children to keep track of during play.
    c. It should be limited to short twenty-second stretches of instruction interspersed with long periods of play.
    d. It should be given in written form so children can read it at their leisure.

4. Which of the following is a healthy lifestyle habit for children?
    a. Getting eight hours of sleep every night
    b. Keeping their emotions to themselves
    c. Following safety procedures like wearing a seat belt
    d. Brushing their teeth once a day before bed

5. Educators should teach students about the importance of visiting a doctor for all EXCEPT which of the following reasons?
    a. Routine medical care and check-ups
    b. Consistent feelings of sadness, anxiety, loneliness, and stress
    c. Pains or aches that do not go away
    d. When insurance coverage changes

6. Health insurance status, safety and injury prevention education and care, nutritional meal planning and diet composition, social dynamics and stress, and culture around leisure time are all potential health behavior influences related to which factor?
    a. Family
    b. Peers
    c. School
    d. Media

7. Which of the following is true regarding motor skill development in children?
    a. Motor skill development shouldn't begin until after kindergarten.
    b. Sports skills are learned more readily than generalized body movements such as skipping.
    c. Gross motor skills are mastered before fine motor skills.
    d. Students benefit from formal movement training rather than free play.

8. Which of the following is NOT a general category of basic movement skills?
    a. Locomotor skills
    b. Sports-specific skills
    c. Non-locomotor skills
    d. Manipulative skills

9. In a kindergarten classroom, physical education should include a focus on all EXCEPT which of the following?
    a. Hitting targets
    b. Weight transfer
    c. Following objects with the eyes
    d. Running and stopping

10. Which of the following age groups is likely to be most interested in the health-based benefits of physical activity?
    a. Two- to four-year-old children
    b. Five- to seven-year-old children
    c. Seven- to nine-year-old children
    d. Nine- to twelve-year-old children

11. Which of the following are the major categories of the arts that educators should focus curricular activities on?
    a. Music, dance, theater, visual arts
    b. Music, performing arts, visual arts, sculpture
    c. Painting, drawing, woodworking, visual arts
    d. Language arts, music, theater, visual arts

12. The youngest children just beginning in art tend to create art with a focus on which of the following?
    a. Self-expression
    b. Narrative storytelling
    c. Scientific and sensory observations
    d. Creative and artistic ideas

13. Which of the following is true of art education for children?
    a. Children should focus on learning about art from their own culture and time-period.
    b. It is important for children to see professional art before creating their own works.
    c. It is important for children to study art theory before beginning their own projects.
    d. Children should experiment with a variety of methods and materials to create art.

14. Which of the following is a way for young students to easily learn rhythm in music class?
    a. Have students memorize each song on multiple instruments.
    b. Have students sit still and focus intently on the music.
    c. Have students read the lyrics before they listen to the music.
    d. Have students accompany music with simple instruments like tambourines.

15. Which of the following is performed by teachers and students using curriculum material or social issues?
    a. Puppetry
    b. Participation Theater
    c. Reader's Theater
    d. Theater-in-Education (TIE)

16. The main skills in theatrical arts for children include all EXCEPT which of the following?
    a. Staging
    b. Literary
    c. Technical
    d. Performance

17. A three- to four-year-old child would likely create a drawing emphasizing which of the following?
    a. The emotions expressed in their work.
    b. The figural accuracy of the drawing.
    c. The symbolic meaning of their work.
    d. The colors they use and how they look.

18. Which of the following is a technique used to make flat objects look as though they have depth?
    a. Balance
    b. Perspective
    c. Optical illusion
    d. Abstraction

19. Art serves all EXCEPT which of the following main functional categories?
    a. Religious functions
    b. Personal functions
    c. Social functions
    d. Physical functions

20. Which of the following is a principle in art that highlights the similarities in separate but related parts of a composition?
    a. Contrast
    b. Harmony
    c. Movement
    d. Balance

Answer Explanations

Reading and Language Arts

1. D: Teachers use directed reading-thinking activities before and after reading to improve critical thinking and reading comprehension. Metacognitive skills are when learners think about thinking. Self-monitoring is when children are asked to think as they read and ask themselves if what they have just read makes sense. KWL charts help guide students to identify what they already know about a given topic.

2. C: Asking oneself a comprehension question is a metacognition skill. Readers with metacognitive skills have learned to think about thinking. It gives students control over their learning while they read. KWL charts help students to identify what they already know about a given topic.

3. A: Reading fluency involves how accurately a child reads each individual word within a sentence, the speed at which a child reads, and the expression the child applies while reading. Therefore, accuracy, rate, and prosody are the three key areas of reading fluency.

4. D: During the Emergent Spelling stage, children can identify letters but not the corresponding sounds. The other choices are all fictitious.

5. A: Reciprocal teaching involves predicting, summarizing, questioning, and clarifying. The other choices are all fictitious.

6. B: KWL charts are an effective method of activating prior knowledge and taking advantage of students' curiosity. Students can create a KWL (*Know/Want to know/Learned*) chart to prepare for any unit of instruction and to generate questions about a topic.

7. D: Flashback is a technique used to give more background information in a story. None of the other concepts are directly related to going back in time.

8. A: Graphic organizers are a method of integrating knowledge and ideas. These include many different visual tools for connecting concepts to help students understand information.

9. B: Making inferences is a method of deriving meaning in writing that intended by the author but not explicitly stated. A flashback is a scene set earlier than the main story. Style is a general term for the way something is done. Figurative language is text that is not to be taken literally.

10. C: Genre is a means of categorizing text by its structure and literary elements. Fiction and non-fiction are both genre categories. Plot is the sequence of events that make a story happen.

11. A: Scanning future portions of the text for information that helps resolve a question is an example of self-monitoring. Self-monitoring takes advantage of a natural ability of students to recognize when they understand the reading and when they do not. KWL charts are used to help guide students to identify what they already know about a given topic. Metacognitive skills are when learners think about thinking. Directed reading-thinking activities are done before and after reading to improve critical thinking and reading comprehension.

12. C: The five basic components of reading education are phonemic awareness, phonics, fluency, vocabulary, and comprehension.

13. A: If a child can accurately read text with consistent speed and appropriate expression while demonstrating comprehension, the child is said to have reading fluency skills. Without the ability to read fluently, a child's reading comprehension (Choice *C*) will be limited.

14. B: Phonics is the ability to apply letter-sound relationships and letter patterns in order to accurately pronounce written words. Phonemic awareness is the understanding that words are comprised of a combination of sounds. Fluency is an automatic recognition and accurate interpretation of text. Vocabulary is the body of words known to a person.

15. C: Comprehension is the level of content understanding that a student demonstrates after reading. Orthographic development is a cumulative process for learning to read, with each skill building on the previously mastered skill. Fluency is an automatic recognition and accurate interpretation of text. Phonics is the ability to apply letter-sound relationships and letter patterns in order to accurately pronounce written words.

16. A: Poems are an effective method for teaching fluency, since rhythmic sounds and rhyming words build a child's understanding of phonemic awareness.

17. C: Phonics allows readers to effectively translate print into recognizable speech. If children lack proficiency in phonics, their ability to read fluently and to increase vocabulary will be limited.

18. D: Cross-curricular integration is choosing to teach writing projects that include the subjects of science, social studies, mathematics, reading, etc.

19. B: Students should carefully read what they've written during the Evaluating stage of the POWER strategy.

20. B: Graphic organizers are used during the Organizing stage of the POWER strategy. They help students to examine, analyze, and summarize selections they have read and can be used individually or collaboratively in the classroom. Graphic organizers may be sequencing charts, graphs, Venn diagrams, timelines, chain of events organizers, story maps, concept maps, mind maps, webs, outlines, or other visual tools for connecting concepts to achieve understanding.

21. D: 6+1 Traits is a model for teaching writing that uses common language to explain writing standards. The 6+1 Traits are the characteristics that make writing readable and effective no matter what genre of writing is being used. These seven traits are ideas, organization, voice, word choice, sentence fluency, conventions, and presentation.

22. D: Organization is the trait that teaches students how to build the framework of their writing. Students choose an organizational strategy or purpose for the writing and build the details upon that structure. There are many purposes for writing, and they all have different frameworks.

23. C: Ideas ultimately form the content of the writing. The Ideas Trait is one of the 6+1 Traits model and is where students learn to select an important topic for their writing. They are taught to narrow down and focus their idea before further developing it.

24. A: Voice is the primary trait that shows the individual writing style of an author. It is based on an author's choice of common syntax, diction, punctuation, character development, dialogue, etc.

25. B: Word choice is the trait that teaches the use of precise language. Teachers can enhance this trait in students by helping them to use exact language that is accurate, concise, precise, and lively.

26. D: Intentional writing practice for the purpose of communicating refers to purposeful writing. Students can use this as a method of thinking through issues and solving problems related to writing.

27. C: Considering prior knowledge before instruction is part of Acknowledgement. For teachers, it begins with understanding where students are coming from and the experiences they bring with them to the classroom. When a teacher considers prior knowledge before beginning instruction, they are being considerate of each student's time and intellect.

28. B: Providing feedback is a way to build positive self-image and encourage success. A positive self-image is fostered by repeated success. Giving clear and effective feedback communicates to the student that her or his work is worthwhile, and that someone cares enough to review and consider it.

29. A: Demonstration includes the four steps: Preparation, Presentation, Application and Evaluation. Demonstration is when a teacher not only models and explains how to do a task but also engages in thinking through the task with the students. Effective teachers narrate their thinking processes when modeling a strategy.

30. D: Autonomy and self-motivation are the goals of giving assistance. Students need assistance and guidance in a classroom; however, knowing how much help to offer is always a balancing act. If teachers give too much assistance, they end up doing the work for students, who then do not learn. If teachers do not offer enough assistance, students become lost, overwhelmed, and do not learn.

31. B: Conversational reading and language priority are premises of the Abecedarian Approach. Conversational reading involves a conversational-style of reading instruction in which the educator plays an active role by partnering in shared reading activities. By emphasizing language throughout the day, the language priority strategy creates endless occasions for meaningful conversations. Educators work to extend conversations from a variety of different angles, promoting higher cognitive thinking and engagement.

32. C: Speaking, Listening, Reading, and Writing are the four elements of literacy development. As social beings, children begin to recognize that with effective literacy skills, their social, emotional, and physical needs can be met, and their curiosity can be satisfied.

33. D: Four concepts that teach listening skills are focusing, looking, non-verbal cues, and verbal cues. Behaviors that enable good listening skills should not be expected. They need to be taught. Students need to learn the difference between what an excellent listener does and what poor listening behaviors are.

34. A: Teachers must master conventions because they are communicators, educators, evaluators, models, and agents of socialization. Teachers serve several key roles in the classroom. Students will not be able to learn properly unless their teachers have mastered these conventions.

35. C: Synonyms, Antonyms, and Homonyms are examples of semantic relationships. There are five types of semantic relationships, including the three noted in the question. The other two are Hyponyms and Meronyms.

36. B: Pre-teaching is the most valuable strategy for helping children understand new words. Educators select what they evaluate to be the unfamiliar words in the text and then introduce them to the class before reading. Educators using this method should be careful not to simply ask the children to read the text and then spell the new words correctly.

Social Studies

1. B: John White does not have an important historical influence to the state of Georgia. White was the leader of the Roanoke colony founded under the authority of Sir Walter Raleigh in what was then called Virginia and later became North Carolina. White went back to England for supplies in 1587 and when he returned, all of the colonists had mysteriously disappeared.

Choice *A* is incorrect because after Andrew Jackson was elected President in 1828, he worked with Georgia officials to extradite the Cherokee Indians and other Native American tribes from the state. Choice *C* is incorrect because during the Civil War, Union Major General William T. Sherman led over 60,000 soldiers through Georgia in his famous *March to the Sea*. Finally, Choice *D* is incorrect because in 1895, Booker T. Washington delivered a speech at the Cotton States and International Exposition in Atlanta, declaring that African Americans should focus on vocational education.

2. A: James Oglethorpe convinced King George II to colonize the area that is now Georgia with individuals from Britain's overflowing debtor's prisons. Button Gwinnett, George Walton, and Lyman Hall were the three Georgians who signed the Declaration of Independence in 1776. Thus, Choices *B*, *C*, and *D* are incorrect.

3. C: At the time of the Constitutional Convention, Thomas Jefferson was in Paris serving as America's foreign minister to France. Therefore, he is not a good fit for this project. George Washington led the meeting, and Alexander Hamilton and James Madison set the tone for debate, rendering *A*, *B*, and *D* incorrect.

4. A: Plains Indians followed the buffalo across the prairies, living in tent-like teepees that were easily moved from place to place. Choice *B* is incorrect because Indians in the Southwest relied on farming for much of their food and built adobes, which are houses made out of dried clay or earth. Indians in the Eastern and Northwest sections of North America survived by hunting, gathering, farming, and fishing, and lived in wooden longhouses, plank houses, or wigwams. Thus, Choices *C* and *D* are incorrect.

5. C: Established in 1607, Jamestown, Virginia was the first permanent British settlement in the New World. Plymouth was founded a bit later in 1620 when a group of Pilgrims founded the first permanent European settlement in New England, making Choice *A* incorrect. Choice *B* is incorrect because although the Roanoke Colony was founded in 1585, it isn't considered permanent – the colony's leader, John White, went back to England for supplies two years later, and he returned to find that all of the colonists had mysteriously disappeared. Choice *D* is incorrect because L'Anse Meadows was an area in Newfoundland that was briefly settled by Scandinavian Vikings around 1000 A.D.

6. D: The British issued the Townsend Act in 1767, which taxed imported lead, glass, paints, paper, and tea, and increased the colonists' anger and further strained the relationship between England and the colonies. Choice *A*, the Stamp Act of 1765, taxed printed items, including playing cards and newspapers printed in the colonies. Choice *B*, the Sugar Act of 1764, placed import duties on items such as molasses, sugar, coffee, and wine. Choice *C*, the Currency Act, banned the issuing of paper money in the colonies and mandated the use of gold in business dealings.

7. C: The first shot took place on Lexington Green. When the British heard that colonists were stockpiling weapons they sent troops to Concord to seize them. However, a group of approximately seventy Minutemen confronted the British soldiers on Lexington green. British troops killed five protesting colonists during the Boston Massacre in 1770, but this is not considered the first shot of the Revolution. Thus, Choice *A* is incorrect. Choice *B* is incorrect because the Boston Tea Party was when colonists dumped 342 chests of expensive tea into the Boston Harbor in defiance of the tea tax. The Revolution had already started when the Battle of Trenton took place on December 25, 1776, making Choice *D* incorrect.

8. A: British General Lord Cornwallis surrendered to Washington's troops at Yorktown, Virginia. No battles occurred at Valley Forge, but Washington's troops suffered major losses as a result of starvation, disease, and exposure to the cold, making Choice *B* incorrect. Choice *C* is incorrect because the Battle of Trenton was the first major battle of the Revolution, which occurred when Washington led his troops across the Delaware River to wage a surprise attack on British and Hessian soldiers stationed in Trenton on December 25, 1776. Choice *D*, Saratoga, New York, was the site of a major victory by General John Burgoyne in October 1777 and prompted European countries to help support the American cause.

9. C: British soldiers burned the White House during the War of 1812. Neither the Washington Monument nor the Statue of Liberty – Choices *A* and *D* – were built at the time, and Philadelphia's Independence Hall, Choice *B*, escaped conflict during this war.

10. B: Jefferson Davis was elected president of the Confederate States of America in November 1861. Choice *A*, General Robert E. Lee, was the leader of the Confederate Army. Choice *C*, William T. Sherman, was a union general famous for his march through Georgia and the burning of Atlanta in 1864. Choice *D*, Abraham Lincoln, was President of the U.S. during the Civil War.

11. D: This period was called the Gilded Age since it appeared shiny and golden on the surface, but was fueled by undercurrents of corruption led by big businessmen known as robber barons. Choice *A*, Manifest Destiny, is the concept referring to the pursuit and acquisition of new lands by the U.S., which led to the purchase of Alaska from Russia in 1867 and the annexation of Hawaii in 1898. The Columbian Exchange, Choice *B*, was an era of discovery, conquest, and colonization of the Americas by the Europeans. The New Deal, Choice *C*, was a plan launched by President Franklin Delano Roosevelt to help rebuild America's economy after the Great Depression.

12. C: The Declaration of Independence occurred during the American Revolution, so it should therefore be considered an effect, not a cause. Similarly, slavery was a cause for the later Civil War, but it was not a primary instigator for the Revolutionary War. Although a single event can have many effects long into the future, it is also important to not overstate the influence of these individual causes; the civil rights movement was only tangentially connected to the War of Independence among many other factors, and therefore it should not be considered a primary effect of it. The French and Indian War (which was part of the Seven Years' War) and the Bill of Rights, on the other hand, were respectively a cause and effect from the American Revolution, making Choice *C* the correct answer.

13. A: The Soviet Union was invaded by Germany in 1941 and allied with Britain and subsequently the U.S. President Roosevelt, British Prime Minister Winston Churchill, and Soviet director Joseph Stalin met in 1945 to plan their final assault on Germany and discuss postwar strategies. Germany aligned with Italy and Japan in 1940 to form the Axis Alliance. Their goal was to establish a German empire in Europe and place Japan in control over Asia. Thus, Choices *B*, *C*, and *D* are incorrect.

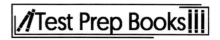

14. B: The North Atlantic Treaty Organization (NATO) was formed between Western Europe, Canada, and the U.S. in defense of Soviet hostility after the Soviet Union introduced Communism into Eastern Europe. The Soviet Union countered by creating the Warsaw Pact.

15. C: The G.I. Bill was a government program started in the 1950s that gave military veterans a free education. In the revolutionary 1954 case, *Brown vs. the Board of Education,* the Supreme Court ruled that school segregation was illegal, thereby setting the Civil Rights Movement in motion, making Choice *A* incorrect. *Freedom Rides*, Choice *B*, and the Montgomery bus boycott, Choice *D*, were among the non-violent protests against segregation that took place in the U.S. in the 1960s.

16. B: President Reagan advocated *peace through strength*, building up the U.S. military and launching the Strategic Defense Initiative (SDI), also called *Star Wars*. Choice *A*, the Strategic Arms Limitation Talks (SALT I and II), negotiated between 1972 and 1979, resulted in limits on nuclear weapons for both the U.S. and Russia. Choice *C*, the Iran-Contra Affair, was a scandal involving the secret sale of weapons to Iran in exchange for American hostages. Choice *D*, *Glasnost*, was a policy of political openness launched by Soviet leader Mikhail Gorbachev.

17. A: Afghanistan was the site of the bombing raids. Bush invaded Iraq, Choice *B*, in 2003 when Iraqi dictator Saddam Hussein defied the terms of the truce agreed upon in 1991 after the Gulf War. Kuwait, Choice *C*, was invaded by Iraq in 1990, sparking the Gulf War. Pakistan, Choice *D*, is where Osama bin Laden was killed by a group of Navy SEALs under orders from President Obama.

18. B: The Mississippi and the Missouri are the two largest rivers in the U.S., winding through the Great Plains in the center of the country. The Colorado and Ohio Rivers are about half the length of the Mississippi and Missouri.

19. C: Latitude – imaginary lines covering the globe from east to west – and longitude – imaginary lines running north to south – are used to pinpoint location on a map. Scale is used to show the relationship between the map measurements and the equivalent distance on the world's surface. Contour lines are used to show detailed elevation on a map.

20. D: Under America's democratic form of government, voting is a *right*, but it is not an *obligation*. U.S. citizens are *obliged* to obey the law, pay taxes, and serve on a jury if asked to do so, making Choices *A*, *B*, and *C* incorrect.

21. D: There are twenty-seven amendments to the U.S. Constitution. The 14th Amendment was adopted in 1868 to abolish slavery. The 18th Amendment was passed in 1919 and prohibited the production and sale of alcoholic beverages, but the 21st Amendment repealed it in 1933.

22. **B:** Microeconomics looks at the interplay of consumers, households, and companies within individual markets and the relationships between them. Macroeconomics, Choice *A*, is the study of entire economies. Booms and busts, Choice *C*, are terms used to describe the cyclical nature of economic activity, typically prompted by extreme changes in the economy. Economic output, Choice *D*, is the total amount of goods and services produced by an ***economy.***

23. A: President Franklin Roosevelt is notorious for his Fireside chats during his presidency, particularly surrounding WWII. A recording of one of these radio broadcasts is a good example of a primary source. Primary sources are context-specific, first-hand accounts. They don't have to be in the form of written words, so a radio recording that is a first-hand account of life during that time would be a great example for a third grade class. Choices *B* and *C* might be useful during WWII lessons, but they are not examples of primary sources. Moreover, Choice *C* is not about life in the United States. Choice *D* is incorrect because Eisenhower took to office after WWII had ended.

24. C: The tertiary sector provides consumer or business services, including industries such as entertainment, retail sales, and restaurants. The primary sector, Choice *A*, takes raw materials from the Earth, such as coal, timber, copper, and wheat. The secondary sector, Choice *B*, converts raw materials into goods, such as textile manufacturing, food processing, and car manufacturing. The quaternary sector, Choice *D*, provides informational and knowledge services, such as education, business consulting, and financial services.

25. B: Opportunity cost is the term used to describe the choices that determine how consumers spend or save their money. Choice *A*, the circular flow model, is used by economists to describe the movement of supply, demand, and payment between businesses and consumers. A savings account, Choice *C*, is considered low-risk because the bank will pay the saver a low interest rate to keep it safe. Assets, Choice *D*, are valuable items purchased by investors in the hopes that they will increase in worth over time and yield returns or profits.

Mathematics

1. B: This inequality can be seen with the use of a number line. $\frac{3}{7}$ is close to $\frac{1}{2}$. $\frac{5}{6}$ is close to 1, but less than 1, and $\frac{8}{7}$ is greater than 1. Therefore, $\frac{3}{7}$ is less than $\frac{5}{6}$.

2. A: Using the order of operations, multiplication and division are computed first from left to right. Multiplication is on the left; therefore, multiplication should be performed first.

3. B: A factor of 36 is any number that can be divided into 36 and have no remainder.

$$36 = 36 \times 1, 18 \times 2, 9 \times 4, \text{and } 6 \times 6$$

Therefore, it has 7 unique factors: 36, 18, 9, 6, 4, 2, and 1.

4. A: This would be an appropriate activity to address the concept of understanding and visualizing volume and how to calculate it. The sugar cubes could serve as the unit cube and then the volumes of different boxes could be calculated.

5. C: Each number in the sequence is adding one more than the difference between the previous two. For example:

$$10 - 6 = 4, 4 + 1 = 5$$

Therefore, the next number after 10 is $10 + 5 = 15$. Going forward:

$$21 - 15 = 6, 6 + 1 = 7$$

The next number is:

$$21 + 7 = 28$$

Therefore, the difference between numbers is the set of whole numbers starting at 2: 2, 3, 4, 5, 6, 7....

6. A: (-3, 2). The coordinates of a point are written as an ordered pair (*x*, *y*). To determine the *x*-coordinate, the student can trace a line directly above or below the point until reaching the *x*-axis. This step notes the value on the *x*-axis. In this case, the *x*-coordinate is -3. To determine the *y*-coordinate, the student can trace a line directly to the right or left of the point until reaching the *y*-axis, which notes the value on the *y*-axis. In this case, the *y*-coordinate is 2. Therefore, the ordered pair is written (-3, 2).

7. C: The perimeter is found by calculating the sum of all sides of the polygon.

$9 + 9 + 9 + 8 + 8 + s = 56$, where *s* is the missing side length

Therefore, 43 plus the missing side length is equal to 56. The missing side length is 13 cm.

8. A: A mixed number contains both a whole number and either a fraction or a decimal. Therefore, the mixed number is $16\frac{1}{2}$.

9. A: The place value to the right of the thousandth place, which would be the ten-thousandth place, is what gets used. The value in the thousandth place is 7. The number in the place value to its right is greater than 4, so the 7 gets bumped up to 8. Everything to its right turns to a zero, to get 245.2680. The zero is dropped because it is part of the decimal.

10. B: This is a division problem because the original amount needs to be split up into equal amounts. The mixed number $12\frac{1}{2}$ should be converted to an improper fraction first.

$$12\frac{1}{2} = \frac{(12 * 2) + 1}{2} = \frac{23}{2}$$

Carey needs to determine how many times $\frac{23}{2}$ goes into 184. This is a division problem:

$$184 \div \frac{23}{2} = ?$$

The fraction can be flipped, and the problem turns into the multiplication:

$$184 \times \frac{2}{23} = \frac{368}{23}$$

This improper fraction can be simplified into 16 because:

$$368 \div 23 = 16$$

The answer is 16 lawn segments.

11. C: Numbers should be lined up by decimal places before subtraction is performed. This is because subtraction is performed within each place value. The other operations, such as multiplication, division, and exponents (which is a form of multiplication), involve ignoring the decimal places at first and then including them at the end.

12. A: The additive and subtractive identity is 0. When added or subtracted to any number, 0 does not change the original number.

13. B: 100 cm is equal to 1 m. 1.3 divided by 100 is 0.013. Therefore, 1.3 cm is equal to 0.013 m. Because 1 cm is equal to 10 mm, 1.3 cm is equal to 13 mm.

14. C: $\frac{1}{3}$ of the shirts sold were patterned. Therefore, $1 - \frac{1}{3} = \frac{2}{3}$ of the shirts sold were solid. Anytime "of" a quantity appears in a word problem, multiplication needs to be used. Therefore:

$$192 \times \frac{2}{3} = \frac{192*2}{3} = \frac{384}{3} = 128 \text{ solid shirts were sold}$$

The entire expression is:

$$192 \times \left(1 - \frac{1}{3}\right)$$

15. B: A rectangle is a specific type of parallelogram. It has 4 right angles. A square is a rhombus that has 4 right angles. Therefore, a square is always a rectangle because it has two sets of parallel lines and 4 right angles.

16. D: Area = length x width. The answer must be in square inches, so all values must be converted to inches. $\frac{1}{2}$ ft is equal to 6 inches. Therefore, the area of the rectangle is equal to:

$$6 \times \frac{11}{2} = \frac{66}{2} = 33 \text{ square inches}$$

17. C: The teacher would be introducing fractions. If a pie was cut into 6 pieces, each piece would represent $\frac{1}{6}$ of the pie. If one piece was taken away, $\frac{5}{6}$ of the pie would be left over.

18. B: Each hour on the clock represents 30 degrees. For example, 3:00 represents a right angle. Therefore, 5:00 represents 150 degrees.

19. D: There are no millions, so the millions period consists of all zeros. 182 is in the billions period, 36 is in the thousands period, 421 is in the hundreds period, and 356 is the decimal.

20. A: Every 8 ml of medicine requires 5 mL. The 45 mL first needs to be split into portions of 8 mL. This results in $\frac{45}{8}$ portions. Each portion requires 5 mL. Therefore:

$$\frac{45}{8} \times 5$$

$$\frac{45*5}{8} = \frac{225}{8} \text{ mL is necessary}$$

21. D: Division can be computed as a repetition of subtraction problems by subtracting multiples of 24.

22. C: Volume of this three-dimensional figure is calculated using length x width x height. Each measure of length is in inches. Therefore, the answer would be labeled in cubic inches.

23. A: This student made a mistake in adding fractions in that a common denominator was not found. In the initial problem, the least common denominator is 15 because it has both 5 and 3 as factors. The fractions must be rewritten using 15 as the denominator.

$$\frac{2}{3} + \frac{3}{5} = \frac{10}{15} + \frac{9}{15}$$

$$\frac{19}{15} = 1\frac{4}{15}$$

If the student was then asked to add $\frac{1}{4} + \frac{1}{3}$ and neglected to find a common denominator, the student would incorrectly determine that $\frac{1}{4} + \frac{1}{3} = \frac{2}{7}$, when it should be $\frac{7}{12}$.

24. B: A number raised to an exponent is a compressed form of multiplication. For example

$$10^3 = 10 \times 10 \times 10$$

25. B: The perimeter of a rectangle is the sum of all four sides. Therefore, the answer is:

$$P = 14 + 8\frac{1}{2} + 14 + 8\frac{1}{2}$$

$$14 + 14 + 8 + \frac{1}{2} + 8 + \frac{1}{2} = 45 \text{ square inches}$$

26. C: Inches, pounds, and baking measurements, such as tablespoons, are not part of the metric system. Kilograms, grams, kilometers, and meters are part of the metric system.

27. C: It shows the associative property of multiplication. The order of multiplication does not matter, and the grouping symbols do not change the final result once the expression is evaluated.

28. B: $12 \times 750 = 9,000$. Therefore, there are 9,000 milliliters of water, which must be converted to liters. 1,000 milliliters equals 1 liter; therefore, 9 liters of water are purchased.

29. A: According to order of operations, the operation within the parentheses must be completed first. Next, division is completed and then subtraction. Therefore, the expression is evaluated as:

$$(3 + 7) - 6 \div 2$$

$$10 - 6 \div 2 = 10 - 3 = 7$$

In order to incorrectly obtain 2 as the answer, the operations would have been performed from left to right, instead of following PEMDAS.

30. A: Operations within the parentheses must be completed first. Then, division is completed. Finally, addition is the last operation to complete. When adding decimals, digits within each place value are added together. Therefore, the expression is evaluated as:

$$(2 \times 20) \div (7 + 1) + (6 \times 0.01) + (4 \times 0.001)$$

$$40 \div 8 + 0.06 + 0.004 = 5 + 0.06 + 0.004$$

5.064

31. B: The formula for the volume of a rectangular solid would need to be used. The volume of the first box is:

$$V = 3 \times 5 \times 10 = 150 \text{ cubic inches}$$

The second box needs to hold cereal that would take up the same space. The volume of the second box is:

$$V = 5 \times 6 \times h = 30 \times h$$

In order for this to equal 150, h must equal 5 inches.

32. C: The measure of two complementary angles sums up to 90 degrees.

$$90 - 54 = 36$$

Therefore, the complementary angle is 36 degrees.

33. C: A compass is a tool that can be used to draw a circle. The circle would be drawn by using the length of the radius, which is half of the diameter.

34. C: A dollar contains 20 nickels. Therefore, if there are 12 dollars' worth of nickels, there are:

$$12 \times 20 = 240 \text{ nickels}$$

Each nickel weighs 5 grams. Therefore, the weight of the nickels is:

$$240 \times 5 = 1,200 \text{ grams}$$

Adding in the weight of the empty piggy bank, the filled bank weighs 2,250 grams.

35. B: Katie eats $\frac{1}{3}$ of $\frac{3}{4}$ of the pizza. That means she eats:

$$\frac{1}{3} \times \frac{3}{4} = \frac{3}{12} = \frac{1}{4} \text{ of the pizza}$$

Therefore, $\frac{3}{4} - \frac{1}{4} = \frac{2}{4} = \frac{1}{2}$ of the pizza remains. This problem involves subtraction of fractions with like denominators.

36. D: 3 must be multiplied times $27\frac{3}{4}$. In order to easily do this, the mixed number should be converted into an improper fraction.

$$27\frac{3}{4} = \frac{27 * 4 + 3}{4} = \frac{111}{4}$$

Therefore, Denver had approximately:

$$\frac{3x111}{4} = \frac{333}{4} \text{ inches of snow}$$

The improper fraction can be converted back into a mixed number through division.

$$\frac{333}{4} = 83\frac{1}{4} \text{ inches}$$

37. B: Each nickel is worth $0.05. Therefore, Joshua deposited:

$$12{,}345 \times \$0.05 = \$617.25$$

Working with change is a great way to teach decimals to children, so this problem would be a good introduction to multiplying decimals.

38. B: Ordinal numbers represent a ranking. Placing second in a competition is a ranking among the other participants of the spelling bee.

39. D: This problem would be most appropriate in a lesson about the order of operations. According to the order of operations, multiplication and division must be completed first from left to right. Then, addition and subtraction are completed from left to right. Therefore:

$$9 \times 9 \div 9 + 9 - 9 \div 9$$

$$81 \div 9 + 9 - 9 \div 9$$

$$9 + 9 - 9 \div 9$$

$$9 + 9 - 1$$

$$18 - 1 = 17$$

If instead, students completed the operations as written strictly from left to right (without considering the order of operations), the incorrect solution of 1 would be found.

40. B: When giving an answer to a math problem that is in fraction form, it always should be simplified. Both 3 and 15 have a common factor of 3 that can be divided out, so the correct answer is:

$$\frac{3 \div 3}{15 \div 3} = \frac{1}{5}$$

Science

1. C: Reactivity. Chemical properties describe the behavior of substances, while physical properties describe their appearance. Reactivity is a behavior, and therefore it's the correct answer.

2. D, E: Smell and texture. Length and width can be measured with a ruler, and mass can be measured with a balance. Qualitative data involves the observations garnered via the five senses. These measurements do not involve making measurements with numbers. Therefore, smell and texture are valid examples.

3. C: An observation typically kicks off the scientific method. The first step is to identify a problem based on an observation—the who, what, when, where, why, and how. An observation is the analysis of information using basic human senses: sight, sound, touch, taste, and smell. In this step of the scientific method, the problem is identified—the who, what, when, where, why, and how. Recall that designing a science investigation is based on the scientific method, which consists of the following steps making an observation, forming a question, conducting an experiment, collecting and analyzing data, and forming a conclusion.

4. C: If light exposure increases, then plant height will increase. Choices *A* and *B* are not good choices because it's impossible to measure a cat's happiness, and there's a subjective factor involved in determining the softness of pants. Feeling more comfortable isn't objective enough, and measuring growth should be clarified—will height or mass be measured? Measuring purring would also be difficult to do quantitatively; cats either do purr or don't purr. Volume could be measured with a scientific device, but that would have to be specified. Choice *C* has a valid independent and dependent variable, both which can be measured, so it's the correct choice.

5. D: Dimitri because weather involves the water cycle. The other suggestions (ad thus, answer choices) reflect are misunderstandings. It's weather that's day-to-day and depends on wind and heat patterns, while seasons depend on proximity to the Sun. Weather patterns such as rain and snow definitely involve the water cycle, so that's the correct choice.

6. C: Modeling with flashlights and tennis balls. Early childhood educators should know that PowerPoint isn't an effective teaching method, and while going outside is fun, without modeling, the activity will be meaningless. The book idea would not be an effective teaching tool in this case because it's unable to model nearness, closeness, and general location. Modeling is the best option.

7. C: Alaska is farther from the equator. Climate has nothing to do with the size or shape of a state; it relates to exposure to the Sun. Places closer to the equator are hotter, so the answer is *C*.

8. B: Mountains. The other choices all involve breaking down rocks; mountains are the only landform that is created.

9. B: Tornados. Hurricanes and rain are liquid precipitation, and snow is solid precipitation. Tornadoes only involve wind, so *B* is the correct answer.

10. A: Causing volcanoes. Plate tectonics involve movement in the Earth's crust that exposes areas for volcanic activities. Plates have nothing to do with evaporation or delta formation; both of those processes involve the water cycle. Plate movement also has nothing to do with tornado and wind movement.

11. B: Metamorphic. These rocks change due to pressure and heat. Hardened magma and igneous rocks are the same, and sedimentary rock is compressed layers of weathered sediment.

12. A: Sedimentary. Sedimentary rock layers contain fossils. Igneous and hardened magma are the same, and they are from the Earth's surface and wouldn't contain fossils. Metamorphic rock is on the bottom of the crust and melting and reforming, so it also wouldn't contain fossils.

13. B: Footprint. Trace fossils are *evidence* of an organism as opposed to the *remains* of an organism. Bones, shells, and teeth were all once part of an organism and are true fossils.

14. B: Moves. All organisms grow, reproduce, and have DNA, but not every organism moves. Plants aren't mobile like animals, yet they are alive, as are mushrooms and other fungi.

15. C: Plant. A producer is an organism that makes its own food, and from the list, only plants can do that. Humans and insects eat for food, and fungi, like mushrooms, decompose organisms for food.

16. D: Butterfly. This is the only organism on the list that has a larva that changes into a pupa. Neither humans nor chickens undergo metamorphosis, and frogs have the intermediate tadpole phase, not the larval phase.

17. C: Diagnostic assessment. Often referred to as "pretests," diagnostic assessments evaluate students' background knowledge prior to the learning process. Therefore, it would be normal and not indicative that a student is not understanding the taught material if he or she did not know what species has a tadpole stage. Standardized tests create controlled conditions and consistent scoring procedures to evaluate a particular aspect of student learning. Formative assessments are frequent, structured assessments that are carried out throughout the learning process; they can be formal or informal, and they help quantify learning and guide instruction. Summative assessments evaluate learning at the end of the learning process; they are cumulative and can be used to assess the quality of instruction and the progress of student learning. Incorrect answers on these other types of assessments, while not alarming or uncommon, should signal to the teacher that the child may need further explanation and review of the concepts.

18. D: Protons have a positive charge. An atom is structured with a nucleus in the center that contains neutral neutrons and positive protons. Surrounding the nucleus are orbiting electrons that are negatively charged. Choice *D* is the only correct answer.

19. B: It makes them less visible to predators. The other choices may or may not be true (they aren't), but regardless, the only one that increases the chance of survival is Choice *B*.

20. A: Zero. This particular food chain fails to show any omnivores, or animals that eat both meat and plants.

21. B: Competitive. As both the warthog and the gazelle eat the same organism (the shrubs), they are competing for that organism as a resource. They aren't eating each other, and they also aren't helping or hurting each other.

22. C: Musical achievements. Although musicianship in general might be somewhat inherited, the number of achievements certainly isn't. Eye color, blood type, and heart disease are all inherited.

23. D: All of the above. All listed factors are altering ecosystems and putting species at risk of extinction.

Health Education, Physical Education, and the Arts

1. B: Nutrition recommendations for children include replacing higher fat foods with lower-fat alternatives, reducing the intake of sugary beverages, and replacing more refined foods like applesauce with foods in their natural form, such as a fresh, whole apple. Answer Choice *B* is incorrect because fiber is beneficial in the diet because it increases the feeling of satiety, which can lower caloric intake, and fiber can also reduce LDL cholesterol by binding to it and helping the body excrete it. Lower fiber refined grains have the bran stripped away and should be replaced by higher fiber options.

2. A: The optimal physical education curriculum for five- to six-year-old children should focus on movement for enjoyment. Children at this age are motivated by fun and playing and will be active if it is fun. They are not necessarily ready to focus on sports-specific skills requiring significant hand-eye coordination. They do best with moderate- and high-intensity activities with adequate rest.

3. C: When teaching new skills, especially to toddlers and young children, instructions lasting longer than twenty seconds or containing more than just a couple of steps or cues will lead students to losing interest or getting overwhelmed. It is typically advantageous to have very short instructional periods interspersed between longer breaks to play and try out the introduced skills. Reading material is likely not appropriate for this age group, many of whom do not yet know how to read.

4. C: Following safety procedures like wearing a seatbelt is the best choice. Experts recommend that children get over nine hours of sleep per night. Also, children should brush their teeth after every meal, not just before bed. Finally, it is important for children to learn how to express their emotions in a healthy way and let a trusted adult know if they are struggling with persistent feelings of sadness or anxiety.

5. D: Teachers should educate students on the importance of visiting doctors for routine medical care and check-ups (every six months or so); consistent feelings of sadness, anxiety, loneliness, and stress; and pains or aches that do not go away. Research has found that even at the preschool level, talking about the importance of visiting the doctor can positively impact health behaviors in adulthood.

6. A: Family influences on health behaviors include health insurance status, safety and injury prevention education and care, nutritional meal planning and diet composition, social dynamics and stress, and the family's culture around leisure time.

7. C: Gross motor skills are mastered before fine motor skills. Students begin developing basic motor skills like walking, balancing, and manipulating objects from a very early age. They master gross motor skills before they move on to fine motor skills. Sports skills are not learned more readily than generalized body movements, because sports skills require more fine motor skills, complex motions, and cognitive abilities (e.g. locating and aiming for targets). Also, what looks like play actually helps children develop movement patterns and abilities.

8. B: The general categories of basic movement skills include locomotor skills like walking, running, and skipping; non-locomotor skills such as squatting and twisting; and manipulative skills such as throwing and catching.

9. A: In a kindergarten classroom, hitting targets is not an appropriate focus for physical education because children at this age have not mastered the fine motor abilities and complex skills to aim and hit targets. Hitting targets is more appropriate for fifth grade students. In kindergarten, activities should focus on foundational skills such as weight transfer, balance, following objects with the eyes, and basic skills like jumping and skipping.

10. D: Of the listed age groups, nine- to twelve-year-old students are likely to be more interested in health-based benefits of physical activity than younger children, who are primarily interested in movement for fun and enjoyment. As children mature, they gain a deeper understanding of physiology and healthy lifestyle choices and they become more interested in the health benefits of exercise.

11. A: Educators should focus curricular activities on the major categories of arts: music, dance, theater, and visual arts (painting, drawing, sculpture, pottery, etc.).

12. C: The youngest children tend to create art with a focus on the scientific and sensory aspects of the project rather than artistic creativity, self-expression, or conveying a narrative or story. They enjoy art more as a means to which explore the textures they make (for example, making texture rubbings with crayon on paper), the contrast of colors they use, and the various shapes they make as they move the drawing utensil around (although they are not making shapes for symbolic reasons, they are simply enjoying and exploring what they make when they use the supplies).

13. D: Children should experiment with a variety of methods and materials to create art. Educators should provide children with a wide range of materials like finger paint, glitter, and felt so that children experiment with different textures. *A* is not the best answer because art education should expose students to the historical and cultural context of art beyond that of their everyday experiences. Students can learn about famous artists and art history, but those lessons can be incorporated into creative coursework; they are not a prerequisite for student experimentation.

14. D: Have students accompany the music with simple instruments like tambourines. Students can easily beat along to simple songs using rhythmic instruments like tambourines, maracas, or small drums. Young children enjoy moving around more than sitting and focusing on one thing for an extended time, so learning rhythm through actions like shaking rhythmic instruments or stomping and clapping is more effective for students at this age. Also, *C* is not the best answer because many young children are not yet strong readers.

15. D: Theater-in-education (TIE) is performed by teachers and students using curriculum material or social issues. Participants take on roles, which enable them to explore and problem-solve in a flexible structure, yet in an educational theatrical way. In Readers' Theater, readers perform a dramatic presentation sitting on stools reading the lines typically from children's literature, enabling performance opportunities in the absence of elaborate staging or script memorization. Puppetry can be used for creative drama with either simple puppets and stages made of bags, cardboard, socks, or more elaborate, artistic materials.

16. A: The main skills in theatrical arts for children include literary (reading and writing the script and memorizing lines), technical (includes the staging, lighting, sound effects, etc.), and performance elements (such as the set design and the musical score). Staging is part of the technical elements.

17. D: A three- to four-year-old child's drawing usually emphasizes his or her color choices. At this young age, children typically do not use art for self-expression, symbolism, or realistic figural accuracy. These are all artistic skills that students develop when they are older. Young students tend to focus on sensory exploration involving color, shape, and texture.

18. B: Perspective is a technique used to make flat objects look as though they have depth. Balance is using size, position, color, shape and lighting in the artwork so that all of the elements are equally present with no particular component overpowering. Abstraction is unrealistic artwork that typically has geometric lines or patterns.

19. A: Art has personal (self-expression, gratification, narrative functions), social (collective meaning for a group of people such as symbolic art honoring a god or political art), and physical functions (such as a pottery mug for tea) that often overlap in a project. Religious functions fall under the realm of social functions.

20. B: Harmony is a principle in art that highlights the similarities in separate but related parts of a composition to show how different things can actually be similar and blend together. Balance is positioning objects or using size, color, shape and lighting in a way that makes all of the elements equally present. Contrast is exemplifying differences between two unlike things such as loud and soft music, major and minor tones, fast and slow dancing movements, and light and dark colors.

Dear GACE Early Childhood,

We would like to start by thanking you for purchasing this study guide for your GACE Early Childhood exam. We hope that we exceeded your expectations.

Our goal in creating this study guide was to cover all of the topics that you will see on the test. We also strove to make our practice questions as similar as possible to what you will encounter on test day. With that being said, if you found something that you feel was not up to your standards, please send us an email and let us know.

We have study guides in a wide variety of fields. If you're interested in one, try searching for it on Amazon or send us an email.

Thanks Again and Happy Testing!
Product Development Team
info@studyguideteam.com

FREE Test Taking Tips DVD Offer

To help us better serve you, we have developed a Test Taking Tips DVD that we would like to give you for FREE. **This DVD covers world-class test taking tips that you can use to be even more successful when you are taking your test.**

All that we ask is that you email us your feedback about your study guide. Please let us know what you thought about it – whether that is good, bad or indifferent.

To get your **FREE Test Taking Tips DVD**, email freedvd@studyguideteam.com with "FREE DVD" in the subject line and the following information in the body of the email:

    a. The title of your study guide.

    b. Your product rating on a scale of 1-5, with 5 being the highest rating.

    c. Your feedback about the study guide. What did you think of it?

    d. Your full name and shipping address to send your free DVD.

If you have any questions or concerns, please don't hesitate to contact us at freedvd@studyguideteam.com.

Thanks again!

Made in the USA
Columbia, SC
13 September 2021